THIS
I KNOW
FOR SURE

Taking God at His Word

A Bible Study by
BABBIE MASON

ABINGDON PRESS

Nashville

THIS I KNOW FOR SURE: TAKING GOD AT HIS WORD
A BIBLE STUDY BY BABBIE MASON

Copyright © 2013 Abingdon Women

All rights reserved.

This book is printed on acid-free paper.

ISBN 978-1-4267-7245-0

13 14 15 16 17 18 19 20 21 22—10 9 8 7 6 5 4 3 2 1

MANUFACTURED IN THE UNITED STATES OF AMERICA

Contents

Introduction

Do you long to know God more intimately? Do you desire a rock-solid faith to believe Him for the challenges, questions, and doubts you are facing regardless of how you may feel? Though there are things we cannot know or understand this side of heaven, there *are* some things we can know beyond a shadow of a doubt—even in the most uncertain times.

This study comes as a result of my own desire to establish an unshakable confidence in Christ. Life is constantly changing. In spite of it all, I've made the determination to trust in the God who never changes. This is a call for you to join me. I invite you to examine your relationship with God and make up your mind to believe God and take Him at His Word regardless of your circumstances.

Together we will take hold of some nonnegotiable principles of our faith, discovering what it means to know God intimately, with certainty and assurance, which is deeper than just knowing *about* Him. With the Bible as our textbook, we will discover that just as God worked in the lives of His people in Bible days, He is real and present in our lives today.

During the course of our study, we will meet people from the Bible who, like us, struggled with doubts and questions and still chose to trust God and His promises. They show us what it looks like to walk with God even when we aren't sure of our next step. And we'll see how they made up their minds to follow God in all His ways in spite of their circumstances. In some cases, we'll shine the spotlight on those who missed God's direction so that we may learn from their example as well. And when we reach the end of our study, our faith in God will be stronger, our confidence in Him will be higher, our love for Him will be sweeter, our compassion for others will be deeper, and our joy in the Lord will be complete.

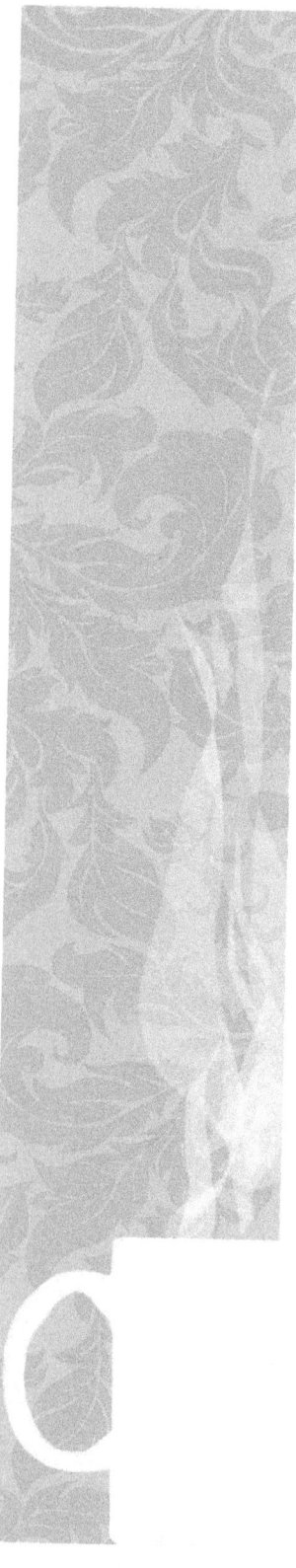

Our Theme Song and Scripture

As I began thinking about the things I know for sure about the God I love, was inspired to write a song. Let me share the words of the chorus with you:

> *There is a God in heaven*
> *And I am in His plan*
> *He will forsake me never*
> *My life is in His hands*
> *His boundless love will lead me*
> *As long as time endures*
> *Oh, this I know*
> *This I know for sure*

Within the first five lines of the chorus are five biblical assurances that lead to an unshakable faith. I call them landmarks of the faith—uncompromising truths we can agree upon and affirm with certainty regardless of our culture, where we grew up, or where we may go to church. These truths, which provide the framework for our study, will help us to follow Christ without compromise. Undergirding it all is a foundational truth from the Scriptures that I've found to be a source of strength and encouragement for believing God and His Word:

> *I know whom I have believed, and am persuaded that he is able to keep*
> *that which I have committed unto him against that day.*
>
> 2 Timothy 1:12 KJV

The apostle Paul wrote these words to his beloved disciple Timothy to spur him on in the faith. After all Paul had endured—shipwrecks, beatings, hunger, nakedness, imprisonment, torture, and more—these words were an inspiring and victorious message to his younger counterpart. They also serve as a sure foundation for us in the trying times in which we live. For this reason, we will use this powerful declaration as our theme Scripture and memory verse.

I find it easier to remember 2 Timothy 1:12 if I sing it to the tune of the hymn "I Know Whom I Have Believed," composed by Daniel Whittle and James McGranahan. If you, like me, find it easier to memorize this verse by singing the chorus of this classic hymn, I encourage you to lift your voice in song! If you don't know the tune, you can find an arrangement of the hymn on the DVD (or the companion music CD, available at www.babbie.com). Whether you sing it or recite it, I pray that 2 Timothy 1:12 will remind you that you can know and believe God and find that He always keeps His promises!

Preparing for the Journey

As we prepare to begin our journey, it's helpful to know the route we'll be taking and the navigational tools we'll be using. Our route consists of personal Bible study, which you will do throughout the week, and a weekly group session. This book and your Bible will serve as your navigational tools. You also might want to use a journal to document your journey in greater detail (optional).

For each week of study, you will find a brief introduction that presents the landmark for that week followed by five daily readings with interactive Bible study. Each day's reading can be completed in about 20-30 minutes. Let me encourage you to think of this daily routine not as mere homework but as an opportunity to know Jesus more intimately. Completing these readings will not only prepare you for the discussion and activities during the group session; you'll find your own faith beginning to soar. Now, let me rehearse the daily format with you.

Read God's Word

Each reading begins with a passage of Scripture that emphasizes the theme of the day. Read this passage through before you proceed to the next section.

Reflect and Respond

Next we will study a Bible character or story from which we have much to learn on a particular topic, as well as dig into other related Scriptures. I'll also share insights from my life that illustrate Scripture lessons and their application in our daily lives. Throughout this section you'll find questions and exercises (highlighted in bold) to help you dig deeper and respond to what you're learning.

Go to God

Finally, we will close in prayer. I've always believed that if you want to know something, you just have to ask. James 4:2b says, "[We] have not because [we] ask not" (KJV). So each day's entry concludes with an opportunity for personal inventory and reflection. During this time of soul searching, we'll use the acronym ASK from Jesus' words in Matthew 7:7 as our guide:

> **A**sk and it will be given to you;
> **S**eek and you will find;
> **K**nock and the door will be opened to you. (NIV, emphasis added)

Ask

This is your opportunity to inquire of the Lord in prayer as you think about what you have read. This section guides you in asking God, "What does this

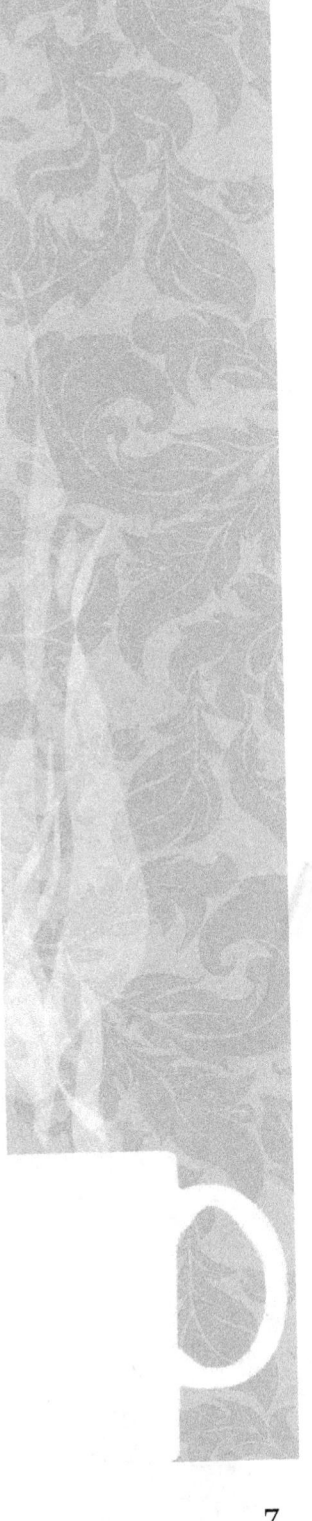

daily reading *mean*?" You will be guided to pray about what you are learning. You may want to record your thoughts in this book or a prayer journal to track your prayer requests or make note of a point of interest you want to remember.

Seek

To seek means to search for or to pursue. This section guides you in asking, "What does this daily reading mean to *me personally*?" As you think about each day's reading, meditate on what you have read throughout the day. As you meditate on God's Word, the Holy Spirit will speak to your heart about its meaning and prompt you to apply what He is teaching you. In addition to responding to any prompts in this section, you may want to make notations in your Bible or write in a journal about what lessons you may be learning.

Knock

To knock means to ask and seek, but with greater intensity. This section helps you to ask God, "How can I apply what I've learned to my life?" When you are knocking, you are standing by the door waiting for an answer. Expect God to answer. This is your opportunity to discover not only who God is but also the power of God within you personally! Your response to His answer is obedience. Nothing pleases God more than a life that is dedicated to pleasing Him.

A Blessing

Dear one, I can't tell you how honored and excited I am to take this journey with you. My heart is already singing a song of expectation as I anticipate how God is going to speak to us during our study. May you be blessed as you declare your unwavering confidence in the promises of God!

I'd like to start by asking for God's help. We dare not embark on this journey without His loving guidance.

> *Kind Father,*
>
> *My sister and I come before You now with hungry hearts. We make ourselves available to You, and we thank You in advance for how Your truth will change us over the next six weeks. Speak to my sister's heart, Lord, in unmistakable ways, and help her to grow deeper in her faith in You. Thank You, Lord, for all that You are going to do. In the mighty name of Jesus. Amen.*

Jabbré

Week 1

There Is a God in Heaven

It was art day in a little kindergarten boy's class. As he took out his paints and brushes, he announced, "I'm going to color a picture of God."

"But no one knows what God looks like," responded his teacher.

"They will when I get finished," the little boy said with certainty.

I like that little fellow's attitude. He has found a childlike confidence in God that is truly admirable. You know, it's easy to play it safe as a Christian—to stand among the crowd and blend in. Then one day, without warning, your name is called and you are shoved to the front of the crowd. I don't know if God has ever called you in for inspection, but one summer day my life was interrupted and my comfortable faith was shaken to the core. That day changed my life.

After church one Sunday my husband, Charles, and I headed to my friend Donna's house. That afternoon I would join our friends to throw her a bridal shower. It was a beautiful day, and I was on my way to celebrate one of the biggest moments in my friend's life, enjoying lighthearted conversation with Charles as we drove.

I was driving that day. I got off the freeway and stopped at the light at the end of the exit ramp. We sat in the center lane of traffic and waited for the light to turn green. My view to the left was obstructed by a van. When the light turned green, I approached the intersection when the driver of that van suddenly slammed on his brakes and blew his horn. Instinct kicked in and I slammed on my brakes as well, although at the moment, I didn't know why. Just then, a car came racing from the left, speeding through the intersection and running the light. Had I not stopped precisely at the moment that I did, that speeding vehicle would have T-boned our car. I shudder to think about it. Things could have turned out so differently that day, but God in all His grace and mercy saw fit to spare our lives.

I was shaken by that moment. I sat frozen in the intersection, unable to move. All I could do was call on the name of Jesus. Later on that day and in the moments

and days that followed, that incident replayed over and over in my mind. The narrow miss thrust the issue of my mortality to the forefront. I began to review my life and take inventory of my faith, my relationships, and my work, as we often do in times of crisis or challenge.

I made Jesus my Savior and Lord a long time ago, but that near miss caused me to recommit every area of my life to Him. I realized with a keen awareness that every moment is a blessing from God not to be taken for granted. Even our times of play, rest, and leisure are to be lived with purpose and intent. Our relationship with God through His Son, Jesus Christ, gives us our reason for living. And from that relationship springs our assignment to serve God and others.

In light of that revelation, I have determined to give Jesus my absolute best, not what's left—just as the apostle Paul described: "Yes, everything else is worthless when compared with the infinite value of knowing Christ Jesus my Lord. For his sake I have discarded everything else, counting it all as garbage, so that I could gain Christ and become one with him" (Philippians 3:8-9a NLT). Today is a gift from God. What I do with today is my gift to Him. I am to take nothing for granted—not my family, my friends, or my church; not my work, my play, or my worship; not even my next breath, because all of it could be gone in an instant. I have a new desire to live with purpose and confident faith. No more compromise. No more second-guessing what God has said. I've asked God to grant me many more opportunities to say like that little boy in art class, "People will know what God looks like when I'm finished."

If you've ever experienced a "near miss" in your life, then maybe you understand how it can bring life sharply into focus. But you don't need a "near miss" experience to appreciate the fact that every day on this planet is a blessing from God and an opportunity to enjoy His presence. Why not live every one of those days with hope by placing your confidence completely in God and His Word?

That's what this journey is all about—deciding that you believe God, not just believe in Him, and that you'll take Him at His Word. Each week we will explore what I call a landmark of the faith—a foundational and unshakable promise of God that we can know and believe with confidence—with a final week to tie it all together. This week we begin our journey by exploring this landmark: *There is a God in heaven.* It is my prayer that as we study together, you will join me in believing this with all confidence.

Scripture Memorization

During the next six weeks, you will be memorizing 2 Timothy 1:12, the core verse for this study:

I know whom I have believed, and am persuaded that he is able to keep that which I have committed unto him against that day. (KJV)

Write the verse on several index cards and place them in highly visible areas, such as your bathroom mirror, refrigerator, car dashboard, and bedside table. Read the verse when you get up, throughout the day, and at bedtime. Another great way to memorize this verse is to sing it (you can find an arrangement of the hymn "I Know Whom I Have Believed" on the DVD and companion music CD).

Day 1: Confidence in God's Providence

Read God's Word

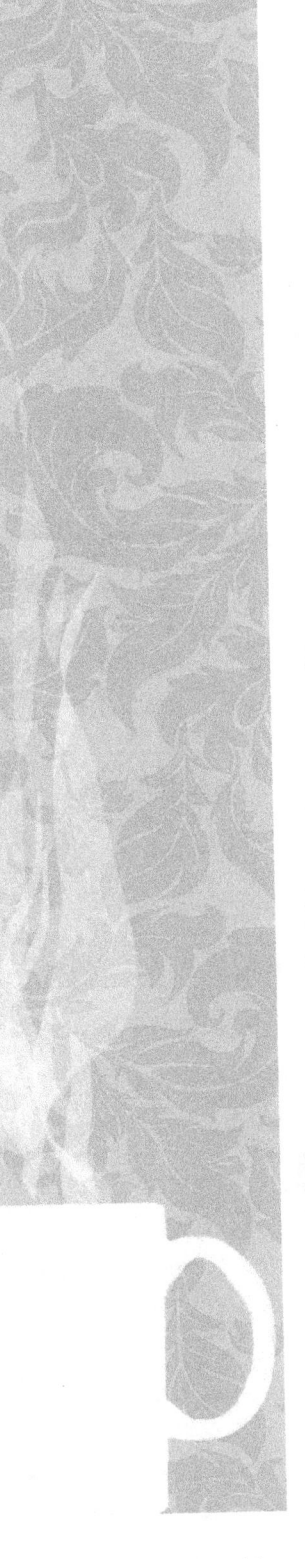

¹In the thirty-sixth year of the reign of Asa, Baasha king of Israel came up against Judah and built Ramah, that he might let none go out or come in to Asa king of Judah. ²Then Asa brought silver and gold from the treasuries of the house of the LORD and of the king's house, and sent to Ben-Hadad king of Syria, who dwelt in Damascus, saying, ³"Let there be a treaty between you and me, as there was between my father and your father. See, I have sent you silver and gold; come, break your treaty with Baasha king of Israel, so that he will withdraw from me."

⁴So Ben-Hadad heeded King Asa, and sent the captains of his armies against the cities of Israel. They attacked Ijon, Dan, Abel Maim, and all the storage cities of Naphtali. ⁵Now it happened, when Baasha heard it, that he stopped building Ramah and ceased his work. ⁶Then King Asa took all Judah, and they carried away the stones and timber of Ramah, which Baasha had used for building; and with them he built Geba and Mizpah.

⁷And at that time Hanani the seer came to Asa king of Judah, and said to him: "Because you have relied on the king of Syria, and have not relied on the LORD your God, therefore the army of the king of Syria has escaped from your hand. ⁸Were the Ethiopians and the Lubim not a huge army with very many chariots and horsemen? Yet, because you relied on the LORD, He delivered them into your hand. ⁹For the eyes of the LORD run to and fro throughout the whole earth, to show Himself strong on behalf of those whose heart is loyal to Him. In this you have done foolishly; therefore from now on you shall have wars." ¹⁰Then Asa was angry with the seer, and put him in prison, for he was enraged at him because of this. And Asa oppressed some of the people at that time.

2 Chronicles 16:1-10

Reflect and Respond

Almost thirty years ago I was a middle school music teacher, and I didn't know whether I should continue teaching or quit my job and step out in faith to pursue a growing music ministry. Charles and I had been married a few years,

and we were raising two growing boys. The word had spread about my singing, and I was receiving invitations to visit churches and civic groups on weekends and during the summer months. Little by little, my calendar was beginning to fill up with singing engagements, but I was still hesitant to quit my day job and leave the security that came with it. The Lord knew that deep in my heart I dreamed of launching a music ministry as a full-time vocation. But that wasn't practical because Charles had started his own small business, and my position as a teacher gave us the health benefits we needed. Together, Charles and I prayed about me quitting my job. I sought the advice of family and friends and the counsel of our pastor, but ultimately it seemed that the decision was mine to make.

One night my dear friend Barb dropped by for a visit. She wanted me to meet an evangelist friend of hers along with his wife. We chatted for a while. Before we ended our conversation, the evangelist asked if I had any prayer requests. I excitedly told him about my desire to quit my job and my reluctance to leave it. He prayed a simple prayer and I said "Amen," believing that God had heard our requests. Then an amazing thing happened. That preacher, whom I had met just moments before, volunteered to buy our health insurance for a year so that I could quit my job without any concerns. What a mighty God we serve! What amazing blessings come when we have confidence in God's guidance and care!

Look with me now at a story from the Bible about the importance of having confidence in God's guidance and care. It is the story of King Asa found in Second Chronicles. You may have never heard of King Asa before now because he is not among the great and remembered kings of the Old Testament. However, there is much for us to glean from his rise and fall related to having confidence in God. You see, Asa was a man who had confidence in God and then lost it, resulting in a very sad ending to his story. He started out trusting God but did not end well—even after God had brought him great success.

You might remember that following the reign of King Solomon, the nation of Israel was divided into the Northern Kingdom, called Israel, and the Southern Kingdom, called Judah. Asa was the third king of Judah, and he had many years of prosperity and success because he sought the Lord.

Read 2 Chronicles 14:1-15. How would you describe Asa's relationship with God?

Now read 2 Chronicles 15:1-19 and answer the following questions.

What warning did Asa receive? (vv. 1-7)

Acting out of bravery, what did Asa do? (vv. 8-11)

How would you describe Asa's confidence in God in this passage?

We see in these chapters that Asa had great confidence in God's providence. He trusted God to take care of his kingdom and was about as devout as a man would be—that is, until he felt threatened and unsure of his kingdom. Then he lost his confidence in God and took matters into his own hands.

Review 2 Chronicles 16:1-10.

What caused Asa to lose his confidence in God? (v. 1)

How did Asa take matters into his own hands? (vv. 2-4)

What were the consequences of his actions? (vv. 7-9)

Let's "unpack" the story together. Early in Asa's kingly rule, he sought after God's heart. He trusted that God would lead and guide his reign. In our reading from 2 Chronicles 14, we saw in verse 2 that Asa "did what was right and good in the eyes of the LORD his God," and in verse 4 of that same chapter we saw that he ordered all of Judah to "seek the LORD." Then, in verse 11 we saw how Asa prepared for battle with faith-filled words.

Reread 2 Chronicles 14:11 below. Circle every time Asa referred to God using the words LORD, God, You or Your.

"LORD, it is nothing for You to help, whether with many or with those who have no power; help us, O LORD our God, for we rest on You, and in Your name we go against this multitude. O LORD, You are our God; do not let man prevail against You!"

It is clear that Asa placed his trust in God! So what happened? What caused him to act according to his own will when he learned of an impending invasion? Was it panic? Lack of confidence? Pride? Had he forgotten all that God had done for him? Surely all of these contributed to his inability to trust God.

God sent a seer named Hanani to deliver rebuke. Hanani recounted God's great and mighty deeds during Asa's reign. He scolded Asa for taking matters into his own hands and disregarding his God. I can almost feel the dagger in Asa's heart when Hanani declared this piercing message:

> *"For the eyes of the LORD run to and fro throughout the whole earth, to show Himself strong on behalf of those whose heart is loyal to Him. In this you have done foolishly; therefore from now on you shall have wars."*
>
> 2 Chronicles 16:9

According to this verse, why is God scanning the whole world? (What does He want to do, and to whom?)

How is King Asa described in this verse?

Years before, Asa had been committed to God with his whole heart. But now he was the foolish one. No longer would he be seen as one committed to the Lord, and no longer would his kingdom live in peace.

The next verse tells us that Asa reacted in anger, throwing Hanani in jail and treating some of the people badly. Later when he contracted a severe foot disease, he consulted doctors rather than God, refusing to seek God's help. In a tragic ending, Asa died with a hard heart. Most of his life he had put all his trust and hope in God; then fear and pride became too much to keep at bay. And in choosing fear and pride, Asa made the choice to abandon a life with God altogether.

Sister, it comes back to having confidence in God and relying upon Him. Asa lost his confidence in God's ways. Instead of trusting God's plan for his reign, he decided to make his own way. What about you? Do you trust God to provide in miraculous ways? Are you totally confident in God's providence? To answer that question, let's look a little deeper into the theme of God's providence.

Providence can be thought of in different ways. First is a general providence that describes God's overall care and supervision of His creation. Nave's Topical Bible defines it like this: "The universal sovereign reign of God; God's preserving and governing all his creatures, and all their actions.… General providence includes the government of the entire universe, especially the affairs of men."[1]

Another way to understand providence is a more particular care and guidance that God exercises on behalf of those who seek Him with their whole hearts.
Again, Nave's defines this as "God's particular care over the life and activity of
the believer."[2] Let's consider each understanding of providence more carefully.

• **God's overall care and supervision of His creation**

What do these Scriptures teach us about God's overall care for creation?

Psalm 104:14, 19-21

Matthew 5:45*b*

• **A more particular care and guidance that God exercises on behalf of those
who seek Him with their whole hearts**

**What do these Scriptures teach us about God's particular care for those who
seek His heart?**

Psalm 37:23

Romans 8:28

**How do the following Scriptures help to give you confidence in God's
particular care and guidance for** *you*?

Philippians 4:19

Matthew 6:25-33

I have great confidence in God's ability to care for my every need, and I am
gaining more and more confidence as I take each step with Him. This confidence
is expressed in the theme song for this study, "This I Know for Sure," which I will
sing for you in the video during this week's group session. The first verse and
chorus are so appropriate for this moment.

Providence:
1. God's overall care
   and supervision of
   His creation

2. A more particular
   care and guidance
   that God exercises
   on behalf of those
   who seek Him with
   their whole hearts

When life is uncertain
Questions come and go
I'll not be moved by how I feel
But trust in what I know

There is a God in heaven
And I am in His plan
He will forsake me never
My life is in His hands
His boundless love will lead me
As long as time endures
Oh, this I know
This I know for sure

God will provide the way for you. I'm sure of it! I know this because He has provided a way for me. Regardless of our circumstances, we can count on God to faithfully guide and care for us, providing for all our needs.

Go to God

Ask

Ask God if there is anything that may be preventing you from enjoying a more intimate relationship with Him. Like King Asa, have you distrusted God? Have you walked away from God, attempting to do things your way? Have you placed faith in others, only to be let down or heartbroken? Ask God for forgiveness in each area and commit to rely completely on Him. Thank Him for restoring your relationship with Him.

Seek

What is one thing you know for sure after completing today's reading?

Choose to believe what you know to be true, and practice walking in that promise regardless of how you may feel.

Knock

What is one area of your life that you need to surrender to God today?

Whatever it is, surrender it to Him now and trust that He knows all about our situation today. Watch and wait for what He will do.

Dear heavenly Father,

Thank You for reminding me that my confidence does not lie in my ability but in my availability to You. You are my confidence, and I make myself available to You today. Forgive me for attempting to step out in my own strength. I can't do anything without Your help. This I know for sure. In Jesus' name. Amen.

Day 2: Confidence in God's Power

Read God's Word

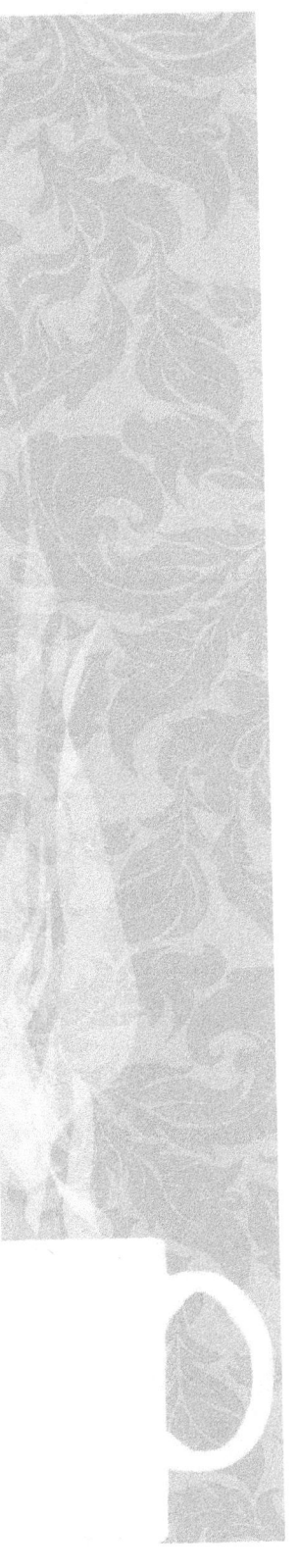

²⁰*And when he came to the den, he cried out with a lamenting voice to Daniel. The king spoke, saying to Daniel, "Daniel, servant of the living God, has your God, whom you serve continually, been able to deliver you from the lions?"*

²¹*Then Daniel said to the king, "O king, live forever! ²²My God sent His angel and shut the lions' mouths, so that they have not hurt me, because I was found innocent before Him; and also, O king, I have done no wrong before you."*

²³*Now the king was exceedingly glad for him, and commanded that they should take Daniel up out of the den. So Daniel was taken up out of the den, and no injury whatever was found on him, because he believed in his God.*

Daniel 6:20-23

Reflect and Respond

Certain stories in the Bible stand out as added proof that there is, most certainly, a God in heaven. I think of Moses parting the Red Sea, the three boys saved from a fiery furnace, miraculous healings, and the ultimate demonstration—the Resurrection of Jesus Christ. The story of Daniel found in Daniel 6 is one of those stand-out examples of God's power. Surely Daniel lived every single day with all confidence that not only is there a God in heaven, but God's presence is in the earth. He is real and powerful, operating in the lives of those who seek Him.

Daniel was certain that God could make a way for him. He had unwavering confidence in the power of God. Daniel was a man of noble lineage, but more than that, he was a man of noble character. Daniel was a brilliant man who had found

favor with God and kings because of his excellent character and keen ability to conduct himself in governmental matters. Because he was a great man before his God, God exalted him before men. King Darius appointed Daniel as one of his three administrators who would supervise the chief administrators throughout the kingdom. In fact, King Darius was so impressed with Daniel's integrity and dedication that he planned to put Daniel over the affairs of the entire kingdom of Babylon. Clearly, this was a man of incredible integrity and character.

Of course, when one person flies up the ladder of success, there will always be those who swarm at the bottom, stewing in jealousy and envy. That's what happened to Daniel. Jealous because of Daniel's promotion and favor, the other administrators and officials tried to dig up dirt concerning Daniel's character. They thought they could expose a scandal or trip him up in some way. Unfortunately for them, they came up with nothing against him.

Read Daniel 6:5. When they ran out of ideas, what did Daniel's accusers decide to use against him?

Can you see that no ground is sacred to your enemies? These evil men conspired against Daniel and convinced King Darius to issue a law and enforce it, saying that anyone who prays to any god or man, except the king, would become dinner for a den of lions. Daniel, a man of lionhearted valor, would rather have disobeyed the king's edict than dishonor his God.

Daniel was a man of great power, because he was a man of great prayer. Even after the edict had been decreed, Daniel not only defied the decree; he did so openly and with the same fervor he had always demonstrated.

Read Daniel 6:10. What did Daniel do—and how often?

Daniel continued to pray three times daily with his window open toward Jerusalem, his homeland. He even fashioned a room in his home for this act of devotion. Daniel was not ashamed of his godly heritage, and he was not ashamed of his God. If he couldn't be at home in Jerusalem to worship, he would at least open up a window and look in that direction. No doubt, his accusers heard him praying through his open window and determined to put an end to him.

Here is a man who wanted to do right by pleasing God with his life. But his enemies saw to it that Daniel would put his life on the line for what he believed. He demonstrated that just because we are living for God doesn't mean that everything is always going to go smoothly in life. After all, hundreds of years later, just outside that same city of Jerusalem, Jesus would be brutally beaten and nailed to a Roman cross—and He did nothing wrong. What makes us think we can escape unscathed?

Why do you think we often feel that life should go more smoothly for those who live for God?

What perspective do we gain from considering the life of Jesus?

After Daniel defied the king's decree, his enemies went straight to the king and pressured the king to follow through with sentencing. The king wanted to rescue Daniel, but in accordance with the law of the land, the decree could not be annulled.

What does Daniel 6:16-17 tell us that the king did next?

Daniel was sentenced to the lions' den, and into the den he went! The king even covered the entrance of the den with a large stone and sealed it with his ring. After spending a restless night in the palace, the king rushed to the lions' den the next morning to find out what had become of Daniel.

Reread Daniel 6:20-22. What did the king discover, and what explanation did Daniel give for this miraculous outcome?

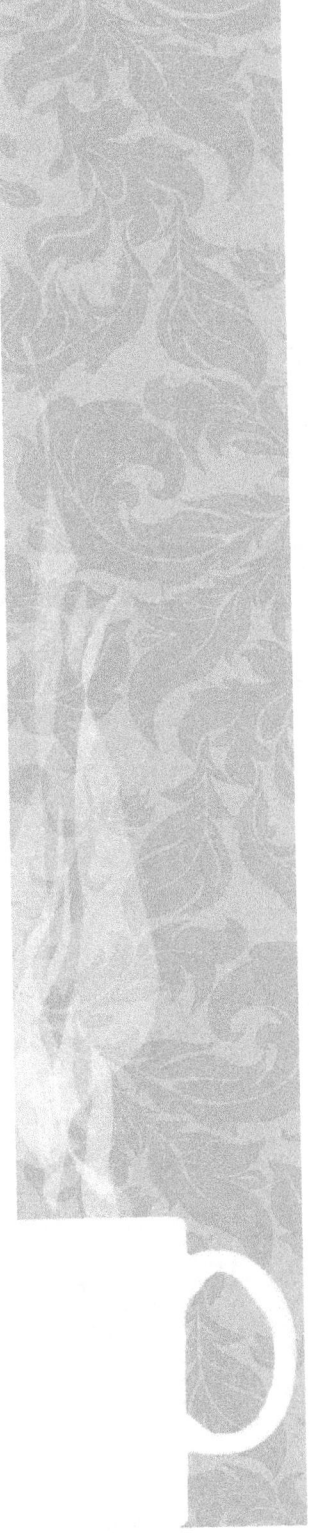

Daniel survived a night in the lions' den without so much as a kitten's scratch. How is that possible? God shut the mouths of the lions!

We see in the remaining verses of chapter 6 that the king decreed that all the people of his kingdom must revere the God of Daniel. And as for Daniel, he was hailed as a celebrity. The king admired him, the people applauded him, and God honored him. His confidence in the power of his God not only saved his life but also led other people to know and love this all-powerful God!

Let's revisit Daniel 6:5 and look a little more closely at this verse. Daniel's accusers couldn't find anything to fault him except his relationship with his God. What a testimony! Can your naysayers say of you, *"The only problem with that woman is her relentless faith in God"*? I don't know about you, but when my enemies examine my life, I want them to find a woman who unequivocally puts God first! Oh, how this girl longs to be a person of incredible faith like Brother Daniel—a person of great character and integrity, loyal to God and possessing an unwavering love for God no matter the cost.

Skim Daniel 4–6 and list words that describe Daniel's character. Then circle those characteristics you've listed that you would like to work on in your own life.

Now consider your witness. What would your "accusers" find to bring against you? Would they have to use a last resort by going after your relationship with God?

Write a few thoughts about how this story is speaking to you today.

God's power is a predominant theme of Daniel's story. Read the following Scriptures and write down any insights you gain from each related to gaining confidence in God's power.

Isaiah 40:28-31

Ephesians 1:19

Ephesians 3:20-21

Philippians 4:13

2 Timothy 1:7

Friend, do you see how wonderful it can be to put our full confidence in God's great power? God's great power is what we need when we face the "lions' den" situations in our lives. God's power in us is exactly what we need when we face trials of every kind.

Now, let me suggest that Daniel might have had cause to be a little full of himself. Reading about him reveals that lesser men might have fallen prey to egotism and self-centeredness. He was loved, revered, handsome, and successful. He was somewhat of a political celebrity—that is, until he climbed the ladder just a little too high for his colleagues' comfort. Then he became a target.

Imagine how a person might struggle with a desire to take all of the accolades without ascribing any praise to God. Imagine Daniel walking out of the lions' den and claiming the credit for God's powerful act. The story would be much different, wouldn't it? But we do that sometimes. We forget that it is God's strength on which we rely—not our own. God's power in us is what saves us from our enemy's schemes. Our confidence is not in our own power or might but in God's alone. God's strength in us is perfect when our strength is gone. I don't know about you, but any confidence I have in myself is only due to my total confidence in the mighty God I serve.

Our confidence is not in our own power or might but in God's alone. God's strength in us is perfect when our strength is gone.

Go to God

Ask

Daniel's confidence in God's great power gave him assurance when trouble knocked on his door. It was as if the whole world was against him, but because God was for him, he prevailed. I'm wondering what your lions' den situation is right now. What fears, doubts, or sins are prowling around your heart, ready to attack? Ask God to search your heart and reveal those things right now.

What are the "lions" that threaten your confidence in God?

Seek

When Daniel heard of the king's decree that his people should pray only unto him, Daniel ran to his God. He didn't do it to make a stand or a statement. He ran to God in prayer because that is what he did every day, several times a day, and this day would be like every other. He sought God and had all confidence that God would be with him, no matter what came his way.

Friend, as you face your trials today, run into the arms of your heavenly Father. He cares for you so very much.

How can you actively pursue a deeper trust in God's power to keep and sustain you?

Knock

Confess to God any lack of trust you carry. Commit to total confidence in God's power right here and now.

> *Most gracious and heavenly Father,*
> *I have not always trusted You with my whole heart. At times I have lacked confidence in Your ability to lead me and taken matters into my own hands. I want to have every confidence in Your love for me, Your power in my life, and Your protection over me. Help me to seek and trust You like Daniel did. In Jesus' precious name I pray. Amen.*

Day 3: Confidence in God's Presence

Read God's Word

25Then King Darius wrote:

To all peoples, nations, and languages that dwell in all the earth:

Peace be multiplied to you.

26I make a decree that in every dominion of my kingdom men must tremble and fear before the God of Daniel.

> *For He is the living God,*
> *And steadfast forever;*
> *His kingdom is the one which shall not be destroyed,*
> *And His dominion shall endure to the end.*
> *27He delivers and rescues,*
> *And He works signs and wonders*
> *In heaven and on earth,*
> *Who has delivered Daniel from the power of the lions.*

28So this Daniel prospered in the reign of Darius and in the reign of Cyrus the Persian.

Daniel 6:25-28

Reflect and Respond

Our Scripture reading today tells the ending of the story of Daniel in the lions' den, which we began yesterday. Daniel's confidence in God and God's faithfulness to deliver Daniel from the lions led King Darius not only to believe in God but also to decree that his entire kingdom must worship God alone. The king boldly declared the proof of his new knowledge that there is a God in heaven. His proof was that God rescued Daniel right before his eyes.

Friend, I hope that you will come to know God like Daniel knew God. The heart of the matter is that God is looking for people with a strong confidence in Him. He is searching all over for people who not only believe *in* Him but also *believe* Him and will keep on believing Him no matter what circumstances they may face. He's looking for you, dear friend. Have you opened wide the window of your heart to look His way? He's searching for someone He can depend on no matter what may come.

Recall King Asa's story from Day 1. What were the words Asa heard in 2 Chronicles 16:9?

"For the eyes of the LORD run to and fro throughout the whole _____, to show Himself strong on behalf of those whose _____ is _____ to Him." **(NKJV)**

Daniel's heart was completely God's. He had every confidence that God was with him no matter what would come his way. As I look at Daniel's life, there's so much to learn. First, I will never discount the power of God's presence. No matter how deep my pit of despair may be, I know that the arm of God's grace is longer still. Second, no matter how many times people let me down, God will always lift me up. And finally, when I find myself staring at a mountain of problems, God reminds me that He is with me and that there's no problem or situation He can't handle. There's no relationship problem, no financial challenge, no health struggle, and no personal battle that God can't overcome.

God is so awesome that He is beyond our comprehension.

Read Isaiah 55:8-9. What do these verses tell us about God's thoughts and ways?

"For My thoughts are not your thoughts, Nor are your ways My ways," says the LORD. "For as the heavens are higher than the earth, So are My ways higher than your ways, And My thoughts than your thoughts." Isaiah 55:8-9

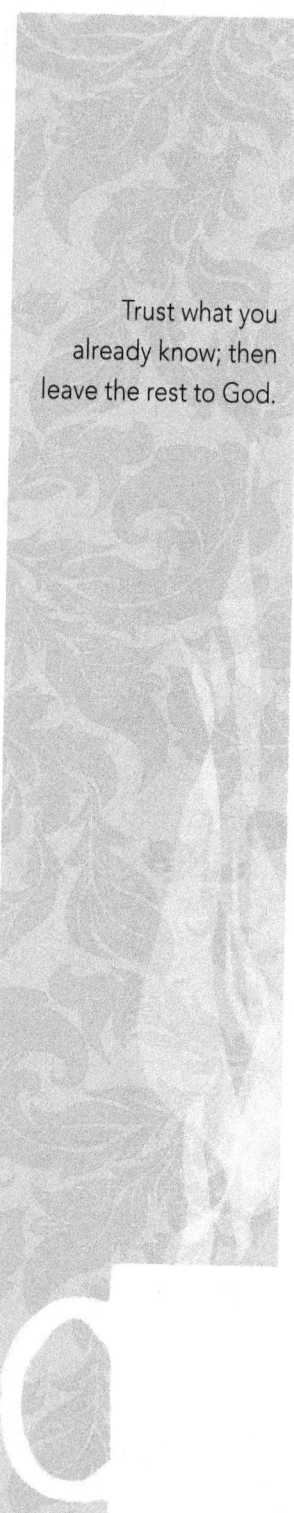

Let me encourage you not to trip up on the things you don't know. Sometimes we let the stuff we don't know occupy too much of our thought process. You might be worried about your job. You may be concerned if you'll qualify for a home loan or if your car will make it to work. You might be stressed, worrying if the kids will get over their colds or how you'll pay the taxes. We worry way too much about the things we don't know. Too often we speculate and theorize and even play out imaginary scenarios in our minds over what *might* happen. Well, what might happen and what the Lord plans are two totally different things. Remember, God is in control and is present with you through whatever happens. Believe that. Trust in what you already know; then leave the rest to God.

Look again at our opening verses from Daniel 6:25-28 to complete the following statements. Claim each one as a promise.

He is the _____ _____ . (v. 26)

God is _____ forever. (v. 26)

His kingdom shall not be _____. (v. 26)

His dominion shall _____ to the _____ . (v. 26)

He _____ and _____. (v. 27)

He works _____ and _____ in heaven and on earth. (v. 27)

He delivered Daniel from the _____ of the _____. (v. 27)

Daniel's confidence in God's power and presence led King Darius to decree that all the people in his kingdom would worship Daniel's God. Daniel's confidence in God led an unbelieving king to love God and declare that God be worshiped, and it serves as a wonderful witness to us as well.

A similar story of confidence in God is found just a few chapters earlier in the Book of Daniel and involves Daniel's friends Shadrach, Meshach, and Abednego. The story has characteristics similar to Daniel's story and is yet another example of God's presence with us through thick and thin.

Read Daniel 3. Compare the story of the three friends to Daniel's story by completing the chart on the next page. (Review yesterday's reading and Daniel 6 as necessary.)

	Shadrach, Meshach & Abednego	Daniel
Social/Political status		
Decree from the king		
Response to the decree		
Consequence of their response		
God's miraculous act		
Result of God's action		

As you can see, the experience the three friends had in the furnace is somewhat similar to Daniel's experience in the lions' den. All of them were leaders. All of them fell victim to the manipulation of jealous peers. All of them chose obedience to God over loyalty to the king. All of them faced dire consequences. All of them witnessed God's rescuing presence and power in miraculous ways.

I want to point out something. With Daniel in the lions' den, God demonstrated His presence by shutting the mouths of the lions. King Darius didn't see God with his eyes, but he attributed Daniel's safety to God. For the three boys in the furnace, however, God demonstrated His presence in another way.

Read Daniel 3:25 and fill in the blanks below:

"Look! I see _____ men, unbound, walking around inside the fire, and they aren't hurt! And the fourth one looks like one of the _____." **(NIV)**

King Nebuchadnezzar noticed a fourth figure in the furnace. God was with these young men right there in the furnace! Here is an example of God's presence in such a time of trial. God was visible as a fourth "person" in the fire.

You know, I have experienced trials in my own life when God has shown up in mighty way. I may not have seen Him with my eyes, but His nearness has bee unmistakable. His presence in those times has brought me the confidence I no have in Him.

I want you to experience God's promise of His presence, just as H promised to the prophet Isaiah. Write your name in each of the blank below and read the verses aloud so that your ears can hear the promise.

But now, says the LORD—
the one who created you, _____,
the one who formed you, _____:
Don't fear, for I have redeemed you;
   I have called _____ by name;
   _____ [is] mine.
When _____ pass[es] through the waters,
   I will be with _____;
   when through the rivers,
      they won't sweep over _____.
When _____ walk[s] through the fire,
   _____ won't be scorched
   and flame won't burn _____....
Don't fear,
   I am with _____.

                                    Isaiah 43:1-2, 5 CEB

Now read Psalm 139:1-18. Where can you go to escape God?

What is your response to God's promise to be present in your life?

I hope you are experiencing God's very real power and presence in your life right now. I pray that you will gain more and more confidence in God as we study His Word together. So, how do you increase your confidence in God? I'd like to suggest three don'ts and dos.

   1. Don't confuse facts and feelings; ground your faith in the truth. Sometimes you might be tempted to base your facts on your feelings, but you should always base your feelings on the facts. A fact is something that is true, and as Christians we believe that God's Word and God's Living Word, Jesus Christ, reveal what is true. So, we can *be* confident in our faith without always *feeling* confident. We can even make a mistake and still have the confidence to start over, because our confidence is not in ourselves but in Christ. You can fall flat on your face and still have the confidence in the Lord to get up and try again. You may have a question, but you can remain confident in faith as you look for answers, knowing that God has all the answers you need. Confident faith does not come as a result of your success; it comes from knowing the Lord.

Read Isaiah 33:6. What reasons do you find in this verse for placing your confidence in God?

2. Don't get caught up in what other people are doing; stay focused on God's plan for your life. Be careful not to allow the successes of others to distract you from what God has called you to do. Becoming distracted is a sure way to become defeated. Stay focused on the assignment God has given you. Remember this powerful promise from God's Word: "So let's keep focused on that goal, those of us who want everything God has for us" (Philippians 3:15 *THE MESSAGE*).

What is God calling you to do at this time in your life? What can help you to stay focused on this assignment?

3. Don't make excuses for yourself; remember who you are—a child of God! You might say, "I'm too old." Not true! Daniel was over eighty years old when he was thrown to the lions. You could be thinking, "I'm too young." I beg to differ! You are never too young to be used by God. Mary the mother of Jesus was a young teenager when she gave birth to our Lord Jesus. You may say, "I'm different." You're not different; you're unique! There's much more value in being unique. You may say, "I'm just a mom" or "I'm just (fill in the blank)." You are not "just" anything! You are a child of God! You are valuable and precious to Him. He has a unique and beautiful plan for you. Proverbs 14:26 says, "In the fear of the LORD there is strong confidence, And his children will have refuge" (NASB).

How does remembering that you are a valued, protected child of God help to eliminate excuses and increase your confidence?

We can *be* confident in our faith without always *feeling* confident.

Don't confuse facts and feelings; ground your faith in the truth. Don't get caught up in what other people are doing; stay focused on God's plan for your life. Don't make excuses for yourself; remember who you are—a child of God! These three reminders will help you to avoid the pitfalls of doubt and grow in your confidence in God. God's Word always causes our faith to rise. Even as you take small steps, move in God's direction and put your faith into practice. You will find that your love for Christ will develop into a deeper, sweeter, more trusting relationship.

Go to God

Ask

Seek the Lord right now. Invite His presence into this moment. Give thanks to God for this time to be with Him. Ask the Lord to give you confidence in His loving presence every step of the way.

Seek

What keeps you from realizing more confidence in God? Pride? Fear? Doubt? Lack of faith?

List below the things that hold you back from all-out trust in God's providence, power, and presence. When you have your list, seek God's assurance to overcome each barrier, crossing out each word as you pray.

Knock

Confess any of those times when you have forgotten to look for and rely upon God's power and presence. Ask God to give you confidence like Daniel to stand boldly on the promises of God this week.

Heavenly Father,
Thank You for Your sweet presence that walks with me, leads me, comforts me, protects me, and guides me. Help me to put all my confidence in Your promises. You are truly awesome. In Jesus' name I pray. Amen.

Day 4: Confidence in God's Plan

Read God's Word

¹⁶*Now Laban had two daughters: the name of the elder was Leah, and the name of the younger was Rachel.* ¹⁷*Leah's eyes were delicate, but Rachel was beautiful of form and appearance.* ¹⁸*Now Jacob loved Rachel; so he said, "I will serve you seven years for Rachel your younger daughter."*

¹⁹*And Laban said, "It is better that I give her to you than that I should give her to another man. Stay with me."* ²⁰*So Jacob served seven years for Rachel, and they seemed only a few days to him because of the love he had for her.*

²¹*Then Jacob said to Laban, "Give me my wife, for my days are fulfilled, that I may go in to her."* ²²*And Laban gathered together all the men of the place and made a feast.* ²³*Now it came to pass in the evening, that he took Leah his daughter and brought her to Jacob; and he went in to her.* ²⁴*And Laban gave his maid Zilpah to his daughter Leah as a maid.* ²⁵*So it came to pass in the morning, that behold, it was Leah. And he said to Laban, "What is this you have done to me? Was it not for Rachel that I served you? Why then have you deceived me?"*

²⁶*And Laban said, "It must not be done so in our country, to give the younger before the firstborn.* ²⁷*Fulfill her week, and we will give you this one also for the service which you will serve with me still another seven years."*

²⁸*Then Jacob did so and fulfilled her week. So he gave him his daughter Rachel as wife also.* ²⁹*And Laban gave his maid Bilhah to his daughter Rachel as a maid.* ³⁰*Then Jacob also went in to Rachel, and he also loved Rachel more than Leah. And he served with Laban still another seven years.*

Genesis 29:16-30

> Like fabric in the hands of a tailor who cuts away everything that doesn't look like a dress, our Father molds and shapes us into His image, cutting away anything that doesn't resemble Him.

Reflect and Respond

Do your kids have your trademark brown eyes or dry sense of humor? Did they inherit your artistic ability or your love for sports? Have you ever looked at a family photo only to realize those striking inherited traits? I've seen them in my family for sure. I can trace those almond shaped eyes, those high cheekbones, and that perpetual widow's peak all the way back to my great-grandfather. I can see inherited traits in the family of others too. Where I live, folks say that children "take after" their parents.

The same can be said of us and our resemblance to our Father God. Like fabric in the hands of a tailor who cuts away everything that doesn't look like a dress, our Father molds us and shapes us into His image, taking away anything that

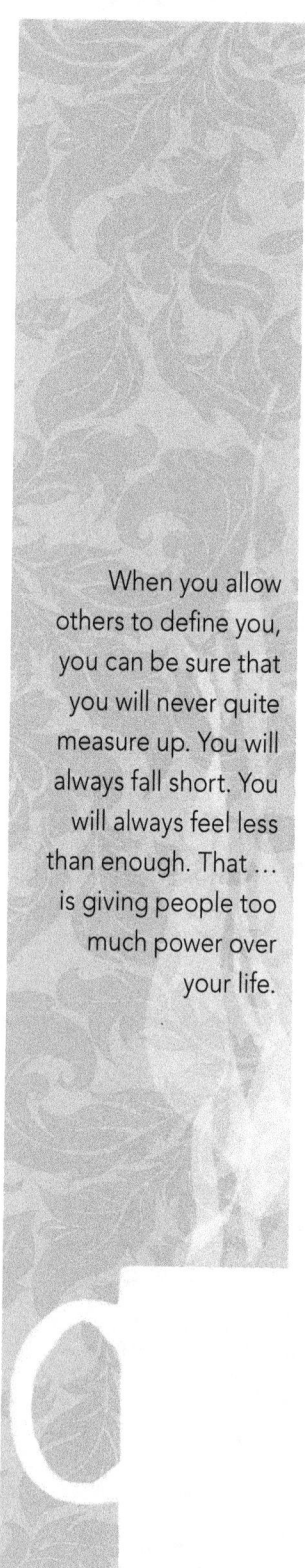

doesn't resemble Him. There is something we possess as humans that separates us from all of God's other creatures. God made us with the ability to relate to Him and others on a spiritual level. We bear His mark by virtue of the fact that we have a changed nature. His plan for us is that we begin to "take after Him" in the way we act, by the words we say, through our personality, by the love we share, and through our ability to worship Him. Others are sure to say, "No doubt about it. She's a child of God."

So, who are you deep down on the inside? Who do you resemble? Far too often, this question is difficult to answer because we tend to allow other people to become our point of reference. I've made the mistake of comparing myself to others, or worse yet, granting people permission to define who I am instead of allowing God to define my identity. Have you permitted people to offer their opinions or to pass judgment, deeming you beautiful or not beautiful, acceptable or unacceptable, fit or unfit? The problem with this is that people's standards and opinions are constantly changing. It's a system that is set up for failure. When you allow others to define you, you can be sure that you will never quite measure up. You will always fall short. You will always feel less than enough. That, my friend, is giving people too much power over your life.

There is one dear sister in the Bible who was slow to realize the powerful truth that a strong identity and inner confidence comes from God and not from the validation of others. This dear one's name was Leah.

Review today's Scripture, Genesis 29:16-30. Then read Genesis 30:1-24. What are your thoughts about Leah after reading her story?

The Bible says in Genesis 29:17 that "Leah's eyes were delicate." Some Bible translations and references interchange *tender*, *delicate*, and *soft* in that verse. But other references use the words *weak* or *dull*, or say that her eyes "had no sparkle." One Bible reference uses the word *nice*. Now, no girl that I know ever considers the word *nice* a favorable compliment. Some have suggested that Leah, the older sister, was matronly and frumpy, a bit gawky, with lightly colored eyes. The name Leah means *weary*. Any way you look at it, she lacked an outer quality—those feminine features that we consider beautiful and desirable—compared to her younger sister, Rachel.

Rachel, on the other hand, was "beautiful of form and appearance" (Genesis 29:17). *THE MESSAGE* Bible says that she was "stunningly beautiful." She likely possessed lovely features, a beautiful countenance, and striking, penetrative eyes. If Rachel were living today, she'd likely be well-suited for Hollywood's silver screen. It's easy to imagine that every woman desired to be like her while every man wanted to be with her—especially this man named Jacob, Laban's nephew.

Sidebar: When you allow others to define you, you can be sure that you will never quite measure up. You will always fall short. You will always feel less than enough. That ... is giving people too much power over your life.

Jacob had recently arrived at his Uncle Laban's home, and his heart was set on having Rachel as his wife from the moment he laid eyes on her. It seemed like a match made in heaven. The Hollywood beauty and the new kid on the block seemed perfect for each other. But we know that when relationships are based on outward appearances, the love affair is teetering on shaky ground. For Jacob, it was love at first sight. He would stop at nothing until the day that Rachel would become his bride.

Laban seemed to like the idea of having a robust, good-looking son-in-law for his daughter, and it didn't hurt that he had a strong back to help with the herds. The two men agreed. Jacob would work for Laban for seven years.

When that seven-year stint was complete, it was time for Jacob and Rachel to be married. So Jacob said to his father-in-law, "Give me my wife so that I may sleep with her" (Genesis 29:21 NLT). In those days it was customary on the evening of the wedding that the heavily veiled bride was brought into the darkened bridal chamber and presented to her husband.

I imagine that all the wine Jacob drank at the marriage banquet must have gone to his head, for surely if he had been sober he would have been aware of Laban's bait and switch. Certainly he would have distinguished some kind of difference between Leah and Rachel. Jacob had been engaged to Rachel for seven years and was smitten by her in every way. So even in the dark of night a man who was deeply in love should have recognized his own wife's voice.

Then Jacob also went in to Rachel, and he also loved Rachel more than Leah.
Genesis 29:30a

It leaves you to wonder if Leah was a willing co-conspirator in this charade. Imagine her whispers of sweet nothings into Jacob's ear at the risk of being discovered. Being the oldest daughter and yet unmarried, it's quite possible that Leah was just as excited to seize the moment as her father was. Dishonesty and trickery seem to have worked their way all through both sides of this dysfunctional family. After all, Jacob had tricked his brother Esau out of his birthright years before. (You can read that story in Genesis 25:29-34 and Genesis 27.)

So, when Laban tricked Jacob, Jacob got a taste of his own medicine! The sordid details are the makings of a television miniseries. Either way, the marriage was consummated, but it wasn't until the next morning and the effects of much wine had worn off that Jacob realized he had not slept with Rachel. Instead, he had taken Leah as his bride.

Jacob was furious! Reluctantly, he agreed to work for Laban seven more years to have Rachel. At the conclusion of Leah's bridal week, Laban gave Rachel to Jacob as his wife. It was culturally acceptable in those days, so Jacob became the husband of two wives at the same time.

Read Genesis 29:30a in the margin. Who did Jacob love more?

Thus began the battle between the sisters. These two women, having to share the same husband, found themselves in a head-to-head competition for the man they both loved. However, Leah found herself in a painstaking position—having to fight to win the affections of a man who loved her sister more.

One way to get Jacob to love her, Leah thought, was to give him children. In the Hebrew culture, parents would pray and ask God for just the right name—a name that would typify the kind of life they envisioned that child would lead. This is very significant as we look closely at the names Leah gave her children.

Read Genesis 29:31-34 and fill in the meanings of the names of Leah's sons.

Leah's first son _____, **meaning** _____.

Leah's second son _____, **meaning** _____.

Leah's third son _____, **meaning** _____.

What do you think is the significance of the names Leah chose for her sons?

Can you hear the cries of rejection from Leah's heart? Real rejection is when you love a man but he doesn't love you back. Real rejection is when you conjure up the nerve to say *I love you* only to be left hanging. Real rejection is when you spend your money, time, and heart only to come up empty. That is what it means to be dissed—disrespected, disregarded, disenchanted, and dismissed. I'd say this could do damage to a woman's confidence and cause her to question God's plan. I can imagine Leah's frustrated words to Jacob just before bed.

"Hey, Jake! What am I, chopped liver? I cook your meals. I'm a great wife and mother. I give you plenty of good lovin'. I give you many sons to bear your name. You could at least tell me you love me! What's up with this?"

Ever been there? Can you feel Leah's pain? More importantly, can you see a pattern here? I once heard that the definition of insanity is doing the same thing over and over again expecting different results.

Try as she might, Leah's efforts were futile. She grew weary of trying to win Jacob's love and approval. It was then that she came to the end of herself. Sister Leah finally heard the wake-up call. But it was not too late. When God is in the picture, it's never too late! Leah had a fourth son.

Look up Genesis 29:35 to discover his name.

Leah's fourth son _____, **meaning** _____.

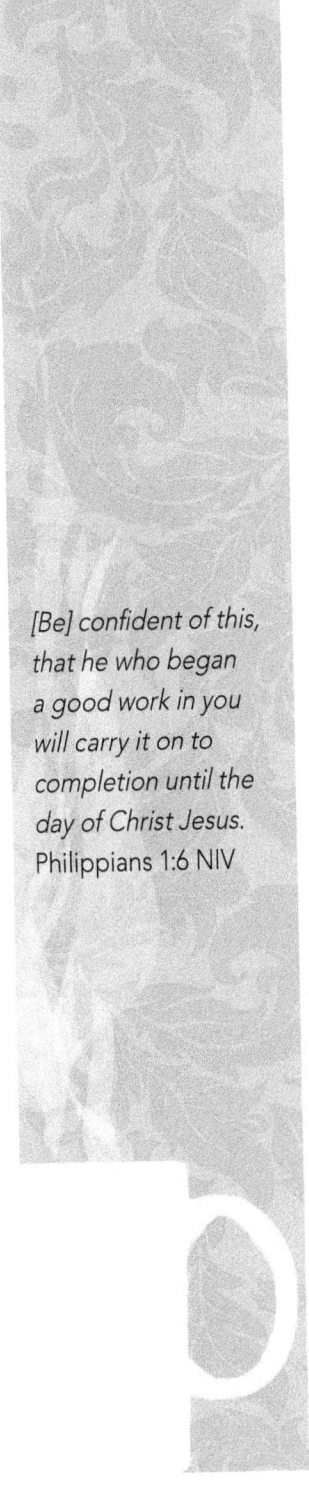

So what can we take away from this saga of two sisters?

First, there is always a danger when we compare. I know what it feels like to compare yourself to others. I've tried to sing like other singers and write songs like other writers. But I've found that when I try to be someone else, I lose myself and dishonor God. I've learned that just being myself is far better than trying to be a replica of someone else.

Yes, Rachel was the beautiful one, but it was Leah, not Rachel, who gave birth to Judah, through whose bloodline our Savior, Jesus, came. After giving birth to Judah, Leah praised the Lord and stopped trying to bear children.

There is confidence in your heart when you stop comparing yourself to everyone else and decide that you are going to be happy with yourself—with the person God has made you to be and the plan He has for your life.

Read Psalm 28:7. According to this verse, what are the results of trusting God?

I want to have a heart that greatly rejoices and leaps for joy! I want to be so taken with my Savior and so focused on His plan for my life that I am not distracted by what others are doing. As the psalmist says, this attitude fills us with songs of praise.

Second, it is always detrimental when we compete. God has something wonderful in store for you—a plan that is just for you. What God has for you, no one can take away from you. Though Leah was in some ways despised by her husband, she was highly regarded by God. She later had two more sons (and a daughter), and her sons would represent six of the twelve tribes of Israel. We can learn a great lesson from Leah. Don't waste time trying to compete with others. The only person who can stop your progress is *you.* Cease your striving and anxiety. Rest in the promise that God has something wonderful in store for you.

Read Philippians 1:6 in the margin. What does this verse promise?

God will not leave you stranded, to go it alone. He won't let you slip between the cracks or forget about your circumstances. You are God's very own, uniquely created to express His love on the earth.

Third, there is always a downside when we compromise. You always come out on the losing end when you sell out or lower your standards. God will never require you to compromise the truth of His Word. Nor will He ever ask you to compromise your integrity, your character, or your personal value.

[Be] confident of this, that he who began a good work in you will carry it on to completion until the day of Christ Jesus.
Philippians 1:6 NIV

With God's help, we can walk in a way that is pleasing to God. The Ne Living Translation of Philippians 2:13 expresses it so well: "For God is workir in you, giving you the desire and the power to do what pleases him." When w invite and allow God to work in us, we do what pleases Him and bring respe to ourselves.

Just as God had a plan for Leah, God has a plan for each of us. His desire that you would "take after Him" and show the world that you are His child. Yo can know for sure that there is a God who is on your side, leading and guidin you every step of the way!

> God has a plan for each of us. His desire is that you would "take after Him" and show the world that you are His child.

Go to God

Ask

Reflect on the word *confidence*. Have you let your trust in God slip? Is there pull toward old ways of thinking or behaving? Are you struggling with doubts o issues you settled awhile back? This is your moment to pray about these things.

Seek

Our adversary originated identity theft. Your enemy has been stealing the identities of countless people since the beginning of time and is on a mission tc steal everything that is near and dear to your heart, starting with your dedicatior to God. Seek the Lord today. Are there any areas in your life where comparison, competition, or compromise have crept in? Submit those areas to the Lord.

Knock

Starting now, celebrate the fact that your identity comes as a result of the fin-ished work of Jesus Christ. "So if anyone is in Christ, there is a new creation: everything old has passed away; see, everything has become new!" (2 Corinthians 5:17 NRSV). Determine that you will not think like the world, talk like the world, or act like the world. Rejoice in the fact that you resemble your heavenly Father. As you encounter others, allow the fragrance of Christ to linger where you are.

> Most gracious Father,
> As I linger in Your presence, I realize that everything I need, You already have. My salvation in Christ, the answers to my questions, my gifts and talents, my confidence and identity—all are found in You. I know You want only what is best for me. Give me a clear picture of anything that prohibits me from being my best for You. Thank You for equipping me with confidence for the journey. With You, I am ready for anything. In the name of Jesus I pray. Amen.

Day 5: Confidence in God's One and Only Son

Read God's Word

¹Therefore, having been justified by faith, we have peace with God through our Lord Jesus Christ, ²through whom also we have access by faith into this grace in which we stand, and rejoice in hope of the glory of God. ³And not only that, but we also glory in tribulations, knowing that tribulation produces perseverance; ⁴and perseverance, character; and character, hope. ⁵Now hope does not disappoint, because the love of God has been poured out in our hearts by the Holy Spirit who was given to us.

⁶For when we were still without strength, in due time Christ died for the ungodly. ⁷For scarcely for a righteous man will one die; yet perhaps for a good man someone would even dare to die. ⁸But God demonstrates His own love toward us, in that while we were still sinners, Christ died for us. ⁹Much more then, having now been justified by His blood, we shall be saved from wrath through Him. ¹⁰For if when we were enemies we were reconciled to God through the death of His Son, much more, having been reconciled, we shall be saved by His life. ¹¹And not only that, but we also rejoice in God through our Lord Jesus Christ, through whom we have now received the reconciliation.

Romans 5:1-11

Reflect and Respond

This week we've considered the story of Asa, who showed us the importance of trusting God to take good care of us so that we can be confident of His loving providence. We visited Daniel as he faced a den of lions with all manner of courage, bravery, and assurance that God's presence and power would hold him fast and never, ever leave him. We saw how Jacob, Rachel, and Leah learned how important it is to trust God's plan, even when things don't go the way we hoped they would. And now, we are here at the end of our first week together to claim our confidence in Christ.

To wrap up this week of study, I want to bring it all back to Jesus. The reason we can know God at all is because He came to earth to know us, love us, save us, and be with us. Our confidence doesn't come from ourselves. No, dear one, our confidence comes from Christ alone. We will never grow in our faith in God by relying on our own will or strength. By walking with God through the joys and trials of life, we come to know Him in a greater way and experience His goodness more and more. As a result, our confidence in God grows as He gives us more faith in Him.

I want you to know and claim that there is a great God in heaven who loves you and pursues you. He sent His Son, Jesus, to die for you and to rise again for you. And Jesus is coming back for you. If you want to know what this God in heaven is all about, then look to Jesus. Would you endeavor to know God intimately through a personal relationship with Jesus Christ? Will you take Him at His Word without wavering?

You can be certain that there is a God in heaven, and in Him we can be confident. Long before the foundation of the world was laid, this God—the One and Only True God—knew that you would need a steadfast, unshakable faith to navigate the rough terrains of life. He knew that putting faith in temporal things such as people, money, or things would only set you up for disappointment. He knew your heart would hunger for an assurance that money can't buy. He knew that you would be desperate to know the answers to real questions about your faith and His plan for your life. He also knew you would struggle with the deeds of your past, the challenges of today, and the doubts you have about the future.

Before He hung the moon against the midnight sky and flung every star into space, He knew you and saw you standing on the other side of a brand new century with an insatiable hunger to know a love that no human can satisfy. He saw you with a keen desire to live a life of significance filled with joy and peace that this world knows nothing of. He has known all along who you are, including your greatest fears and your deepest longings. The Lord has heard the cry of your heart and the questions you've been asking. The God who counts every star and knows them all by name knows *your* name, and He wants you to know that in His name, the name of Jesus, every question finds an answer.

While the possibility is great that you don't know the answer to every question you may be facing, God does. You probably don't even know all the right questions to ask, but God knows that too. And He sent the answer to all of life's quandaries in the form of a personal Savior named Jesus. He not only is able to give you confidence in Him; He *is* confidence personified.

Read Proverbs 18:10 and fill in the blanks below.

The name of the LORD *is a fortified* _____; *the righteous run to it and are* _____. **(NIV)**

When you know Jesus, the answers you need in life are just a prayer away. And when the answers are slow in coming, Jesus proves to be all you need while you wait. Remember, you don't need to know *what* when you know *Who*.

If ever a passage was written to give us confidence in Christ, it is Romans 5:1-11. The apostle Paul wrote this masterpiece to declare that through Jesus Christ

> The Lord has heard the cry of your heart and the questions you've been asking. The God who counts every star and knows them all by name knows *your* name, and He wants you to know that in His name, the name of Jesus, every question finds an answer.

e have peace with God. Paul confirms that through Jesus Christ we are recon-
led to God and have all assurance and confidence in Him. In fact, he claims
at we can be confident even in times of trial because Jesus has won our victory.

**Romans 5:1-11 reads like a declaration of confidence in God. Taking each
verse one at a time, write the passage below in your own words.**

According to this passage, what reason do we have to boast?

How can we rejoice in our suffering?

How does our suffering change us?

In what ways does this passage give you confidence in Christ?

Would you claim confidence in Christ with me now? Read aloud the promises
below and on the following page, and commit to confidence in Christ as we close
our week together.

Jesus, our beautiful Savior . . .
He is every journey's new beginning.
He is the finish at every journey's destination.
He is the lamp at my feet and the light on my path.

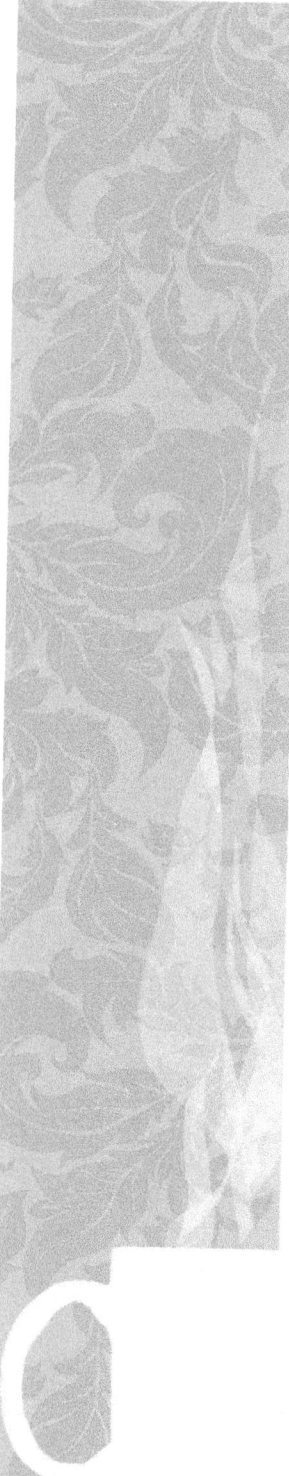

He is the landmark that always points the way homeward.

He is the strong tower, the cornerstone, and the firm foundation.

He is the Prince, the Super Star, the King, and the Rock who will never roll.

He is Lord of all, over all, in all, and through all. He is All in all. He knows a[l] And He knows me.

No one can ever make me doubt Him. I know too much about Him, and cannot live without Him.

Because I know Him, I will not be timid or tentative, shy or shamed, fearful c faint, hesitant or reticent.

Because Jesus lives large on the inside of me, I declare that I am confident. This I know for sure.

Go to God

Ask

Do you need extra confidence today? Have you found yourself doubting tha God could love you enough to send His only Son to die for you? Ask God to giv[e] you belief and cover you with assurance of His work in your life.

Seek

What trials are you experiencing even now that keep you from confidence? How does what you have read today speak into these situations?

Knock

What will you do today to live confidently in the promise that there is a God in heaven who is as close as the mention of His name?

Walk expectantly into your day—whatever comes—with all confidence that God has given you victory!

Most gracious Father,

As I saturate my mind with Your Word, I ask you to replace any trace of fear or despair with confidence and hope, for You are greater than any trial I might face. You are a loving Father, a mighty God, the Author of my life story, and the King of kings. Thank You for the awesome gift of Jesus Christ on my behalf. Thank You for paving the way for me to walk closely with You now and forevermore. In the name of Jesus I pray. Amen.

Week 1

Video Viewer Guide

"We shall not find any _____ *against this Daniel unless we find it against him concerning the* _____ *of his* _____*."*

Daniel 6:5 NKJV

Whenever you want to do something for _____, you're going to always have _____.

When you encounter opposition, you can _____ your ground, _____, and _____ God and His Word.

Daniel _____ with his whole _____ that there is a God in heaven who is much bigger, much _____ than any situation we might face.

We never know how our quiet act of _____ will _____ the lives of others.

Then King Darius wrote:

To all peoples, nations, and languages that dwell in all the earth:

Peace be multiplied to you.

I make a decree that in every dominion of my kingdom men must tremble and fear before the God of Daniel.

For He is the _____ God,

And steadfast forever;

His _____ is the one which shall not be destroyed

And His dominion shall endure to the end.

He _____ and _____.

And He works signs and wonders

In heaven and on earth,

Who has delivered Daniel from the power of the lions.

So this Daniel prospered in the reign of Darius and in the reign of Cyrus the Persian.

Daniel 6:25-28 NKJV

The heart of the matter is that God is looking for people that will have a _____ _____ in Him.

Week 2
I Am in God's Plan

As we begin the second leg of this road trip, let's recall what we hope to accomplish on this journey called *This I Know for Sure*. Our primary objective is twofold: 1) To know God more intimately through a growing personal relationship with Jesus Christ, and 2) To take God at His Word without wavering.

This week we turn our focus to another biblical assurance we can know for sure. Our second landmark of the faith is this: *I am in God's plan*. Friend, God has a specific blueprint for your life. He has taken the guesswork out of executing that plan by giving you His promise to lead you. You can't know every detail about tomorrow, but you *can* trust God because He's already there. He can see the intended destination for you, and He promises to get you there. You may as well exchange worry for anticipation and get ready to enjoy the ride of your life.

I hope you've packed light for this trip. God's Word is all you'll need. Hebrews 12:1 tells us to lay aside all encumbrances and run life's race with determination. Listen with intent to what it says in the New Century Version: "We are surrounded by a great cloud of people whose lives tell us what faith means. So let us run the race that is before us and never give up."

When you're running a race, it's no time for an "I think so" or "I hope so" kind of thinking. The same is true when it comes to running the race of life. If you want to run with endurance, you must have an "I know so" kind of faith. You need to know and believe with confidence that God loves you and has a plan for you that far exceeds your wildest dreams and imaginations. When you discover God's plan, your life will bring glory to Him.

I get excited when I read 1 Corinthians 2:9:

> *No eye has seen, no ear has heard,*
> *and no mind has imagined*
> *what God has prepared*
> *for those who love him. (NLT)*

You need only read the road map. The road map is God's Word! The truth we'll study this week will help to clarify God's plan for *you*!

Scripture Memorization

This week we will continue working to memorize our core Scripture verse for our journey, 2 Timothy 1:12. I'm convinced of this truth now more than ever.

I know whom I have believed, and am persuaded that he is able to keep that which I have committed unto him against that day. (KJV)

Continue using the index cards in visible places throughout the day. Remember that another great way to memorize this verse is to sing it (you can find an arrangement of the hymn "I Know Whom I Have Believed" on the DVD and companion music CD). Lift your voice in song this week as you declare your faith with these beautiful words!

Day 1: Trusting God's Plan

Read God's Word

[11]For I know the thoughts that I think toward you, says the LORD, thoughts of peace and not of evil, to give you a future and a hope. [12]Then you will call upon Me and go and pray to Me, and I will listen to you. [13]And you will seek Me and find Me, when you search for Me with all your heart. [14]I will be found by you, says the LORD, and I will bring you back from your captivity; I will gather you from all the nations and from all the places where I have driven you, says the LORD, and I will bring you to the place from which I cause you to be carried away captive.

Jeremiah 29:11-14

Reflect and Respond

My family loves to fish. When I was a child, my family spent many summer vacations fishing in the Great Lakes, rivers, and streams of Michigan and eastern Canada. It didn't matter if we fished from a boat, along the banks, or from a bridge. We fished in shallow streams and deep rivers, with live and artificial bait, with rods and reels and cane poles. We didn't get concerned if the fish weren't biting. We just found a different spot and kept fishing. Today it's a popular practice for sports fishermen to "catch and release." But that was not our practice. If it was big enough to keep, then it was big enough to eat.

On one vacation we took the family camper for a week of fishing in eastern Ontario, Canada. We arrived at the campsite by midday, and everyone was eager to pitch in and get the site set up before evening. Afterward, Dad and my Uncle Joe ventured out to find a grocery store to buy food, a few supplies, and fishing bait. When they hadn't returned by dusk, we all grew concerned. Eventually Dad and Uncle Joe returned after dark and immediately launched into their story.

On the way to the store, Dad and Uncle Joe enjoyed the view of the green, pristine Canadian landscape. The area around the campsite was densely wooded except for a nearby Native American burial ground and museum that featured the remains of chieftains and historical artifacts. They found the store, did some shopping, and were headed back to the campsite when they took a wrong turn along the way and found themselves lost. When they stopped at a gas station for some directions, neither my Dad nor Uncle Joe could remember the name of the campground, the road it was on, or the direction it was in. Frustrated, they didn't know what to do. Then the gas station owner asked a very key question.

"Can you remember any signs or landmarks you saw along the way?"

My Dad's face lit up as he retold the story. Dad, never off-duty from preaching or teaching and always seeing natural events from a spiritual perspective, said, "Oh yes, now I remember! Our campsite is near some dry bones!"

The gas station attendant recognized the description of the Native American burial ground and museum and sent them off in the right direction. That day, Dad's reference to "dry bones," a term found in Ezekiel chapter 37, was not just an Old Testament Bible story but a road map to his destination.

Have you ever ventured out with sketchy directions? If so, then you know how that is a setup for a setback. Without a well-thought-out plan, you'll find yourself going around in circles, wasting precious time, energy, and resources. Thank goodness my family members knew the value of stopping to ask for help.

The same is true in life. To reach your destination safely, you'll need personal assistance, a navigational aid, a road map, and some landmarks along the way to help you navigate the rough terrain and blind curves that lie ahead.

Reread Jeremiah 29:11. This verse is one of the most beautiful promises concerning God's plan for you. Write the verse below, inserting your name in place of "you." Take it in as a promise from God to you.

To give you the context for this verse, the Babylonians began to deport Jews to Babylon in the year 597 B.C. The prophet Jeremiah wrote a letter to those who were in exile to encourage them. When Jeremiah wrote this letter found in chapter 29, he was reminding God's people of some very important principles when searching for God's direction. He reminded them that times would change, people would change, and circumstances would change. But the principles from God's Word never change; they're still applicable to your life today.

Read 1 Peter 1:24 in the margin. How does this promise related to God's Word strengthen your faith?

Maybe you have found yourself in a certain situation, wondering how you got there or what God could possibly be doing in your life. It may feel hopeless, as if God has abandoned you. Imagine the exiles to whom Jeremiah wrote. They were God's chosen people. God had made a covenant with them. And still they were exiles, strangers in a foreign land. Instead of dashing in with heavenly armies or asking them to just hold tight for a while, God gave them some specific instructions through the prophet Jeremiah.

Read Jeremiah 29:1-14. What are the Lord's instructions in these verses?

v. 5:

v. 6:

v. 7:

God wasn't asking the exiles to wait it out. He was telling them to go about their lives—to plant, marry, build, become part of the city, and create beautiful surroundings. God was promising to be with them right there in the middle of their exile. He hadn't abandoned them in that situation. He wasn't turning His back on them. He was guiding and loving them right where they were.

The Lord told His people not to trust in their own strength but to trust Him for everything. As they continued on with the business of living, they saw God meeting all their daily needs, and their hope began to rise.

Remember this: As long as you have life and breath, you must *always* hope. You see, hope is not wishing on a star or waiting for a chance. Sometimes hope is

"All people are like grass, and all their glory is like the flowers of the field; the grass withers and the flowers fall, but the word of the Lord endures forever."
1 Peter 1:24 NIV

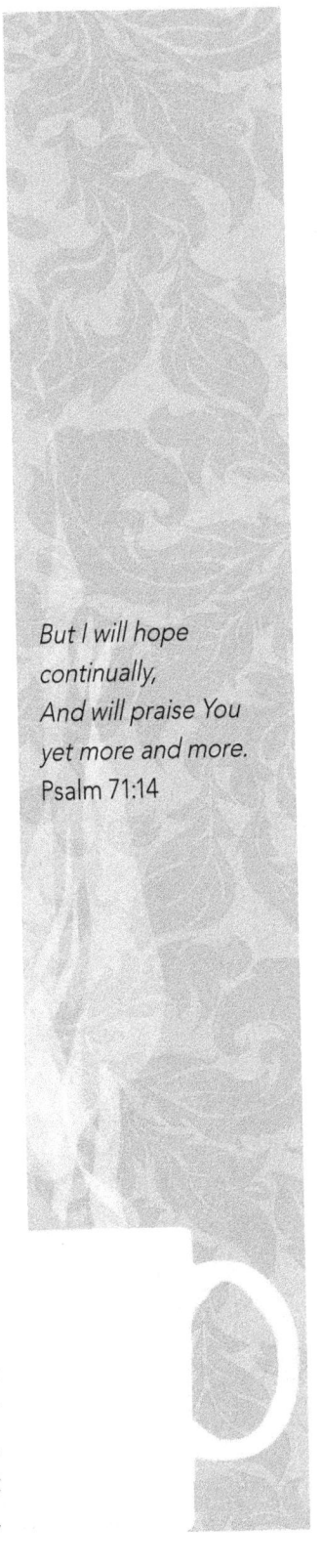

oing the hard thing, because doubting may be easier. Hope is a confident expectation of good. The Hebrew word for hope in Jeremiah 29:11 is *tiqvah*, which means "cord, things hoped for, expectation."[1] I love the idea of hope being like a ord. Hope is something we can hold on to; it ties us securely to what is expected. esus is that cord; He is our hope.

No matter how hard things get, believers in Jesus must always hold on to ope. Hope is the belief that the best is yet to come. Because of the hope we have Christ, we should never hear of a hopeless Christian. That is an oxymoron. he words *hopeless* and *Christian* are two contradictory terms. You have every eason to hope in Christ! You might say, "But, Babbie, the bottom has dropped ut of the economy, and I've got way too much month and not enough money." isten, dear one. Stand on what the Bible says, not what your paycheck says.

Look up Philippians 4:19 and write it here:

Your reply might be, "But, Babbie, I just got laid off from my job. It's all so discouraging. Sometimes I feel like just giving up." Let me challenge you again not to get distracted by what you see or feel.

Read Psalm 71:14 in the margin. What kind of response does this verse encourage?

But I will hope continually, And will praise You yet more and more. Psalm 71:14

Put yourself in the shoes of the exiles as you read the words from our opening Scripture passage, Jeremiah 29:11-14, again. What emotions would you have felt if you had been one of the exiles hearing these words?

How do these words speak to you today?

Are you persuaded that God's plan is the absolute best plan for you? Do you have faith to believe this truth without wavering? You know, God doesn't panic just because you are going through a situation that causes you to panic. You may say, "But God! Life is so hard for me right now! Don't You see me suffering? Hey, God! Are You even up there?" He responds in His still, small voice, "I know what I'm doing. I have it all planned out—plans to take care of you, not abandon you,

plans to give you the future you hope for" (Jeremiah 29:11 *THE MESSAGE*). Yo
see, dear friend, with God, nothing is ever wasted. What appears to be an obst.
cle is really an opportunity to see God at work in your life. Look at your situatio
through the eyes of hope and possibility. What was meant to set you back, Go
will use as a launching pad to propel you into the next level of your faith in Hin
If you are facing an adverse situation today, instead of allowing fear and panic t
overwhelm you, decide that you will place the situation into God's hands with
sense of expectation. You'll be amazed at how panic will be replaced with peac
and that peace will guard your heart and mind (Philippians 4:6-7).

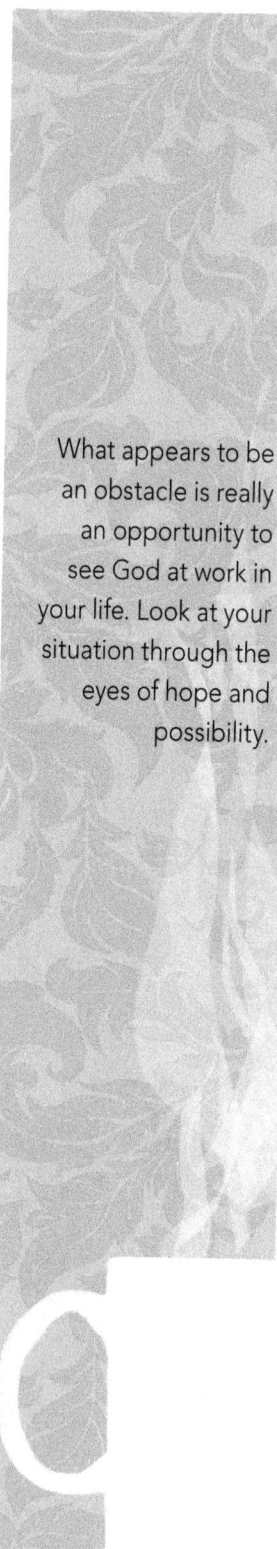

> What appears to be an obstacle is really an opportunity to see God at work in your life. Look at your situation through the eyes of hope and possibility.

Go to God

Ask

Talk to God about your fears and anxieties. Then, regardless of how you may
feel today, ask God to give you faith to believe the promise of Jeremiah 29:11
Reword the verse as a personal prayer, affirming your faith in God's good plans

Seek

Although you cannot see God, you may not feel God, and at times you may
not even see much evidence of Him working in your situation, you must know
that God *is* at work. Nothing can obstruct God's plan. Not people. Not things.
Not even hell itself can keep God's great plan for you from coming to pass. The
psalmist David cried out:

> *The LORD is my rock, my protection, my Savior. My God is my rock.*
> *I can run to him for safety. He is my shield and my saving strength,*
> *my defender.*
>
> 2 Samuel 22:2-3 NCV

Read those words again, and underline all the things God is for you.

What is God saying to you in these verses?

Knock

The Word of God tells us that there is no such thing as a hopeless situation.
There is no hopeless marriage, no hopeless financial problem, and no hopeless
health diagnosis. You can believe this truth from Romans 8:28: "And we *know*

hat all things work together for good to them that love God, to them who are the called according to his purpose" (KJV, emphasis added).

How does this message of hope speak into your current situation? What will your response be this week?

Dear Father in heaven,

Thank You for the great plan You have for me. You are the only One who can be trusted with all the details of life. Help me not to get distracted by the things along the periphery. That is a lesson in futility. I'm certain of this: as I release my stranglehold on life's steering wheel, You will guide me every step of the way. In Jesus' name. Amen.

Day 2: Getting Good Directions

Read God's Word

¹"Let not your heart be troubled; you believe in God, believe also in Me. ²In My Father's house are many mansions; if it were not so, I would have told you. I go to prepare a place for you. ³And if I go and prepare a place for you, I will come again and receive you to Myself; that where I am, there you may be also. ⁴And where I go you know, and the way you know." ⁵Thomas said to Him, "Lord, we do not know where You are going, and how can we know the way?" ⁶Jesus said to him, "I am the way, the truth, and the life. No one comes to the Father except through Me. ⁷If you had known Me, you would have known My Father also; and from now on you know Him and have seen Him." ⁸Philip said to Him, "Lord, show us the Father, and it is sufficient for us." ⁹Jesus said to him, "Have I been with you so long, and yet you have not known Me, Philip? He who has seen Me has seen the Father; so how can you say, 'Show us the Father'?"

John 14:1-9

Reflect and Respond

As a singer, conference speaker, and TV talk show host, I spend a great deal of time in my car. When Willie Nelson wrote the song "On the Road Again," he must have seen me waving to him from the passing lane. Before I walk out of

the door for a trip, I make sure I've got reliable directions in my hand. There's nothing more frustrating than having directions that don't make sense. The same is true in life. In order to stay the course, I have learned to trust that Jesus is the way and that God's Word will guide me, even during my darkest hour.

If you've ever heard me speak or read my book or Bible study *Embraced by God*, then you know I talk a lot about my dad, Reverend Willie G. Wade. Dad was the founding pastor of the Lily Missionary Baptist Church in Jackson, Michigan. I was hired as the church's full-time pianist and choir director at age nine, so you can imagine that Dad and I spent lots of time together. One of the saddest days of my life was March 4, 1986, the day Daddy passed away.

That Wednesday night, just before prayer meeting, Dad sat down and took his last breath. When I received the news, it was as if my heart had been ripped out. I actually felt as if there was a hole in my chest from the grief. But the Lord sustained me, and I realized that even though my dad was gone, my faith was not. As a matter of fact, my faith was strengthened because I have the hope that Dad is in heaven. He taught me that nothing is lost when you know where to find it.

You see, in order to know God's direction for your life, you must begin at the start. You'll only know God's best by first coming face-to-face with the fact that without direction, you'd be truly lost. Jesus said of Himself in John 14:6, "I am the way, the truth, and the life. No one comes to the Father except through Me." *THE MESSAGE* Bible puts it this way, "I am the Road, also the Truth, also the Life. No one gets to the Father apart from me."

Jesus is our starting point and the Way—the Road. With Jesus, a real, vibrant, and life-giving Christian walk is in store. Being a Christian is not about an obligatory visit to church on Sunday. Church pews are plenty filled with folks who go to church because of tradition or because it's the social thing to do. That's nothing more than cold, lifeless religion. There's so much more in store for you than that!

Jesus cares about every detail of your life—the mortgage, the laundry, the grocery list, your job, your bank account, the baby in diapers, and the kid in college. Jesus is concerned about all of it! And He wants to be involved in every aspect of your life, not just those things you decide to make Him a part of. So don't get caught up in dividing your life into "sacred" and "secular" compartments. For the believer, there should be no such thing as sacred thinking and secular thinking. There should be no such thing as your church life and the rest of your life. Jesus doesn't want you to come home from church and put your Christian life up on the shelf with your Bible. He wants you to put it to use! Everything is sacred when you live for Christ. Jesus wants to be Lord of all, or He is not Lord at all.

In what ways have you divided your life into "sacred" and "secular" compartments—whether now or in the past?

What does it mean to say that everything is sacred when you live for Christ?

Do you agree that Jesus is Lord of all or not Lord at all? Why or why not?

If Jesus is Lord of your life, you are never alone on the journey. On Day 1 we studied verses from Jeremiah 29, but I'd like to turn our attention to two verses from that chapter that we didn't focus on.

Read Jeremiah 29:12-13 in the margin. When do we find God? What are the expectations or requirements for finding God?

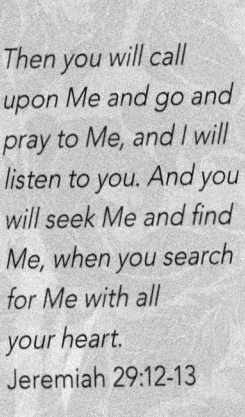

Then you will call upon Me and go and pray to Me, and I will listen to you. And you will seek Me and find Me, when you search for Me with all your heart.
Jeremiah 29:12-13

If we want to find our way in life, we must seek or search for God. The Hebrew word for seek in verse 13 is *baqash*, which means "to seek, require, desire, exact, request."[2] It conveys the idea of finding and securing something that is intensely desired or demanded. The Hebrew word used for search is *darash*, which means "to resort to, seek, seek with care, enquire, require."[3] It implies a persistent or frequent seeking, similar to an investigation. This is the way we are to seek God and God's direction for our lives.

The other day I asked my smartphone for directions. "Please give me directions to Augusta, Georgia," I said. The voice from the phone spoke with confidence: "I don't have directions to Thomas Gusta Sawyer." I had to laugh. But you see, my friend, the point is that you can seek directions from all kinds of sources, but you may or may not get the answer you need; any source other than the Lord may prove unreliable. But God always has the correct answer.

You may not know every detail. That's okay. Leave the details to the One who holds the future in His hands. This is where the rubber meets the road. The Lord promises to give you reliable directions every time!

Look with me at some Scriptures that teach us about getting good directions and having courage to closely follow our Guide.

Read Exodus 13:17-22. What was the reason behind God's choice of directions?

What signs did God use to guide the Israelites?

Read Psalm 25. What do verses 4-5 say about having good directions?

Read John 10:1-5. How do we know how to follow Jesus? (v. 3)

How do you think we get to know the voice of our Guide?

As we follow Jesus, our part is to listen to His familiar voice and let Him lead the way. Jesus' part is to faithfully guide us to our intended destination. As our trustworthy Guide, He commands that we not get discouraged, throw in the towel, and quit when times get tough. When it comes to life's challenges, I've learned this: it may not be okay right now, but it's going to be all right.

Read Psalm 37:25 and fill in the blanks:

I was young and now I am old, yet I have _____ seen the righteous _____ or their children begging bread. **(NIV)**

The psalmist David wrote these words. He surely saw trouble in his life, but he knew firsthand the faithfulness of God. Whatever it is you are facing right now, my friend, Jesus will take care of it. You can trust Him to guide you, to give you good directions forward, and to walk with you every step of the way.

Go to God

Ask

Are you troubled today? Are you bound to burdens that are too heavy to carry? Lay them at the feet of a trustworthy Travel Guide. He knows the way to peace, hope, and joy. Ask Him to guide you right now.

Seek

The Bible says in Isaiah 55:6, "Seek the LORD while He may be found, Call upon Him while He is near."

How are you seeking God as you learn to trust God's plan for your life?

Knock

What is keeping you from a real, vibrant faith in God? List the obstacles:

Ask God to guide you back to the only Road that is the Way, the Truth, and the Life. As you go through the week, believe with confidence that He will be faithful to do it!

Sweet Father,

I am so grateful that You have promised to lead me and guide me. Forgive me when I have become anxious and stepped out on my own. You are so patient with me, Lord! Each and every time, You lead me right back to Your path of righteousness and safety. This is where I find my hope and peace. Yes, this is where I belong. God, You are amazing! Thank You for Your great love for me. In Jesus' precious name. Amen.

Day 3: Standing for Truth

Read God's Word

[3]We give no offense in anything, that our ministry may not be blamed. [4]But in all things we commend ourselves as ministers of God: in much patience, in tribulations, in needs, in distresses, [5]in stripes, in imprisonments, in tumults, in labors, in sleeplessness, in fastings; [6]by purity, by knowledge, by longsuffering, by kindness, by the Holy Spirit, by sincere love, [7]by the word of truth, by the power of God, by the armor of righteousness on the right hand and on the left, [8]by honor and dishonor, by evil report and good report; as deceivers, and yet true; [9]as unknown, and yet well known; as dying, and behold we live; as chastened, and yet not killed; [10]as sorrowful, yet always rejoicing; as poor, yet making many rich; as having nothing, and yet possessing all things.

2 Corinthians 6:3-10

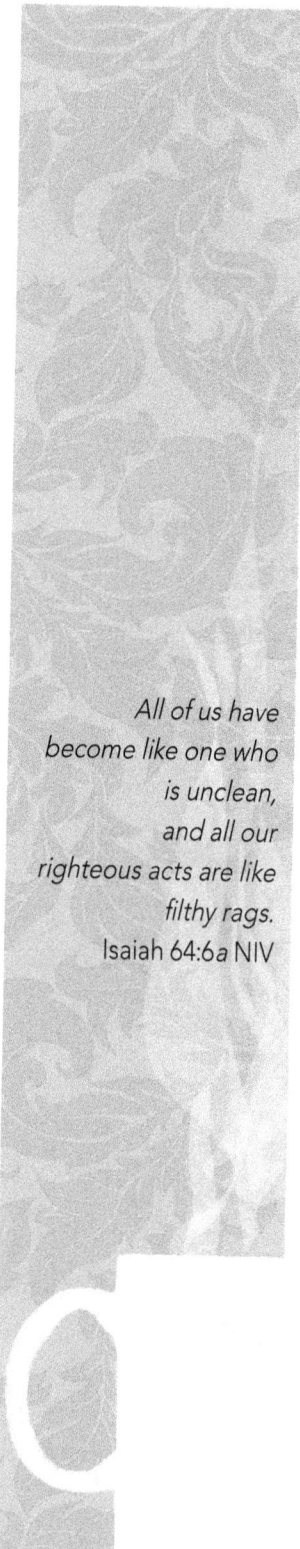

Reflect and Respond

This week we are exploring how we can know with confidence that we are in God's plan. God loves us and promises to fulfill His plan for our lives—and His plan far exceeds our wildest dreams and imaginations. We have seen that God will faithfully guide us on the right path. This is good news! When we seek Him and follow Him, we will discover God's plan for our lives. And as we stand on the truth of God's Word, living our lives with confident faith, we bring glory to God.

Think about this: when we stand *on* the truth, we are standing *for* truth. In other words, when we believe and live out God's Word, we become the living, breathing representatives of God. Let that sink in a moment.

There's a saying that the only Bible some people will ever read is your life. That's an eye-opening statement, isn't it? As humbling as that thought may be, the truth is that people are observing how we live and are continually forming impressions of us. Have you ever said of someone, "She's so sweet! I enjoy being around her"? Or what about this statement: "I can't put my finger on it, but there's something about him that concerns me"? You can learn much about a person's character by how he or she interacts with others. The same can be said of us: our true character is often revealed in the way we encounter other people.

The word *character* describes an individual's essential attributes or moral excellence. Your character is found at the base of your attitude and personality and describes the kind of person you really are. Every one of us has inherent character traits—for good or for bad. You are to be commended if your character is described as kind, patient, generous, faithful, honest, and loyal. And you know you've got work to do if you've ever been described as jealous, manipulative, contentious, conceited, or argumentative.

Let's face it: for the most part, we all possess some good and some not-so-good character traits. This is why we need to know Jesus. Without the power of Christ in our lives, our characters are desperately flawed.

Read Isaiah 64:6a in the margin. To what does this verse compare our best intentions and efforts?

Friend, we need Jesus! And the way we get to know Jesus is through God's Word. Studying the Scriptures to learn more about God and His character helps us to embrace the truth and apply it in our lives, becoming more and more like Jesus. As we do this, we are representing the God we follow, standing for Him in a world that is hungry to know the truth.

What is truth? That's a common question today. As Christians, we believe that God is truth. In Deuteronomy 32:4 we read,

> *He is the Rock, His work is perfect;*
> *For all His ways are justice,*
> *A God of truth and without injustice;*
> *Righteous and upright is He.*

In Jesus Christ, God's one and only Son, we have the embodiment of this God of truth.

Read John 14:6 and fill in the blank:

Jesus said to him, "I am the way, the _____, and the life." (NKJV)

Because God is truth, we can understand the nature of truth by understanding the nature of God.

What does each of the following verses tell us about the nature of God?

Malachi 3:6a

Hebrews 13:8

James 1:17

Every good and perfect gift is from above, coming down from the Father of the heavenly lights, who does not change like shifting shadows.
James 1:17 NIV

These verses tell us that God is unchanging. Because God, who is unchanging, is truth, it follows that truth is unchanging. Truth is firm, faithful, and factual. It is absolute, not obsolete. It is not subjective or based on opinion. It is not biased, prejudiced, or outdated. Truth is objective; it is impartial, fair, just, and based on facts. God is truth, and truth is defined by His character alone.

Here's another important principle for us to believe with confidence. Because God is truth, His Word is truth.

What does Jesus tell us in John 17:17?

Now read Luke 21:33. How long will God's truth last?

When everything else fades away, truth will still be left standing. God has given us the Bible, His words, as our owner's manual for truth. We can stand on it—put our whole lives upon it. It is our textbook for understanding and living truth.

God also has given us another help for determining truth.

Read John 16:13*a* and fill in the blanks:

But when he, the _____ of _____, comes, he will guide you into all the _____. (NIV)

God has given us the Holy Spirit, who leads and guides us into all truth. With the help of the Holy Spirit, we are empowered to live lives that are pleasing to God. Actually, it is the Holy Spirit who enables you to enjoy life to the fullest. And the most miraculous thing of all is that the Holy Spirit desires to dwell in you and help you with every decision and daily challenge. He makes His supernatural strength available to you moment by moment. Don't strike out on your own, dear friend. That is a setup for certain failure. Take advantage of the power the Holy Spirit has already given you so you can live a life of truth and victory.

Let me tell you a story about a man who lived a life of truth. The story goes that a pastor of a large church was in a hurry after finishing up some work at the church office. He had to run to the mall to pick up a few items, pick up his daughter from school and take her home, run to a church meeting, and then spend some time that evening in some counseling sessions. Once he was in the mall, he saw a sign on the music store window that said "2 CDs for $9.99." He went inside and picked up two CDs he had been wanting. Then he went to the register to pay for them. He passed his money to the clerk, all the while talking to everyone around him, as pastors are known to do. After the clerk rang him up, he took his change and his purchase and headed for the parking lot.

When he tossed the bag on the front seat of the car, he noticed for the first time that the clerk had only charged him $1.99 instead of $9.99 for the CDs. His first thought was that he didn't have time to go back into the mall. But a still, small voice kept saying, "You don't have time not to." So he went back into the store and stood in line, waiting for his turn to speak with the clerk.

When he finally made it to the front of the line, he told the clerk, "Look, I'm in a bit of a hurry, but you made a mistake. The sign says, '2 CDs for $9.99,' but you only charged me $1.99. I owe you some money, and I'd appreciate it if you'd make the correction."

"Sir, I didn't make a mistake," she said.

"Yes, you did. There is the sign, and here is my receipt."

"No, sir, I didn't make a mistake."

"What do you mean?"

She paused a minute. "Can I tell you the rest of my story, please? For seventeen years I've not attended any church at all. Recently, however, my life has been falling apart at the seams, and I've felt a need to get back in church. I looked around for a church that was close to my home, and I went there this past Sunday. I slipped into the last row. That day the pastor was speaking on integrity. It just so happened that it was your church I attended. So when I saw you in my line, I wondered if this was something you simply preach on Sunday, or if it is something you actually live on Monday. So I was determined to find out.

"Sir, I don't even know all the right questions to ask. But I know that whatever it is you have, I need."

Then she began to cry. The store manager, who happened to be a Christian, stepped in, took over the register, and dismissed her to speak with the pastor. The pastor then shared the love of Christ with the store clerk, and she invited Jesus to be her Lord and Savior.

Do you think this woman would have stepped foot in a church again if the pastor had not come back into the store? Praise God that this preacher lived the life he preached about![4]

How would you describe good character?

Reread our opening Scripture, 2 Corinthians 6:3-10, and make a list of the apostle Paul's behaviors that displayed good character.

Now Read 2 Corinthians 6:3-10 from *THE MESSAGE.* **Underline the words or phrases that tell when we especially need to stand on God's truth.**

Don't put it off; don't frustrate God's work by showing up late, throwing a question mark over everything we're doing. Our work as God's servants gets validated—or not—in the details. People are watching us as we stay at our post, alertly, unswervingly . . . in hard times, tough times, bad times; when we're beaten up, jailed, and mobbed; working hard, working late, working without eating; with pure heart, clear head, steady hand; in gentleness, holiness, and honest love; when we're telling the truth, and when God's showing his power; when we're doing our best setting things right; when we're praised, and when we're blamed; slandered, and honored; true to our word, though distrusted; ignored by the world, but recognized by God; terrifically alive, though rumored to be dead; beaten within an inch of our lives, but refusing to die; immersed in tears, yet always filled with deep joy; living on handouts, yet enriching many; having nothing, having it all.

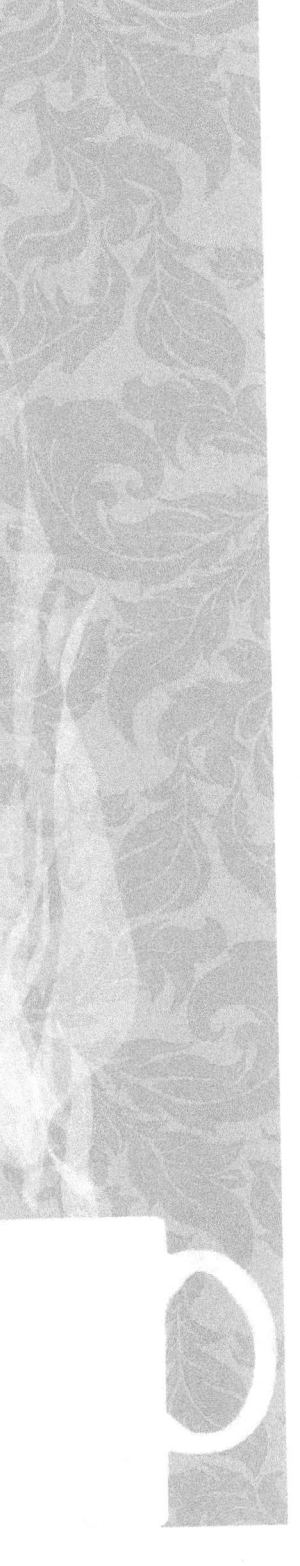

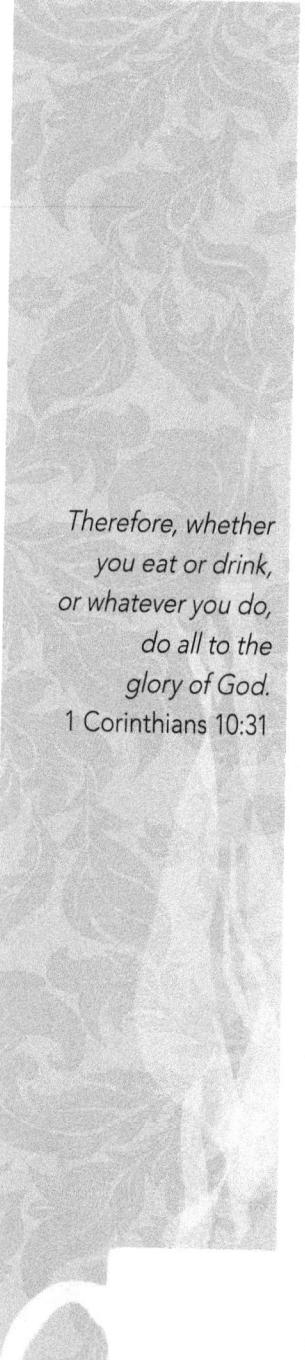

How can your character help to reflect God's kingdom here on earth?

Reflect back to our study of Daniel. Do you recall how he honored God with his life of integrity and faith? God knows our true character. He knows the motives and intents of our hearts, and He rewards those who honor His Word.

Look up Proverbs 2:21-22*a* in your favorite translation and write it below:

Therefore, whether you eat or drink, or whatever you do, do all to the glory of God.
1 Corinthians 10:31

I like the way the New Living Translation says it: "For only the godly will live in the land, and those with integrity will remain in it." These verses tell us that godly character brings reward and glorifies God.

According to the following Scriptures, why were we created?

Isaiah 43:7

1 Corinthians 10:31

Dear friend, we were created to glorify God. Regardless of the details of God's specific plan for your life, you fulfill your ultimate purpose when you live a godly life and bring glory to God. May we always hunger for and live for the Word of God. When we stand *on* the truth, we stand *for* truth in the world. Living godly lives brings glory and honor to God and fulfills God's plan for our lives.

Go to God

Ask

Remember that truth is not relative to your opinion or experiences. Truth is based upon the Word of God. Are you building a life that is firmly planted on the Bible's eternal principles? Ask God for a clear understanding of His truth.

Seek

Romans 12:1 says that you are a living sacrifice. Everything you do for Christ—not only your going-to-church life but also your daily, routine life—is be offered as a sacrifice to God. Don't fit into the world's culture so easily that you allow the world to dictate how you think. Your thoughts, opinions, and lifestyle should all be based on your response to God's Word. The old saying is true: "If you don't stand for what is right, you'll fall for anything." Seek God's heart on how to recognize and stand *on* truth so that you may stand *for* truth.

What do you hear God saying to you?

Knock

As a believer in Christ, you are His representative. People are "taking notes" on your life to determine if you really are who you claim to be. Billy Graham once said, "When wealth is lost, nothing is lost. When health is lost, something is lost. When character is lost, all is lost."[5] God's name will be glorified and you will be blessed as you relentlessly find ways to put God's character on display. Reflect on Matthew 5:16 today: "Let your light shine before people, so they can see the good things you do and praise your Father who is in heaven" (CEB).

How will you let your light shine today?

Dear Loving Father,
I long to be in step with You. Please keep me in the center lane where the lamp of Your Word will be a constant light on my path. As I travel this well-lit road, may I not miss an opportunity to share Your love. Help me to turn a deaf ear to this world's noise and look to You, the author and finisher of my faith. As Psalm 119 instructs, I will hide Your word in my heart so that I will not sin against You. In Jesus' name. Amen.

Day 4: Living with Purpose

Read God's Word

Look carefully then how you walk! Live purposefully and worthily and accurately, not as the unwise and witless, but as wise (sensible, intelligent people).

Ephesians 5:15 AMP

Reflect and Respond

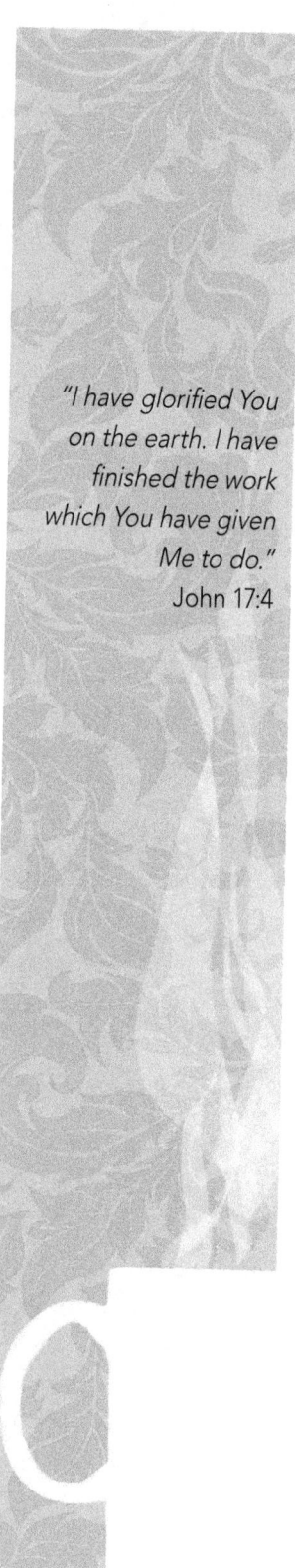

Everything about your life is significant. No matter how remarkable or run-of-the-mill it may seem, everything about you is wrapped up in God's purpose. God has a plan for you. God desires that you live your life on purpose—*with* purpose and *for* a purpose. I hope you are beginning to see that if you are not fulfilling God's purpose for your life, you haven't begun to truly live. You will never achieve your highest dreams and goals apart from God's plan for you. How do we know this? We need only look at the life of Christ, the only One to fulfill His ordained purpose to the letter.

When He was here on earth, Jesus knew how vital it was to live out His Father's specific plan. Just before He went to the cross, Jesus was praying to His Father concerning the work He had completed up to that moment.

Read John 17:4 in the margin. What did Jesus declare?

"I have glorified You on the earth. I have finished the work which You have given Me to do."

John 17:4

What a powerful proclamation! Jesus' only desire was to do the will of His Father and bring Him glory. Can you say the same? Have you earnestly asked God to help you discover His beautiful design for your life with the intention of bringing Him glory?

What does it mean for you to bring God glory with your life? How is your life bringing glory to God now, and how would you like your life to bring God glory?

Read 1 Corinthians 10:31. What additional insights does this verse give you related to how you can bring glory to God with your life?

Bringing glory to God involves *every* aspect of our lives—everything we do. But to help give us a handle for putting this into action, I'd like us to consider three categories or qualities that enable us to bring glory to God. We see these three qualities in the life and teachings of Jesus.

Jesus spent the better part of the last three years of His life teaching His disciples how to live a life that is glorifying to God. He didn't just tell them; He showed them how to walk out God's purpose on the earth. First, Jesus taught the disciples how to grow spiritually by patterning their lives after Him. That's *discipleship*. Second, He taught them to love God and develop intimacy with Him. That's *worship*. And finally, He taught them how to love and serve others with humility. That's *relationship*. These three qualities bring blessing to our lives, encouragement to others, and glory to God. Let's take a closer look at each of these qualities.

1. Discipleship

The Greek word for *disciple* is *mathétés*, which means to be "a learner."[6] A disciple is one who studies or follows another with the goal of emulating the teacher's life and spreading his or her teachings. Discipleship, then, is the process of learning and living out the teachings of another. To be a disciple of Jesus involves not only *learning* what he taught but also *doing* what he taught. A true disciple of Jesus Christ knows Jesus' teachings, lives by them, and passes them on to others.

Read John 15:1-17. What does Jesus teach His followers about what it means to be His disciple? Complete the statements below by searching the verses indicated.

_____ in me. (vv. 4-7)

Remain in my _____. (v. 9)

Keep my _____. (v. 10)

_____ each other. (vv. 12, 17)

Bear _____. (v. 16)

Beloved, these are the marks of true discipleship. To be considered a disciple of Christ is an honor and a privilege. I think of the chosen twelve who followed Christ and dedicated their lives to Jesus. The disciples left everything—their livelihood, their families, their hometowns, their creature comforts, even their safety to follow after Christ. After the resurrection and ascension of Christ, the disciples dedicated their lives to spreading the message of the gospel. Most of them were martyred for the cause of Christ.

Jesus demands that we lay down everything to follow Him. Our own selfish desires, our own dreams and aspirations, our pride and pursuit of worldly ambitions—we must lay it all down to follow Christ. Anything that we could ever lay down or leave behind could never compare to the privilege of knowing Christ.

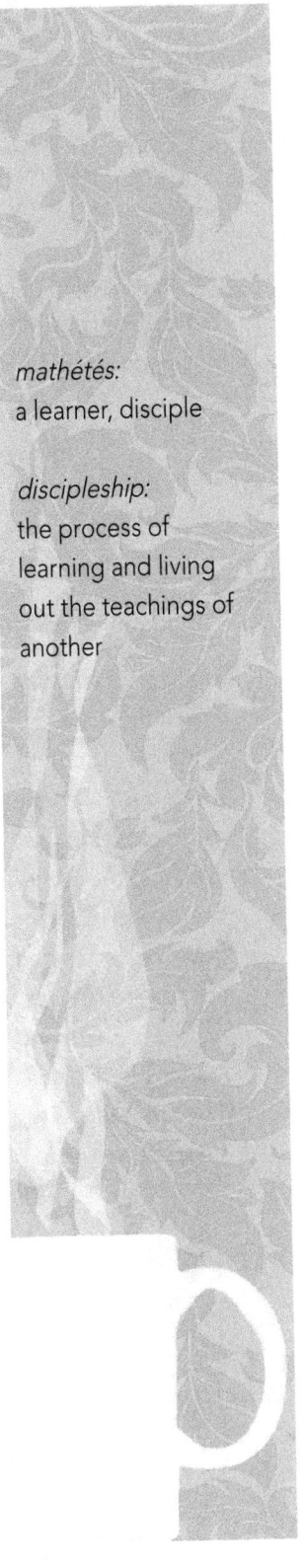

mathétés:
a learner, disciple

discipleship:
the process of learning and living out the teachings of another

In their living and even in their dying, the disciples show us what it looks like to remain in Christ and His love, to keep His commands, to love each other, and to bear fruit. Think about it, dear one. Your dedication to Christ is the fruit of their ministry. Your life is the reward for their work. Now you have the joy and the responsibility to lead others to Christ.

Read the departing words of Jesus spoken to His disciples in Matthew 28:19-20: "Therefore go and make disciples of all nations, baptizing them in the name of the Father and of the Son and of the Holy Spirit, and teaching them to obey everything I have commanded you" (NIV). These same words apply to us today.

In light of this command, consider these questions:

What fruit in your life is evidence of your discipleship?

Who are you leading by example to remain in the love of Christ and keep His commandments (your children or grandchildren, those with whom you work, a neighbor or acquaintance, etc.)? Write their names below.

2. Worship

The word *worship* comes from the Old English *weorthscipe,* which is a combination of *weorth,* meaning worth, and *scipe,* meaning ship.[7] It means showing reverence or adoration to someone worthy of esteem. Though we often use it as a noun, describing a gathering of worshipers, it is first and foremost a verb, describing the act of responding to God's glory with reverence and awe.

So often we get caught up in the *how* and *where* of worship. Jesus had something to say about this.

Read John 4:21-24 in the margin. What did Jesus say about worship?

How did Jesus describe true worshipers?

Jesus said to her, "Woman, believe Me, the hour is coming when you will neither on this mountain, nor in Jerusalem, worship the Father. You worship what you do not know; we know what we worship, for salvation is of the Jews. But the hour is coming, and now is, when the true worshipers will worship the Father in spirit and truth; for the Father is seeking such to worship Him. God is Spirit, and those who worship Him must worship in spirit and truth."
John 4:21-24

Jesus made it clear that the important thing is not where we worship or how we worship—following the worship practices of one group versus another. Regardless of our denomination or our worship style, the important aspect of worship is *Who* we worship.

A songwriter friend of mine, Tony Sutherland, wrote a great book called *Graceworks*. In it he talks about what real worship is:

> So often we focus on the way we worship rather than on the One we worship. In other words, the emphasis is on the mechanics of worship rather than on the Lord of our worship. It is sad to say but many times we give more attention to creativity than we do the Creator! We're not supposed to worship the worship! Jesus alone is the object of our fondest affection! When Jesus (the person of grace) is exalted, people from every walk of life will respond to His unconditional love and surrender to His uncontested Lordship (John 12:32).[8]

When Jesus is the object of our fondest affection, our lives honor God. That is true worship. We can't repay Jesus for all that He has done for us. Our good works can't repay Him. Church attendance can't repay Him. On our best day, our best still falls short. But Jesus paid it all, once and for all! A life of worship focuses on what Christ has already done, not on what we have done. In response, a worshiping heart produces a life of obedience, and obedience is the mark of a true disciple. Worship is not defined by music or the tempo of a song. Worship is not only something you do when you go to church; it is your response for all that Christ has done for you. You were made to worship with your *life*. Therefore, your greatest act of worship is to bring glory to God in all that you do.

Would you say that your heart for worship is growing? Why or why not?

3. Relationship

We learn from the Genesis story that God created us for relationship—relationship with God and relationship with one another. The Scriptures are the grand story of God's love relationship with us and His call for us to love others as He has loved us. In Jesus, we see the pinnacle of this story and the ultimate demonstration of sacrificial love. Jesus gave up everything, even His own life, to demonstrate His love for us and restore our relationship with God. As He taught His disciples, Jesus calls us to follow His example.

Your greatest act of worship is to bring glory to God in all that you do.

"This is My commandment, that you love one another as I have loved you."
John 15:12

Read John 15:12 in the margin. How does Jesus want us to love others?

Jesus demonstrated a humble, sacrificial love that was willing to put the need of others above His own. He was a humble servant.

Read John 13:1-16. What did Jesus do to demonstrate how we are to serv others?

Jesus calls us to follow His example, loving and serving others with humility This is relationship as God intends it to be. When we love and serve others in this way, we give glory to God.

What is your attitude in relationships lately? Do you have a heart to serve others?

I am often encouraged by how God uses my husband, Charles, to show me what discipleship, worship, and relationship actually look like when lived out. One Sunday morning, Charles and I flew home from Florida, where I had been in a concert the night before. I was excited because were going to be able to make it to church later that morning. I was looking forward to enjoying the music and the sermon after being away for several Sundays in a row.

As we were driving to the church, Charles noticed that the car's fuel tank was near empty, and so we stopped to refuel. We had about twenty minutes before the worship service was scheduled to begin, so we would have to hurry to in order to find a parking spot, get inside, and find seats close to the front of the sanctuary. After being away for so long, I didn't want to miss a single word.

Charles pumped the gas and went inside to pay. On the way out, he paused for a moment to notice two young fellows whose car was in distress. One of them pushed the powerless vehicle with all his might while the other tried desperately to steer it to a nearby parking spot. Charles stepped right in behind their car and helped give it a push. After the car came to a stop, Charles nodded his head in response to their thanks and headed back to our truck. I admired my husband's generous spirit. It was nice of him to stop and help those young guys, I thought, but now it was time to get to church. As Charles opened the door to the driver's side, he glanced back to see the two young men struggling to raise the hood of their car. It was obvious these kids didn't know the difference between a headlamp and a tailpipe.

Without missing a beat, Charles hopped into our truck, closed the door, and drove over to lend a hand. I looked at the clock on the truck's dashboard—the worship service would be starting in just a few minutes. All Charles had to do was make a quick determination that the car was beyond his ability to repair, and we could be on our way. One look at their car made it obvious that it didn't need repair; it needed a miracle!

Charles determined there was something he could do to help, and he went right to it. Through the cracked window I could hear the conversation between Charles and the two young travelers. I could hear their distinctive accents, and I recognized those beautiful angular features. I knew that Charles recognized them too and was intrigued by these two strangers who appeared to be from Africa. Having visited Kenya, Uganda, and South Africa, Charles and I have had the opportunity to help dig wells and build churches, schools, and medical clinics in these countries.

Finally I heard Charles say something about the battery. These two young men could tell that my husband knew what he was doing, and they were not about to interrupt him. Like a well-trained surgeon, Charles made his diagnosis and went to work on their ailing vehicle.

I, on the other hand, sat stewing in the truck. There was no way we'd make it to church on time. Gone was my opportunity to hear wonderful music and a great sermon. Gone was my chance to see my friends. I wouldn't have another opportunity to be at our home church to worship for several more weeks. Just then I heard Charles instruct one of the guys to hop in and start the car. Without hesitation, one of the young fellows climbed under the wheel. The car's motor coughed and sputtered a few times but eventually turned over.

I glanced over at the young man behind the wheel. His eyes caught mine as he smiled with pure delight. It was then I saw something I hadn't seen before. I wondered about these young men. Where were they from? How did they get to the United States? Where were their parents? What about their mothers? Could a mother be somewhere praying that very moment that when her son was stranded somewhere along the side of the road, some kind and caring person would come along to help? Maybe their parents had been victims of a civil war. Could these young men, between the ages of my own two sons, be refugees *and* orphans? Tears welled up in my eyes and compassion gripped my heart as I imagined what their stories might be. I've been to Africa enough times to know that whatever the story was, it was probably mingled with pain and loss.

I watched as my husband finished working on their car and told them what part they needed. He spoke to them like a father. They listened like sons. With care and compassion, Charles did as Jesus would do. I watched this powerful scene being played out before me, and I bowed my head under conviction and whispered a prayer, asking for forgiveness. Then I whispered a prayer of thanks for a man like Charles, the Good Samaritan who was kind and willing to help two strangers who were in trouble. Can you imagine the encouragement they received that day from being recipients of Charles's servant heart?

I realized then that I had been to church. I had witnessed a great sermon complete with illustrations. I had prayed a heartfelt prayer and responded to the Lord's invitation. I even sang a song while Charles gave them a few instructions. My heart was as full as it has been after many worship services. Charles was able to put discipleship, worship, and relationship on display in living color.

Like colorful threads of a beautiful garment, discipleship, worship, and relationship are woven together to create the spiritual fabric of your life. These qualities define the mark of a follower of Christ—one who is on a mission for the kingdom of God. The question is, *Are you a missionary or a mission project?* Determine today that you will put your life on display for all the world to see.

Go to God

Ask

Reflect on the fruit of your discipleship, the passion of your worship, and the quality of your relationships. Ask God to help you live a life that fulfills His purpose and brings Him glory.

Seek

God is more interested in who you are than in what you do. He wants you to be who you were created to be, living out your purpose while helping others to discover theirs. This process of following after Christ—learning how He lived and following His example—is called *discipleship*. Seek God's guidance as you commit to grow as a disciple of Jesus Christ.

How is God speaking to you about growing as a disciple?

Knock

Can others tell you are a disciple of Christ? Your Christlike life is your mark of discipleship. Living a life that brings glory to Christ is the quality that sets you apart from the world. This doesn't mean that you won't make mistakes. It means that you look to Jesus to establish the pattern for how you live your life. When we stand before God, He will not ask us if we were good people. All that will matter is whether we followed Christ. The true mark of success is that you are growing up and maturing into the person God has designed you to become.

How will you be more intentional and purposeful as you grow into the person God made you to be?

Dear heavenly Father,

How I love to worship You, to be in Your presence, to feel the warmth of Your sweet Spirit. But I am also aware that worship is living a life that brings You glory. So, I pray that You would create in me a heart for worship and a heart to serve. Make me a humble servant, Lord, so that I may bring glory to Your name. In Jesus' name I pray. Amen.

Day 5: Being Available

Read God's Word

I have been crucified with Christ; it is no longer I who live, but Christ lives in me; and the life which I now live in the flesh I live by faith in the Son of God, who loved me and gave Himself for me.

Galatians 2:20

Reflect and Respond

Yesterday we considered three categories or qualities that enable us to bring glory to God and fulfill His plan for our lives: discipleship, worship, and relationship. Today I'd like us to narrow our focus on relationship—specifically, on the importance of being available to be used by God to bless others.

Each of us has a part to play in God's plan, and this requires us to yield ourselves to God and His purposes. This process of yielding and surrendering ourselves to God's agenda, making ourselves available to carry out God's plans and purposes in our lives, does not come naturally and is seldom easy.

Our world encourages us to "look out for number one," to pursue our dreams and goals at all costs. In fact, the world measures us by our successes and accomplishments—from the classroom to the boardroom and everywhere in between. Ours is a performance-based society. God, however, measures us by our faithfulness and obedience.

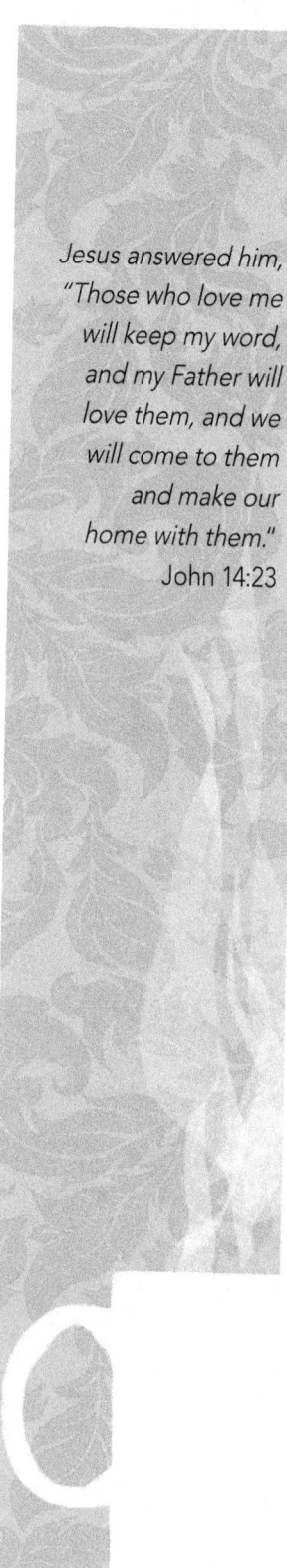

Read 1 Samuel 15:22 and fill in the blanks:

But Samuel replied:

*"Does the Lord delight in burnt offerings and sacrifices
as much as in _____ the Lord?
To _____ is better than sacrifice,
and to _____ is better than the fat of rams."* **(NIV)**

Read John 14:23 in the margin. What did Jesus say that anyone who love Him would do?

God is not interested in our lip service. He wants us to demonstrate our love and commitment to Him through our faithful obedience. In the world's eyes we might be a failure if we do not realize certain goals or accomplishments. You might be considered unsuccessful if you don't live by the world's standards or acquire its status symbols; but in God's eyes, we can fail according to the world's standards and still be a success in His eyes if we are striving to be faithful and obedient to His ways and purposes.

Consider Peter, one of Christ's most devoted disciples. Although he walked with Jesus every day for three years, Peter was a man who had many shortcomings. In the eyes of the world, some might consider Peter a failure.

Read these examples from Peter's life and list his "failures."

Matthew 14:28-33

Matthew 26:51

Matthew 26:69-75

Galatians 2:11-14

Was Peter a failure? Absolutely not. Why? Because even when he fell short, Jesus was there to fully restore him. The same is true for us. With Jesus, we are never on the outside looking in. Even in the midst of life's greatest failures, Jesus still invites us into His presence where we can be fully restored to enjoy intimate friendship with Him.

The world is concerned about religion while Jesus is concerned about relationship. Our relationship with God is integral to our ability to be obedient and available to God. In other words, if we want to build a relationship with Jesus and fulfill His plan for our lives, we have to take time to be connected to Him.

Religious people care more about possessions and status than the condition of the heart. Some people may be more concerned about their standing in the community rather than if their life is pleasing to God. But our position or possessions in life don't matter to Jesus; a heart of devotion is what He is looking for. Relationships take time to develop. They must be nurtured. I created this acronym for the word TIME:

Treasuring
Intimate
Moments
Every day

Are you connected to Jesus, enjoying intimate moments with Him on a daily basis? If so, write about an experience of enjoying an intimate moment with Jesus. If not, what is keeping you from taking time to be connected to Him?

When we take time to cultivate our relationship with Jesus, the outcome is a life of faithful obedience and service. You know, God's plan for us is not to escape to an oasis off by ourselves where we get to mind our own business. No, we were made for relationship—to serve God and serve one another. When we are in God's plan, we can be sure that God will have us serving someone, somewhere.

Did you know that God is not as concerned about your *ability* as He is about your *availability*? Worldly people seek to be served; godly people seek to serve. The person behind the scenes is just as important as the one in the spotlight on center stage. What matters most is that your life is dedicated to serving Christ and giving Him glory with your God-given gifts and talents.

In what area has God assigned you to serve at this time in your life? How are you being faithful to that call?

When the Italian city of Pompeii was destroyed by the volcanic eruption of Mount Vesuvius in the year A.D. 79, many people were buried alive by the hot lava and were later found preserved in its aftermath. Some were found in the streets in an attempt to flee the city. Some were in deep vaults, hoping to find security there. Some were discovered in chambers high above ground, hoping to escape the destructive lava. Where could the Roman sentinel be found? He was found, almost two thousand years later, still standing at the city gate, still at his post of duty, where his captain had placed him.

Each of us has a post of duty where Jesus, our Captain has placed us. Can you be found at your post of duty, relentlessly serving Jesus today?

What insights do you discover in the following Scriptures related to being part of God's plan? (Consider your part and God's part.)

Isaiah 30:21

2 Corinthians 2:14

John 14:12

> But thank God! He has made us his captives and continues to lead us along in Christ's triumphal procession. Now he uses us to spread the knowledge of Christ everywhere, like a sweet perfume.
> 2 Corinthians 2:14 NLT

Your walk talks louder than your talk. So what is your walk saying about you? Is it saying, "I'm determined to get ahead no matter what it takes"? Is it saying, "I'm tired of waiting on God—I'm going to do things my way"? Is it saying, "Why would God use me to do anything? I'm not good at much"?

If you are looking anywhere other than to Jesus for direction, dear friend, you'll be drawing from an empty well. Anything that is isolated and disconnected from its life source will eventually die. I encourage you to make up your mind that you will not live for anything other than Christ. Put His agenda above your own and make yourself available to be used by Him. Make this your declaration today: "I have been crucified with Christ; it is no longer I who live, but Christ lives in me; and the life which I now live in the flesh I live by faith in the Son of God, who loved me and gave Himself for me" (Galatians 2:20).

Go to God

Ask

Be intentional about taking *time*—staying connected to God and nurturing your relationship with Him. Give God the opportunity to say something to you

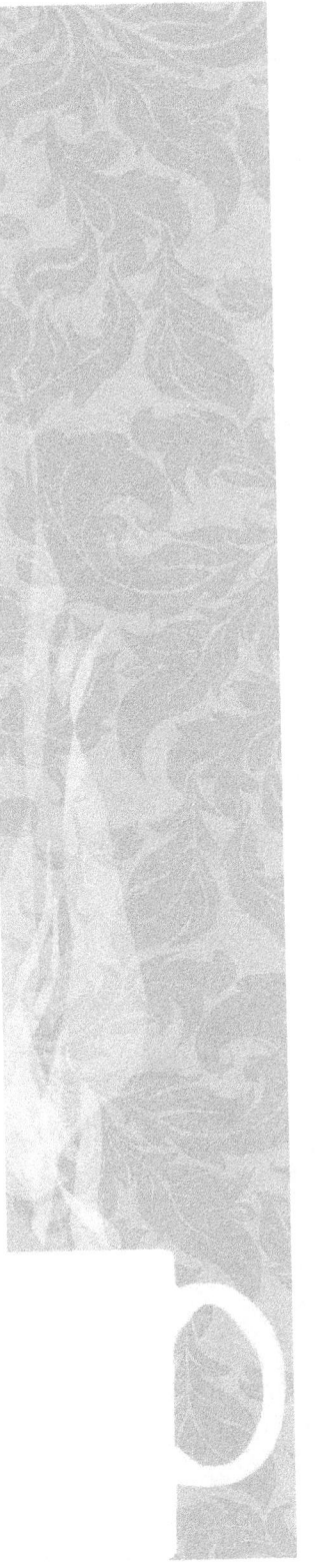

aily through the study of His Word. Consider reading at least one chapter of
e Bible daily. By reading four chapters daily, you will read through the whole
ible in a year.

Write which book of the Bible you will begin to read:

eek

Take the opportunity to say something *to* God daily through devotion and
rayer. Then, take the opportunity to say something *for* God daily. Share your
alvation story with a friend or offer a word of encouragement to someone who
s discouraged.

Who needs to hear your God story? Write their names here:

Knock

Take the opportunity to do something for God daily. Look for ways you can
give God glory by being a blessing to others.

Write an act of blessing you can give to someone this week:

Dear Lord,
I am so grateful to know that You created me for a specific purpose.
I realize that my plans pale in comparison to those You have for me.
My best plans don't even come close! Help me to let go of what I might
consider "good" and trade it in for Your absolute best. Accomplishing
the work You have for me to do and bringing You glory is my only aim. I
am excited about the days ahead. Even if difficult days are in front of me,
I can weather the storms because You are with me. This I know for sure.
In Jesus' name. Amen.

Week 2

Video Viewer Guide

But Ruth said:

"Entreat me not to _____ you,
Or to turn back from following after you;
For wherever you go, I will go;
And wherever you lodge, I will lodge;
Your _____ shall be my people,
And your _____, my God.
Where you die, I will die,
And there will I be buried.
The Lord do so to me, and more also,
If anything but death parts you and me."

When she saw that she was _____ to go with her, she stopped speaking to her.

Now the two of them went until they came to Bethlehem. And it happened, when they had come to Bethlehem, that all the city was excited because of them; and the women said, "Is this Naomi?"

Ruth 1:16-19 NKJV

When we find ourselves in our greatest time of need, we find that God is the _____ of our greatest _____.

God doesn't _____ the qualified; He _____
the called.

Boaz is what you call a *kinsman-redeemer*, a near relative who would
_____ these women from their dreadful predicament—give
them a new _____and a _____ for their future.

So Boaz took Ruth and she became his wife; and when he went in to her, the LORD
gave her conception, and she bore a son. Then the women said to Naomi, "Blessed be the
LORD, who has not left you this day without a close relative; and may his name be famous
in Israel! And may he be to you a _____ of _____ and a
nourisher of your old age; for your daughter-in-law, who loves you, who is better to you
than seven sons, has borne him." Then Naomi took the child and laid him on her bosom,
and became a nurse to him. Also the neighbor women gave him a name, saying, "There is
a son born to Naomi." And they called his name _____. He is the father of
Jesse, the father of _____.

Ruth 4:13-17 NKJV

Where God _____, He _____.

What the Lord wants from us is to _____Him with every single
_____of our lives.

71

Week 3

God Will Never Forsake Me

In recent years we have witnessed the devastation that intense weather-related storms and natural disasters can cause. From hurricanes to tornadoes and floods to wildfires and mudslides, we've seen entire communities in multiple states destroyed in a matter of minutes. Though storms and natural disasters are a phenomenon we've come to expect, even anticipate, the damage that they leave behind can take years to rebuild and cost billions of dollars to clean up.

Personal storms and disasters are also a reality in life. You know as well as I do how storms—in the form of an unexpected diagnosis from a doctor, the foreclosure of a home, the death of a loved one, an assault on a marriage—can bear down on our lives. Any one of these events can bring the best of us to our knees. Whatever the circumstances, when a storm wreaks havoc in your life, there is no insurance company or government agency competent enough to fix the fall-out from the wreckage. But take heart, my friend. You do have a safe place to run for shelter.

Jesus is a refuge from every storm of life. Because Jesus loves you, He will never leave you to face the storm alone. He knows how to speak peace into the torrential winds and waves that dash against you.

This week we will consider how we can face the storms of this life without fear, standing securely and firmly on the Word of God. We will see that regardless of the forces that come against us, God is with us and will never leave us defenseless. Together we will boldly stand upon this landmark of faith: *God will never forsake me.*

Scripture Memorization

This week we will continue working to memorize our core Scripture verse for our journey, 2 Timothy 1:12:

I know whom I have believed, and am persuaded that he is able to keep that which I have committed unto him against that day. (KJV)

Continue using the index cards in visible places throughout the day. Remember that another great way to memorize this verse is to sing it. If you have already memorized the verse, reflect on the strength you get from hiding this word in your heart. When I think about the storms of life that come—those times when answers are hard to find—I know that I know that I know that I can stake my future on the promises of God!

Day 1: Build on the Rock

Read God's Word

²⁴"*Everybody who hears these words of mine and puts them into practice is like a wise builder who built a house on bedrock.* ²⁵*The rain fell, the floods came, and the wind blew and beat against that house. It didn't fall because it was firmly set on bedrock.* ²⁶*But everybody who hears these words of mine and doesn't put them into practice will be like a fool who built a house on sand.* ²⁷*The rain fell, the floods came, and the wind blew and beat against that house. It fell and was completely destroyed.*"

Matthew 7:24-27 CEB

Reflect and Respond

My mother, a very wise and resilient woman, has always taken stormy weather in stride. Years ago she gave me some wise counsel concerning storms. She said, "You're either in a storm, coming out of a storm, or headed for another storm. Rain or shine, the weather doesn't bother me. We're going to have weather whether we like it or not."

My mother is right. Storms in our atmosphere and in our lives are inevitable. It doesn't matter how old you are, where you were born, or your income bracket; if you live on this planet, you're going to encounter some mean times. Storms will blow through your life.

You know how it is. One minute everything is fine and you are cruising through life under sunny skies. The next thing you know, without warning, the skies turn black and the bottom drops out. But here is what I know for sure: every storm I've ever experienced only lasted for a season. The storm didn't come to stay. The storm came to pass.

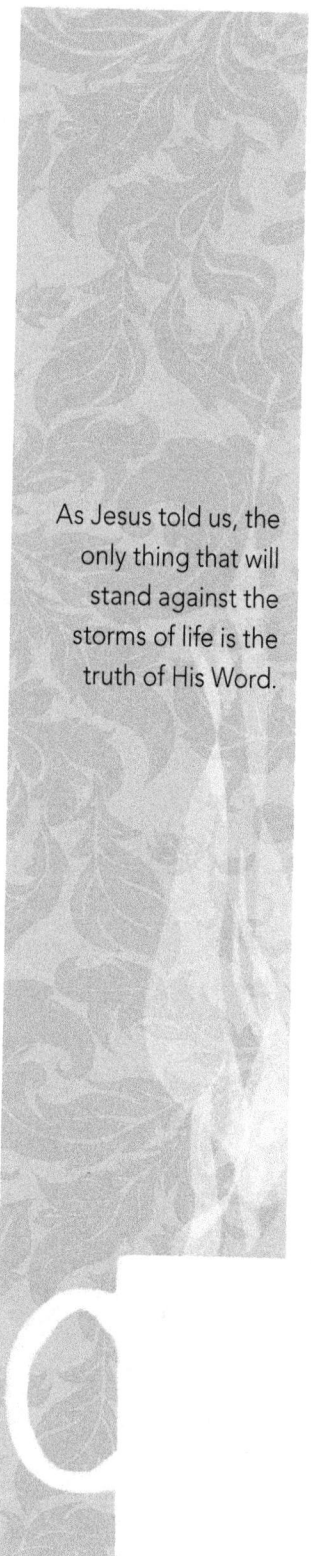

As Jesus told us, the only thing that will stand against the storms of life is the truth of His Word.

About ten years ago, Charles and I moved from the bustling city to a quiet spot in the country. There we built our new home from the ground up. I knew just the kind of house I wanted. I talked about the square-footage, style, color scheme, layout of the kitchen, and number of bedrooms I wanted. What I didn't talk much about was the foundation. There's nothing pretty about a deep hole hewn out of the ground. There's nothing fashionable about concrete walls and steel rods in sturdy construction. But the foundation is the most important part of our home. The foundation bears the weight of our entire house, supporting floors, furniture, appliances, family, guests, and the grand piano my dad gave me when Charles and I got married.

Fortunately, God tells us how to build strong foundations for our lives—foundations that will support us through the approaching storms that are coming. In the Gospel of Matthew, Jesus teaches us a great lesson on how to build a home, a relationship, a family, or a business. Who would know better than a master builder how to storm-proof not only your house but also your life.

Read Jesus' words from Matthew 7:24-27 and describe the two houses in the story.

	House 1	House 2
Foundation:		
How it fared in the storm:		

At the time Jesus spoke this building analogy, He was concluding His famous Sermon on the Mount that begins in Matthew 5. Jesus' words were not just for the select few who heard Him that day; He knew that tough times would impact everyone throughout the ages. And He knew that in every generation, all kinds of people would be searching for truth—for answers to the dilemmas they face in life. People like you and me need a firm place to stand when the gale force winds of life blow, threatening everything that isn't nailed down. And as Jesus told us, the only thing that will stand against the storms of life is the truth of His Word.

Reread Matthew 7:24-26 and fill in the blanks:

"Everybody who hears these _____ of mine and puts them into practice is like a _____ _____ who built a house on bedrock." (v. 24 CEB)

But everybody who hears these _____ *of mine and doesn't put them into practice will be like a* _____ *who built a house on sand.*
(v. 26 CEB)

Have you ever built a sand castle at the beach? Jesus makes the reference that building your life without a strong foundation is like building a house on sand. Get this picture in your mind. It's a beautiful day at the beach, and you spend hours building an impressive and creative sand castle. It looks amazing, glistening in the afternoon sun. But you soon learn that it doesn't take much to level a sand castle. The tidewater comes rolling in, an afternoon rain shower sets in, and that sand castle, as pretty as it is, has no leg to stand on. Gone. In no time there won't even be a sign that it was ever there.

Is this how you want to build your life, placing everything you love and value on nothing more than sand?

How would you describe the foundation of your life right now? Put a checkmark on the line below to indicate whether your life is built like a sand castle, a mighty fortress, or something in between.

Sand castle————————————————————**Fortress**

God has given us His Word, the Bible, as our foundation—our textbook—for godly living. As we discussed in Week 2, Jesus is the way, truth, and life (John 14:6). Jesus is truth personified. This is a foundational faith principle worth repeating. When we set our lives upon a firm foundation, we stand on the truth of Jesus Christ Himself.

According to the following Scriptures, how do we recognize and know the truth?

John 14:17

John 16:13

Jesus said that those who hear but don't act upon God's wisdom are like one who builds a house on the sand. Jesus was sending out a warning: when it rains, it pours—and everybody gets wet.

> *"When He, the Spirit of truth, has come, He will guide you into all truth; for He will not speak on His own authority, but whatever He hears He will speak; and He will tell you things to come."*
> John 16:13

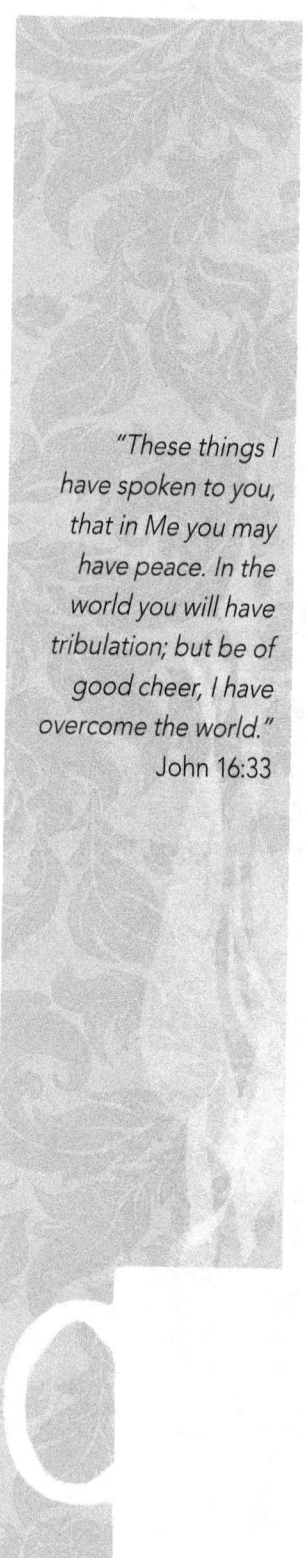

Read Matthew 5:45. What did Jesus say about who gets rained upon?

Sometimes the storms of life show no sign of letting up. Out of frustration you've probably said, "If it's not one thing, it's another." Isn't that true? If it's not the house, it's the car. If it's not your finances, it's your health. If it's not your money, it's your honey. There's always some challenge to face. Jesus is well aware of how life's problems can compound one on top of another.

Read how Jesus described the situation in Matthew 7:27, circling the word *and* every time you come to it:

And the rain descended, and the floods came, and the winds blew, and beat upon that house; and it fell: and great was the fall of it. **(KJV)**

In both scenarios found in Matthew 7:24-27, the rains fell, the floods came, and the winds blew. In both instances the winds beat upon the house. But in the case concerning the fool, not only did the house fall; the fall was great. The foolish builder took shortcuts in order to save time, effort, and money. In the end, that decision cost dearly. The fool lost everything—home, family, and even quality of life—which was damaged beyond repair.

Jesus insisted it is not enough to just hear His words. Anyone can do that. Religious people do that all the time. Even people who don't know Christ personally have heard His words. Scores of churchgoers warm a pew for an hour each week, listen to God's Word, and then choose to build their lives on shaky ground. The mindset that one can build a stable life according to the world's standards will eventually see its foundations crumble. We've all stood helplessly by, holding our proverbial breath while the harsh winds of our times have ravaged our nation's financial, educational, and political systems, and practically every other human-made system or institution.

Jesus, the master storyteller, told the parable of the wise builder and the fool to challenge us not only to hear His words but also to act upon what we have heard. Those who act upon the words of Jesus are wise, admitting in their hearts, "Jesus, I recognize that Your Word is truth. I trust You with my life. I believe Your Word, and I'll do what You say because You know best."

Jesus reveals that it's not a matter of *if* the storms will come against you, but *when*. Just because you're a Christian doesn't mean you won't have difficulties in life. As a matter of fact, the opposite is true. As a Christian, you'll probably experience more difficulty in life not because you did something wrong, but because you did something right.

Read John 16:33 in the margin. What did Jesus tell his disciples?

The disciples followed Jesus and carried His message to the world after His death, but they were not immune from the trouble of the world. In fact, many experienced hardship and persecution because of their faith. The same is true today.

Though we do not face religious persecution in our country as our sisters and brothers in other places in the world do, how do we sometimes experience hardship or difficulty because of our faith?

As followers of Christ, there are some things we choose to do and other things we won't do. There are places we refuse to go with people we refuse to call friends. There are standards we refuse to compromise and unpopular choices we make. The rub is that all of this makes us different than the culture around us. The enemy of our souls knows this, too, and tries to hinder us, keeping us from accomplishing great things for God.

You need to know that your enemy's mission is to put roadblocks in your way to trip you up. Depending on where you live, a thunderstorm, snowstorm, tornado, or some other type of storm could rise up at a moment's notice. The same is true in your life. The pressures of life can come against you at any time. Expect these difficulties and prepare for them. If you are building your life on the wisdom of God's Word, you will be ready for these challenges. You will be reminded that the stakes are higher and there's too much to lose. Regardless of the forces that come against you, never forget that with God on your side, you are never, ever left defenseless. God's Word is a firm foundation on which to build your life!

Go to God

Ask

If you're fortunate enough not to be in a storm right now, praise God! But don't get too comfortable. Build your hope on eternal things by shoring up your foundation with the truth of God's Word. Sooner or later another storm will be headed your way. Remember what my mother used to say: "We're going to have weather whether we like it or not." Then remember what Jesus said: "Everybody who hears these words of mine and puts them into practice is like a wise builder who built a house on bedrock. The rain fell, the floods came, and the wind blew and beat against that house. It didn't fall because it was firmly set on bedrock" (Matthew 7:24-25 CEB). Are you building your life on bedrock? Talk to God about how you can shore up your foundation.

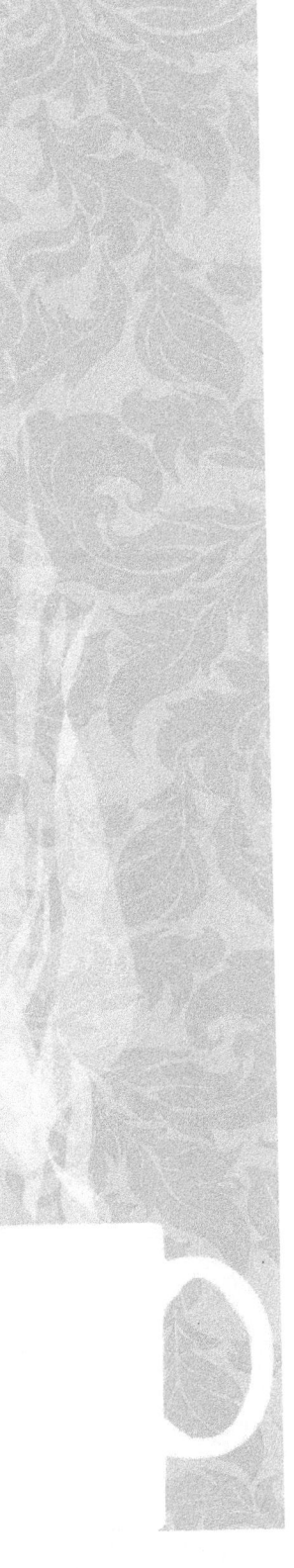

Seek

Read Matthew 7:24-27 once more. Seek God's voice in this passage. This sto[ry] may be so familiar to you that you skim over it. But take a closer look.

What is God saying to you in these verses?

Knock

You may be facing some pretty hard times right now. Or maybe, in a manne[r] of speaking, you've hunkered down in a corner, too afraid to look out the win[-] dow to see if the storm has already passed. Either way, you have nothing to fea[r.] Jesus wants you to know for sure that He loves you and that you can always fin[d] a hiding place in Him. He will never forsake you but will keep you safe until th[e] storm passes.

Now consider what you will do to build a firm foundation. What do yo[u] need—a church community? a daily Bible study routine? a regular prayer time[?] something else?

Create a "blueprint" for your faith foundation by making some notes below[.] Then be sure to start building!

Dear Lord,

Thank You for the solid ground that we stand upon in You. Thank You for making us storm-proof as we live our lives upon Your Word. We know that storms will come, seas will rise and roar, but they cannot tear us away from You. We love You, Lord. In Jesus' name. Amen.

Day 2: Don't Be Afraid; Pray

Read God's Word

¹It happened after this that the people of Moab with the people of Ammon, and others with them besides the Ammonites, came to battle against Jehoshaphat. ²Then some came and told Jehoshaphat, saying, "A great multitude is coming against you from beyond the sea, from Syria; and they are in Hazazon Tamar" (which is En Gedi). ³And Jehoshaphat feared, and set himself to seek the LORD, and proclaimed a fast throughout all Judah. ⁴So Judah gathered together to ask help from the LORD; and from all the cities of Judah they came to seek the LORD.

⁵Then Jehoshaphat stood in the assembly of Judah and Jerusalem, in the house of the LORD, before the new court, ⁶and said: "O LORD God of our fathers, are You not God in heaven, and do You not rule over all the kingdoms of the nations, and in Your hand is there not power and might, so that no one is able to withstand You? ⁷Are You not our God, who drove out the inhabitants of this land before Your people Israel, and gave it to the descendants of Abraham Your friend forever? ⁸And they dwell in it, and have built You a sanctuary in it for Your name, saying, ⁹'If disaster comes upon us—sword, judgment, pestilence, or famine—we will stand before this temple and in Your presence (for Your name is in this temple), and cry out to You in our affliction, and You will hear and save.' ¹⁰And now, here are the people of Ammon, Moab, and Mount Seir—whom You would not let Israel invade when they came out of the land of Egypt, but they turned from them and did not destroy them— ¹¹here they are, rewarding us by coming to throw us out of Your possession which You have given us to inherit. ¹²O our God, will You not judge them? For we have no power against this great multitude that is coming against us; nor do we know what to do, but our eyes are upon You."

2 Chronicles 20:1-12

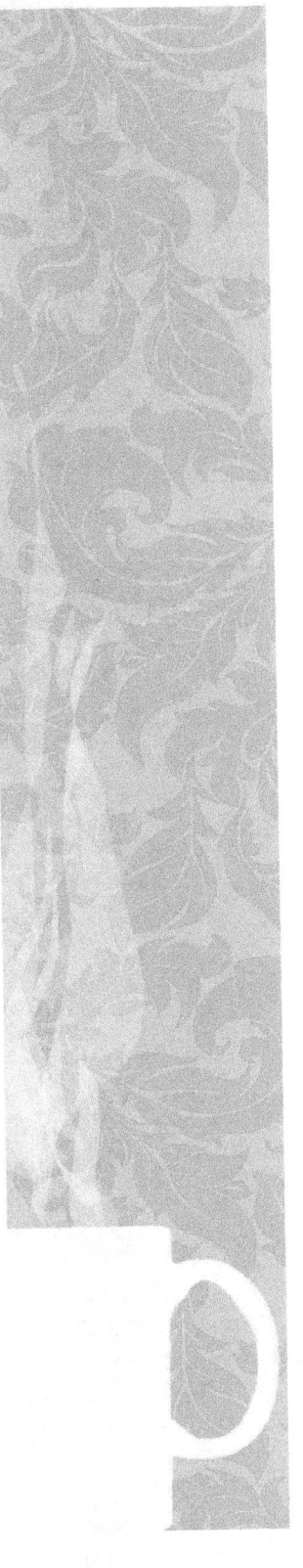

Reflect and Respond

Have you ever found yourself in a situation where you had to wait for a season before an answer came? Did you ever call a customer service line only to be put on hold? Have you ever waited in the emergency room of a hospital? Are you waiting for a child to reach the next developmental level—or return home from college? Are you waiting expectantly for some improvement in your health?

I've done a good bit of waiting in my life, and I know exactly how you feel. I've waited for Christmas mornings, graduations, and a wedding day. I've waited for babies to arrive, and I've waited long into the night while sitting by the bedside

of my husband when he was hospitalized. You probably feel the same way
do when it comes to waiting: I don't like it. Waiting is hard, inconvenient, and
uncomfortable. It's as if time puts itself on hold while life is making up its mind
what it wants to do.

Perhaps you've prayed a prayer like this: "Answer me speedily, O LORD
my spirit fails!" (Psalm 143:7a). We get excited when God answers our prayers
quickly, don't we? Then sometimes it seems that God takes His time and we're
left in limbo. Here's the good news: your waiting is not in vain. In God's economy,
no time is ever wasted. God always has a plan and a purpose for the waiting.

In the in-between times, it may seem as if God has forgotten your request. It
may feel that your life has been put on hold. But hear the words that the Lord
said to Joshua: "I will never leave you nor forsake you" (Joshua 1:5 NIV). In the
in-between times, God is behind the scenes doing His best work on your behalf.

The Word of God gives us specific instructions to follow while we wait on
God's direction. We can learn a great lesson as we face those seasons of uncertainty by reviewing what God has done for His people in the past. Today and
tomorrow we will be studying King Jehoshaphat to discover how to face our
fears and trust God when it would be easier to panic.

Jehoshaphat was a great king of the tribe of Judah who learned firsthand that
God would provide just the right solution at just the right moment. Today we
will see how fear crept into the story and how Jehoshaphat overcame it.

**Review the opening Scripture, 2 Chronicles 20:1-12. What news did
Jehoshaphat receive? (vv. 1-2)**

God's people found themselves between a rock and a hard place. With their
backs against the wall and their enemies breathing down their necks, this great
king knew that without God's help, they were doomed. Jehoshaphat was only
human. When he received the news that their enemies were gaining ground,
initially he was greatly alarmed. Who wouldn't be in that situation? But the king
knew that it was no time for fear. It was time for action.

How did the king handle the matter? (vv. 3-12)

King Jehoshaphat knew the situation was out of his hands, so he placed the
situation into God's hands. This is a critical response. How many heartbreaks
and setbacks we would avoid if only we would seek the Lord by fasting and
praying about a matter rather than taking matters into our own hands.

When we read this story, we find that it is packed full of strategic elements to help the people of God stand strong when they are waiting for the outcome. Even when the outcome is uncertain, even when you have to wait on God and trust Him every step of the way, you can know for sure that He is with you while you seek Him. God instructs you not to run scared. He commands you not to be overwhelmed and paralyzed with fear so that you can't think straight. Instead, He commands you to trust Him and turn the situation over to Him.

Though written hundreds of years later, the writer of Philippians tells us what to do when we are anxious or feeling overwhelmed. What instructions do you find in Philippians 4:6-7?

Just about every book in the Bible speaks to the subject of fear and commands us not to allow fear to control us. There are many "fear not" references in the Bible. As I've studied these "fear nots" of the Bible, I have found an interesting pattern. Wherever the words "fear not" appear, good news always follows close behind. Let's look at some examples.

Look up the following Scriptures and complete the chart.

	Who is afraid?	What is the fear?	What is the promise?
2 Chronicles 20:15			
Genesis 15:1-3			
Isaiah 41:8-10			
Joshua 1:1, 9			
Luke 1:30			
Luke 2:8-10			

Be anxious for nothing, but in everything by prayer and supplication, with thanksgiving, let your requests be made known to God; and the peace of God, which surpasses all understanding, will guard your hearts and minds through Christ Jesus.
Philippians 4:6-7

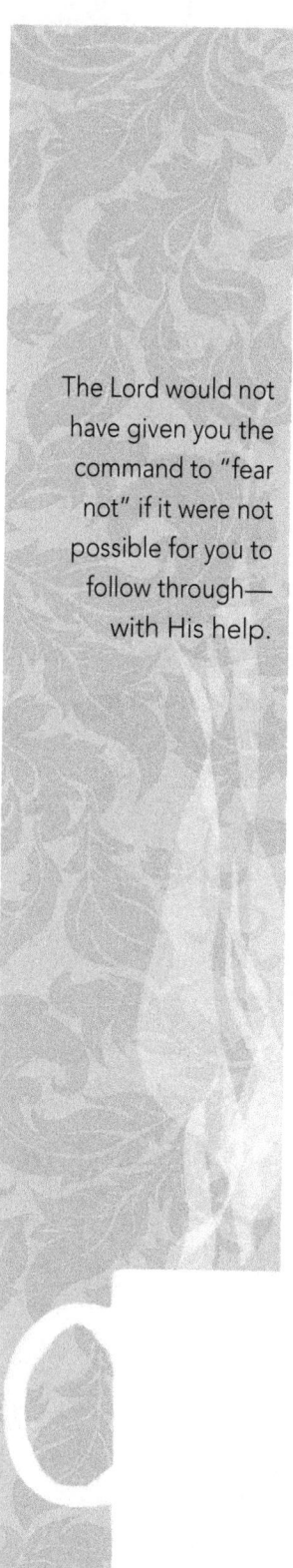

> The Lord would not have given you the command to "fear not" if it were not possible for you to follow through—with His help.

Do you see the pattern? In these and the many other "fear nots" in the Bible, we are reminded that God has commanded us not to fear but to look instead for His powerful promises to come to pass in our lives.

Sometimes the emotion of fear can be a healthy thing. You should have a healthy fear and respect for fire that burns out of control or for wild, dangerous animals. But the spirit of fear is not God's method of operation. The spirit of fear comes only from the enemy as a form of torment. Stand your ground and remember God's command not to fear. You might be thinking, "Well, there are some situations where I just can't help being fearful." Not according to God's Word! Though fear might rise up in you in a moment, you don't have to camp out there. The Lord would not have given you the command to "fear not" if it were not possible for you to follow through—with His help.

Read 2 Timothy 1:7 below to discover a believer's power over fear. Circle the word *not*. Underline what God *has* given us:

For God has not given us a spirit of fear and timidity, but of power, love, and self-discipline. **(NLT)**

This means, then, that it's actually possible not to be fearful—not to allow fear to take up residence.

Let's return now to the story of Jehoshaphat. Every great leader knows the importance of having a strategy for times of war, and that begins with keeping a level head in times of imminent danger. After Jehoshaphat called a national day of prayer and fasting, he called on the forces of heaven to gird them. He didn't fall apart in the face of danger; instead, he pulled it all together. When it counted the most, he didn't emphasize his situation, reminding himself and his people how big their enemies were. He made the Lord the center of attention and reminded the entire nation how big their God was.

Reread Jehoshaphat's powerful prayer in 2 Chronicles 20:5-12. Summarize the prayer below in your own words.

What a great lesson in prayer! Did you notice that Jehoshaphat did not rush into God's presence with a lengthy list of his personal needs, although they were critical? He didn't go to God with complaints or murmurings. Instead, he proclaimed God's attributes, those qualities that tell of God's greatness. It's not that

God needed to be reminded of His greatness; Jehoshaphat and the people were the ones who needed the reminding. In this powerful prayer, the king did not recite what he was feeling about himself but rehearsed what he already knew about God. Jehoshaphat shows us that by approaching God's throne in this manner, we respond to God in faith, not out of our fear or anxiety.

How would your prayer life change if you focused on praying the promises of God instead of praying your problems? Don't worry; pray. Don't wring your hands and pace the floor; pray. Don't take your problems to your friends and talk about them. Take your burdens to the Lord and leave them there. And if you find yourself picking them back up, take them to the Lord once again. Keep doing this and you will develop the habit of prayer. It is a habit we must practice every day.

As a songwriter, I like to keep my eyes peeled for quotations that could inspire a new song. I'll leave you with this great inspiration from a quotation I've seen on more than one church billboard: "Seven days without prayer makes one weak." Amen!

Go to God

Ask

Do your prayers express such a faith and confidence in God that whatever you ask according to His will, you believe He will do for you? It is more important to honor God, who already knows our need, than to selfishly come to God with our agenda. Like King Jehoshaphat, we need to recognize God for His ways, not just for His acts. Spend a few moments praising God and rehearsing His greatness, goodness, power, and faithfulness.

Seek

Does your prayer list read more like a shopping list, expressing your greed rather than your real need? God is well aware that you have many needs. Never forget that your God is the great Need-Meeter. I remember the old saints in my father's church saying this from time to time: "God is rarely early. But He's never late. Now, He may not come when you want Him, but He's always on time." I can say *amen* to that! In between the time you pray and the time you are waiting for an answer, stand on your faith, believing that God will come through for you.

What need in your life are you waiting for God to answer right now?

Knock

"We do not know what to do, but our eyes are upon you" (2 Chronicles 20:12 NIV). Does Jehoshaphat's plea ring true for you today? What situation in your life causes you to run to God? Knock on the door of God's heart, plead with Him, proclaim His greatness, and praise Him. Then, lay out your needs before Him. Trust Him to meet your need.

> Dear heavenly Father,
>   Thank You for Your awesome and mighty power. Thank You for Your sweet and tender mercies. Thank You for your incredible affection. You are so very good. Lord, I lay my needs before You, one by one, and ask You to meet them. I will give You all the praise and glory. In Jesus' name I pray. Amen.

Day 3: Let God Lead

Read God's Word

^{13}Now all Judah, with their little ones, their wives, and their children, stood before the LORD. ^{14}Then the Spirit of the LORD came upon Jahaziel the son of Zechariah, the son of Benaiah, the son of Jeiel, the son of Mattaniah, a Levite of the sons of Asaph, in the midst of the assembly. ^{15}And he said, "Listen, all you of Judah and you inhabitants of Jerusalem, and you, King Jehoshaphat! Thus says the LORD to you: 'Do not be afraid nor dismayed because of this great multitude, for the battle is not yours, but God's. ^{16}Tomorrow go down against them. They will surely come up by the Ascent of Ziz, and you will find them at the end of the brook before the Wilderness of Jeruel. ^{17}You will not need to fight in this battle. Position yourselves, stand still and see the salvation of the LORD, who is with you, O Judah and Jerusalem!' Do not fear or be dismayed; tomorrow go out against them, for the LORD is with you."

^{18}And Jehoshaphat bowed his head with his face to the ground, and all Judah and the inhabitants of Jerusalem bowed before the LORD, worshiping the LORD. ^{19}Then the Levites of the children of the Kohathites and of the children of the Korahites stood up to praise the LORD God of Israel with voices loud and high.

^{20}So they rose early in the morning and went out into the Wilderness of Tekoa; and as they went out, Jehoshaphat stood and said, "Hear me, O Judah and you inhabitants of Jerusalem: Believe in the LORD your God, and you shall be established; believe His prophets, and you shall prosper." ^{21}And when he had consulted with the people, he appointed those who should sing to the LORD, and who should praise the beauty of holiness, as they *went out before the army and were saying:*

> *"Praise the LORD,*
> *For His mercy endures forever."*

²²*Now when they began to sing and to praise, the Lord set ambushes against the people of Ammon, Moab, and Mount Seir, who had come against Judah; and they were defeated.* ²³*For the people of Ammon and Moab stood up against the inhabitants of Mount Seir to utterly kill and destroy them. And when they had made an end of the inhabitants of Seir, they helped to destroy one another.* ²⁴*So when Judah came to a place overlooking the wilderness, they looked toward the multitude; and there were their dead bodies, fallen on the earth. No one had escaped.*

2 Chronicles 20:13-24

Reflect and Respond

Have you ever found yourself beaten, bruised, and battle weary? If so, it's because you are fighting a battle that doesn't belong to you. You have a God who is bigger than your enemies, and He will fight for you. In fact, no matter the size of the battle you're facing, you are to let God fight for you. You do have a responsibility, however. Just as each member of a ball team has an assigned position, so do you. Just as every member of a corporate staff has a specific job description, so do you. Your position is to stand and see the salvation of the Lord.

Let's look more closely at Jehoshaphat's battle.

Review 2 Chronicles 20:14-17.

Who did the Spirit of the Lord come upon? (v. 14)

What did the Lord say through him? (vv. 15-17)

Who did the battle belong to? (v. 15)

What was needed to win the battle? (v. 17)

He who has begun a good work in you will complete it until the day of Jesus Christ.
Philippians 1:6

Jehoshaphat knew that God would deliver them. He knew God was the only One who could save them. When you stand firm on what you know, not on what you feel, you are in the position to receive from the Lord. In addition, you are clearheaded. This allows the Holy Spirit to show you the cunning strategies of the evil one, who only wants to steal everything that is near and dear to you. I'm a witness that the Lord will teach you how to stand strong in the midst of a battle.

One evening while Charles and I were out to dinner with friends, my purse was stolen. I was extremely upset with myself for being careless concerning my belongings. While we were at dinner, having a good time and even talking about the things of God, I looked around and my purse was gone. By evening's end, my heart was heavy with regret.

That night as I was getting into bed, the Lord impressed upon me to grab paper and pencil and to write down the negative emotions I was feeling. It just so happened that they all started with the letter "D." So I wrote as many negative "D" words as I could think of at the time: Disappointment. Discouragement. Denial. Debt. Disbelief. Divorce. Depression. Disease. Disagreement. Discontent. Death. Depravity. Danger. Distraction.

Every one of these words produces a negative emotion. It is quite easy for these words and attitudes to find their way into our thoughts and conversations, causing us to become victimized by them and keeping us from realizing victory in our lives. But I discovered that God's Word has an answer for every negative "D" word we may face. What the enemy thought would cause me *distress*, God used to teach me to put up a *defense*. I'm sharing this now to strengthen you.

When you *doubt*, remember Philippians 1:6. Read the verse in the margin. Write the words that give you faith below. How does this verse equip you against doubt?

When you feel *discouraged*, find hope in Psalm 42:5-6. Look up the verses and write the instructions you find in them below.

Read John 10:10 and complete the following statement:

Your enemy aims to devour your dreams, steal your joy, and destroy your health. But Jesus has come *"that [you] may have _____, and that [you] may have it more _____"* **(NKJV).**

When *disagreement* plagues any relationship, remember 1 Peter 4:8. Write the verse below and read it aloud to yourself.

When you battle with *distraction*, stand on the promise found in Isaiah 26:3. Read the verse in the following translations and circle the words and phrases that are common between them.

You will keep in perfect peace
all who trust in you,
whose thoughts are fixed on you! (NLT)

Those with sound thoughts you will keep in peace,
in peace because they trust in you. (CEB)

You will keep in perfect peace
those whose minds are steadfast,
because they trust in you. (NIV)

For every tool or tactic that comes against you, Jesus has a powerful weapon you can use to fight back: God's Word. Don't give in or let down your guard. Instead take up your rightful position as a redeemed, spirit-filled child of God and stand on the power of God's Word. Your position is one of an equipped and powerful warrior. From head to toe, you are to put on the whole armor of God. "Hanging in there" is not allowed. We must not "hang in there," as some are in the habit of saying casually. The phrase seems harmless, but words have power and life! So I've taken the phrase "hang in there" out of my vocabulary. I refuse to use it, because "hanging in there" is never the stance of the believer. God's Word does not say, "You just hang in there until I can get back with you." No!

Read 2 Chronicles 20:17 in the margin. What command does it give?

> *"'You will not need to fight in this battle [says the Lord]. Position yourselves, stand still and see the salvation of the Lord, who is with you, O Judah and Jerusalem!' Do not fear or be dismayed; tomorrow go out against them, for the Lord is with you."*
> 2 Chronicles 20:17

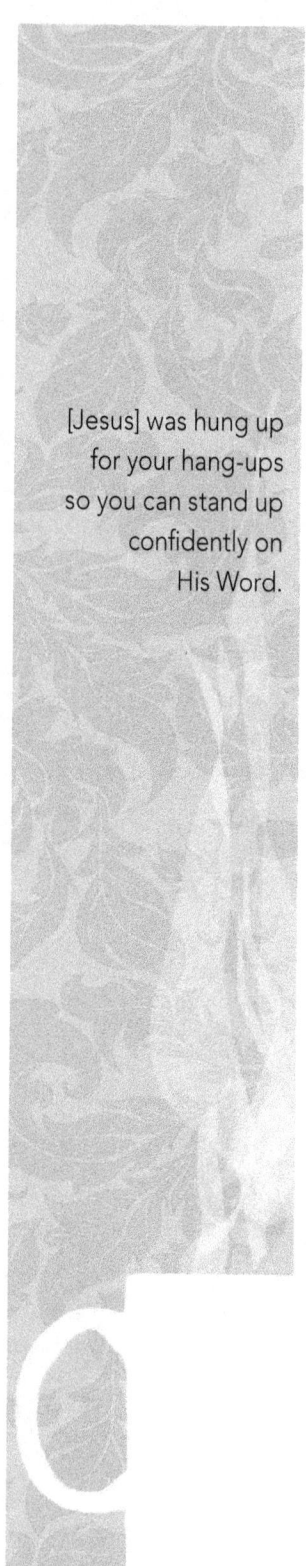

> [Jesus] was hung up for your hang-ups so you can stand up confidently on His Word.

You don't have to hang in there, because Jesus already did that for you when He hung on the cross at Calvary. He was hung up for your hang-ups so you can stand up confidently on His Word. So speak these words to yourself right now: "No longer will I take the position of hanging in there. From now on I'm standing in there!"

Don't let the unknown details concerning tomorrow fill your heart with fear and cause you to trip and fall. God has already taken care of tomorrow. With God on your side, you cannot lose!

Go to God

Ask

The possibility is great that you are facing some sort of conflict today. If there is a challenge in your life, don't run from it, no matter how difficult it may be. With God's help, face it head on.

Write your challenge below and claim God's mighty power through prayer.

Seek

The children of Judah had every reason to run for cover. Instead they received instructions from the Lord on how to endure the battle. Instead of fighting, the Lord told the children of Judah to praise their way out. Why? Praise confuses your enemy. The blessed privilege of praising the Most High God has been given to His children. Shake your fist in the face of the enemy by giving God praise even before you know the outcome. Right now, open up your mouth, speak the praises of God, and watch the enemy run!

Knock

Perhaps you have been asking God to answer a specific request. As you wait on God, *wait* on God—in the sense that a waiter serves a guest in a restaurant. In other words, serve Him. Just as a well-trained waiter would attend to a guest's every need in a fine restaurant, you are to serve the Lord with joy, even anticipating His desires. And just as the guest would reward the waiter for fine service after enjoying a great meal, God will fortify you with just what you need: "But they that wait upon the LORD shall renew their strength; they shall mount up with wings as eagles; they shall run, and not be weary; and they shall walk, and not faint" (Isaiah 40:31 KJV).

If you are waiting on God to follow through on His promise to you, don't worry or become impatient and resort to your own plan. Don't get anxious and get ahead of God. This one thing is for certain: you cannot hurry God. He moves in His own time clock. He loves you so much. You are in His tender care. He wants you to place all your trust in Him and wait patiently for Him. And He will come through right on time. Confess your belief in this assurance right now.

Dear loving Father,

How I thank You for Your mighty power in my life. Thank You for saving me from my enemies. Thank You for lifting me up when I'm down. Lord, give me clear instructions as I face the challenges that lie ahead. I will praise Your awesome name every step of the way. In Jesus' name. Amen.

Day 4: Believe that Jesus Can Heal

Read God's Word

¹¹*Now it happened, the day after, that He went into a city called Nain; and many of His disciples went with Him, and a large crowd.* ¹²*And when He came near the gate of the city, behold, a dead man was being carried out, the only son of his mother; and she was a widow. And a large crowd from the city was with her.* ¹³*When the Lord saw her, He had compassion on her and said to her, "Do not weep."* ¹⁴*Then He came and touched the open coffin, and those who carried him stood still. And He said, "Young man, I say to you, arise."* ¹⁵*So he who was dead sat up and began to speak. And He presented him to his mother.*

¹⁶*Then fear came upon all, and they glorified God, saying, "A great prophet has risen up among us"; and, "God has visited His people." And this report about Him went throughout all Judea and all the surrounding region.*

Luke 7:11-17

Reflect and Respond

Nestled within the pages of the Gospel of Luke is an account so brief that if you weren't looking for it, you might easily overlook it. It is the story of a woman from the town of Nain. As we look at this story together over the next two days, it is my prayer that it will saturate your heart.

When we are down to nothing, God is up to something.

This woman had lost everything she considered valuable. Her husband ha died, leaving her a widow, and then death came knocking on her door again claim the life of her only son way too early in his young adult life. She was o her way to bury the young man, who had been her sole means of support sinc the death of her husband and who no doubt had been the bright spot in a dar season of her life. Without a male family member to meet her needs, the day ahead would certainly be difficult for her. She, like most widows, would fac extreme poverty.

The times had not been kind to this woman. Now she was left alone and lonel in her grief. She had been robbed of her joy, stripped of her dignity, cheated c her dreams, and drained of her hopes; her heart and her arms were empty. Thi nameless widow knew what it was like to be down—down in the dumps an down to her last dime. But this is what I know for sure: God does His best wor when we are down. Yes, when we are down to nothing, God is up to something

Let's look at the verses prior to this story about the widow from Nain. Jesu was on a bit of a healing spree in these few chapters in Luke, and the scenes play like episodes of a great movie.

Read Luke 7:1-10 and answer the questions below.

Where was Jesus? (v. 1)

Who needed healing? (v. 2)

What did the centurion do? (v. 3)

What did Jesus say to the centurion's friends? (v. 9)

What did they find when they returned home? (v. 10)

Shortly before encountering the widow and her deceased son, Jesus entered Capernaum. It was there that He healed a centurion's servant after the centurion heard that Jesus was nearby and sent messengers to plead with Him. The Lord had only to send His word with the messengers, and the miracle occurred. Imagine that. Jesus, the living Word, sent the spoken word with power, and it was accomplished.

Then we come to the story of the widow whom Jesus helped in what must have been her lowest hour.

Review Luke 7:11-17.

Where was Jesus? (v. 11)

Who needed healing? (v. 12)

What did Jesus do? (vv. 13-15)

How did the people respond? (vv. 16-17)

Oh, how I wish I could have been there to witness Jesus raising this young man from the dead! I would love to have been a part of the masses that followed Jesus on His preaching and teaching tour around the Sea of Galilee. Using my imagination, I can visualize large crowds of people following Jesus similar to the way people and paparazzi in Hollywood follow their favorite actors and rock stars as they are out and about on the city streets. Love has a way of drawing people, doesn't it?

Jesus always drew a crowd. A growing number of disciples, the sick and infirm, curiosity seekers, and religious skeptics all followed Him. Jesus had been going about healing the sick, casting out demons, and teaching the multitudes, but this would be the first display of His power to bring the dead to life again. The miracles of raising Jairus's daughter and Lazarus would follow later. Other prophets like Elijah and Elisha had also raised the dead, but it was God who had used them in those circumstances. So when Jesus performed this miracle, the witnesses knew this was no ordinary man but a man sent from God.

Look again at Luke 7:12-13. Why did Jesus heal her son?

This is what I love about Jesus. This woman, so distraught by her loss, so engulfed in her sorrow, so engrossed in her pain, did not even see Jesus as He approached. Oh, but you can be certain He saw her. She did not come to where He was, seeking Him out; He came to where she was. Isn't that just like Jesus?

Read 2 Corinthians 8:9 (in the margin) and Philippians 2:5-8. What did Jesus give up in order to come to us? Why do you think He did this?

> *For you know the grace of our Lord Jesus Christ, that though He was rich, yet for your sakes He became poor, that you through His poverty might become rich.*
>
> 2 Corinthians 8:9

Jesus put on flesh and became like us so we could put on a robe of righteousness and become like Him. From the moment Jesus saw the distraught mother in the funeral procession, He had compassion on her. Jesus always has compassion on those who are grieving or hurting. He has compassion on you and me.

Are you experiencing a painful season in your life right now? Are you overwhelmed with grief or loss today? Take comfort in the fact that Jesus has felt every emotion you are feeling. Hold onto this truth from 1 Peter 5:7: "Give all your worries and cares to God, for he cares about you" (NLT).

Go to God

Ask

Dear friend, whenever you are at a loss, Jesus feels your pain and has compassion for you. As frail human beings, we can only assist in burden-bearing for each other for a little while before we are distracted by our own discomforts. But Jesus not only carries our burdens; He carries our burdens as long and as far as we need—not one moment or one step short of the full distance.

Just as Jesus did for this widow, He will do for you. He will meet you right where you are. And just like a mother who drops whatever she is doing to comfort her hurting child, the first beautiful words He will speak are those He spoke to the widow: "Don't cry." How compassionate and tender our Lord is! Pour out your cries to Jesus and feel the warmth of his compassion today.

Seek

Read these words of the psalmist:

> [1]*Hear my cry, O God;*
> *Attend to my prayer.*
> [2]*From the end of the earth I will cry to You,*
> *When my heart is overwhelmed;*
> *Lead me to the rock that is higher than I.*
>
> [3]*For You have been a shelter for me,*
> *A strong tower from the enemy.*
>
> Psalm 61:1-3

Read Psalm 61:1-3 in the margin, and write it in your own words below. Seek the Rock that is higher as you face your challenges today.

Hear my cry, O God; Attend to my prayer. From the end of the earth I will cry to You, When my heart is overwhelmed; Lead me to the rock that is higher than I. For You have been a shelter for me, A strong tower from the enemy. Psalm 61:1-3

Knock

After a recent concert, I met a precious young lady who stood waiting in line to speak to me. While others waited to get their CDs and books signed, she had nothing in her hand. What she did have was a story. She had recently had a miscarriage and could hardly get the painful words out before she began to cry. I embraced her tightly, comforting her and calling on Jesus to heal her pain. What a privilege it was to bear her burden, if only for a few moments.

Who is carrying burdens that you can help to bear today? Write their names below and pray for them one by one. Then, make a point to call them and share their load.

Healing God,
Thank You for your healing power. Sometimes You heal bodies, sometimes You heal hearts, sometimes You heal relationships. We can't always see the healing happening, but we know You are always working in us. Have compassion on us, Lord. Bring Your healing into the broken places in our lives. We ask You to say the word and heal our brokenness. We will give You all the praise and glory. In Jesus' name. Amen.

Day 5: Celebrate the Healing

Read God's Word

[11]Now it happened, the day after, that He went into a city called Nain; and many of His disciples went with Him, and a large crowd. [12]And when He came near the gate of the city, behold, a dead man was being carried out, the only son of his mother; and she was a widow. And a large crowd from the city was with her. [13]When the Lord saw her, He had compassion on her and said to her, "Do not weep." [14]Then He came and touched

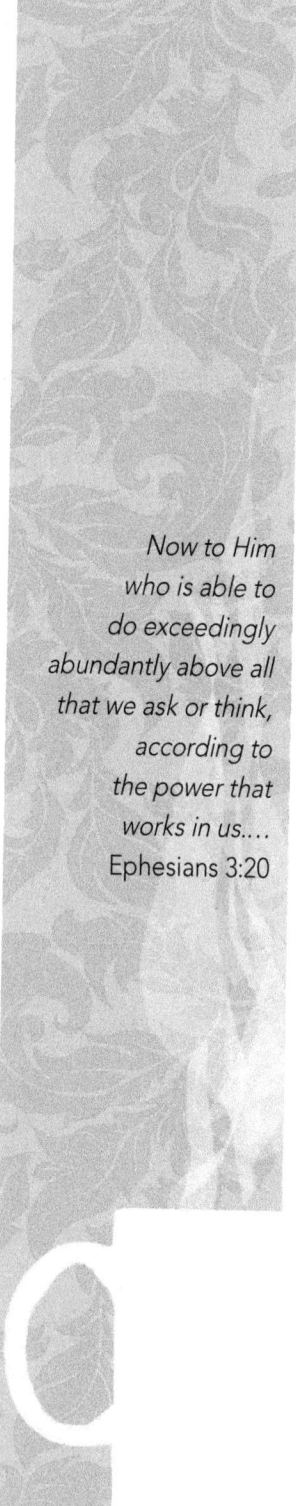

the open coffin, and those who carried him stood still. And He said, "Young man, I s
to you, arise." [15]So he who was dead sat up and began to speak. And He presented him
his mother.

[16]Then fear came upon all, and they glorified God, saying, "A great prophet has ris
up among us"; and, "God has visited His people." And this report about Him we
throughout all Judea and all the surrounding region.

Luke 7:11-1

Reflect and Respond

Yesterday we focused on Jesus' compassion for this widow. Today I want u
to focus on the celebration after the healing. The powerful truth that God neve
forsakes us and is with us through even the darkest hours of life is a message tha
is not meant to be kept to ourselves. In fact, once we experience God's healin
and saving power, we can't help but celebrate and share it with others.

I've sung for a lot of funerals in my lifetime. Singing under those circum
stances is never easy. Choosing just the right song to sing is always a challenge
But if I were in the crowd that day and had been asked to sing at that funeral,
would have had to change my tune. Out with "Nearer, My God, to Thee"! Afte
seeing that young man come back from the dead, I would have led a rousing
rendition of the "Hallelujah Chorus"! You see, Jesus never attended a funera
where the dead stayed dead. He has all power, even power over death; so wher
Jesus went to a funeral, the funeral was over.

Once the dead are raised to life again, there's nothing left to do but celebrate
Sometimes the blessings are so unbelievable that we just have to praise!

**Read Ephesians 3:20 in the margin. What words does this verse use to
describe the ways that Jesus blesses us?**

That's right. Jesus blesses us beyond what we can imagine—with a brand-new
life. On the hand-hewn open coffin lay the body of the widow's son, wrapped
in burial cloths. Jesus did what was unheard of, particularly for a rabbi—he
touched the dead body. Most rabbis wouldn't think of touching the dead for fear
of being contaminated. But with Jesus, the Teacher of teachers, the Resurrection
and the Life, even the dead obey His voice. And the living? They, too, are halted
by His authority. The pallbearers and those in the funeral procession stopped the
procession to experience the demonstration of His power.

*Now to Him
who is able to
do exceedingly
abundantly above all
that we ask or think,
according to
the power that
works in us....*
Ephesians 3:20

Reread Luke 7:14-15. What did Jesus say to the deceased young man? What happened?

Jesus spoke to the deceased young man, and that young man sat up and began to talk! Wouldn't you like to know what that young man's first words were? Maybe he exclaimed something like, "Boy, that was the best nap ever!" Or maybe his words were a series of questions such as, "Who are all these people? Why am I in a casket? What did You say Your name was, Sir?"

Whatever his words, it's easy to imagine that both the mother and son gave endless thanks and praise to Jesus for what He had done. These events caused them and those around them to want to know more about Jesus and the life-changing truths He taught.

Reread Luke 7:16-17. How do these verses describe the crowd's reaction to the healing?

We read that a great fear came upon all the people, and they glorified God, for in Christ they saw the hope they had long been waiting for. They saw the power of possibility that could carry them from where they were to places they had only dreamed of before.

Reflect for a moment on the power that Jesus demonstrated by raising the deceased young man. How does this give you encouragement for the challenges you are facing right now?

Can you imagine how amazed those who were following Jesus must have been when Jesus spoke and that young man sat up? And the widow! Imagine the depth of her joy at the return of her son. This mother had no idea what would happen and who she would meet as she left her home for the grave site that day. One thing I love about Jesus is that He is full of wonderful surprises! When you least expect it, He manifests His presence, bringing light to darkness, life to death, and joy to sorrow.

Jesus still heals today. He may use modern medicine to bring about healing in one's body, or He may bring healing with one divine touch. Either way, we are to respond the same way the people did when the widow's son was brought back to life: with wonder and awe.

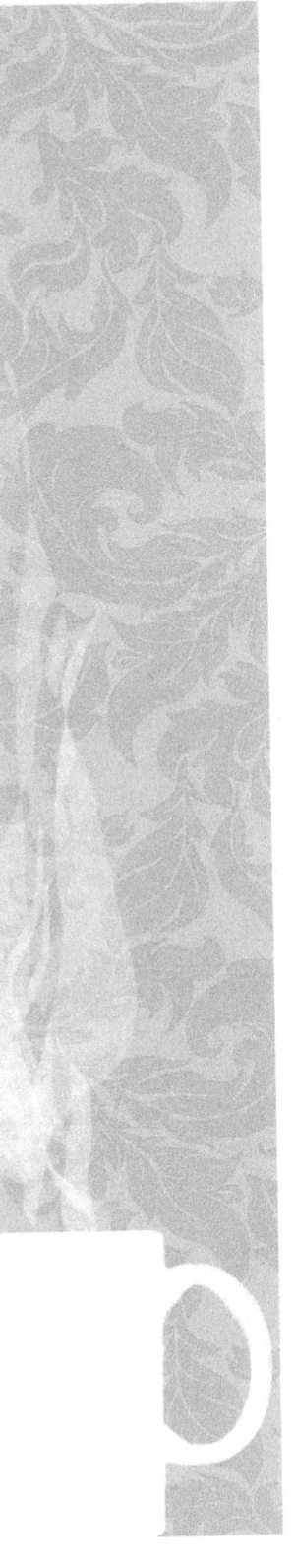

Look with me now at another healing story in the Gospels.

Read Mark 7:31-37 and answer the following questions:

Where was Jesus in this passage? (v. 31)

Who was brought to him for healing? (v. 32)

What did Jesus do and say? (vv. 33-34)

How long did the healing take once Jesus spoke these words? (v. 35)

What instructions did Jesus give to those who witnessed the healing? (v. 36)

What did the people do? (vv. 36-37)

The crowd that witnessed Jesus' healing of this deaf man could not contain their excitement. I love the way the Common English Bible translation reads: "The more [Jesus] tried to silence them, the more eagerly they shared the news. People were overcome with wonder" (vv. 36-37*a*). You can just imagine Jesus telling them to keep quiet, and them responding, "Listen, Jesus, if you want us to keep quiet about how great you are, then you're going to have to have to stop being so amazing!"

When healing comes, there is cause for celebration. The psalmists knew this well.

You have turned my mourning into dancing;
you have taken off my sackcloth and clothed me with joy,
so that my soul may praise you and not be silent.
O Lord my God, I will give thanks to you forever.
Psalm 30:11-12 NRSV

Look up the following verses. After each, write your thoughts or a prayer of response.

Psalm 9:13-14

Psalm 30:11-12

Psalm 103: 1-5

In the song that inspired this study, "This I Know for Sure," my desire is to voice my confidence in the Lord, regardless of the inner longings of the soul. The lyrics to the third verse and the chorus that follows come to my mind at this time. Let them encourage your heart:

> *When the nights are lonesome*
> *Fear comes with dismay*
> *I find peace in His presence*
> *And strength again to say*
>
> *There is a God in heaven*
> *And I am in His plan*
> *He will forsake me never*
> *My life is in His hands*
> *His boundless love will lead me*
> *As long as time endures*
> *Oh, this I know*
> *This I know for sure*

I wrote this song to bring you hope, dear one. Sometimes you may look at your situation and be tempted to give up. But that is not the time for giving up. That is the time for holding fast to what you know to be true.

Can you recall a promise from God's Word right now to speak hope to a difficult situation? Maybe it's our memory verse, 2 Timothy 1:12. Can you quote it from memory now? Close your eyes and recite it; then open your eyes and read it aloud: "I know whom I have believed, and am persuaded that he is able to keep that which I have committed unto him against that day" (KJV).

Go to God

Ask

Is there anything that has "died" in your life? Do you have a dead, passionless marriage? Maybe you've been told your womb is lifeless, causing you to die just a little more each day on the inside. Are you working a dead-end job, or do you have a mountain of debt and not a bit of credit? Relax. Breathing life into situations that have been pronounced "dead on arrival" is Jesus' speciality. He is the One who can resurrect dead hopes and transform dashed dreams. He is able to reignite the fires of faith if you are hesitant to believe. And He can restore your joy if you find yourself in the pit of despair. What has been lost in your life today? Talk to God about it now.

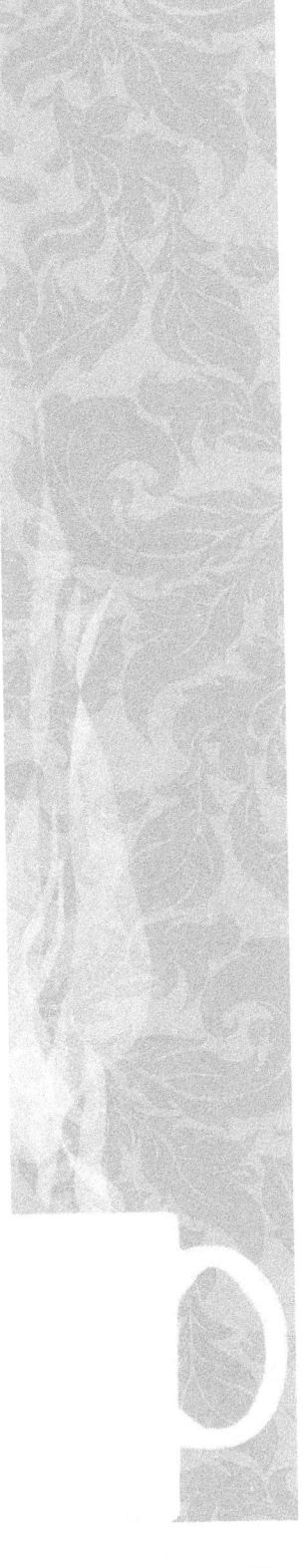

Seek

If you need renewing, relieving, restoring, reviving, or resurrecting, come Jesus and trust in Him for comfort and refuge. When love has died, when th nights are long, and when hope seems all but gone, lean in and listen closely f a still, small voice. Jesus has something He wants you to know for sure: you ar not forsaken. When Jesus is all you have, He is all you need. He is the comforte for those who mourn. He is the healer for those who are sick. He is a shelter i the storm. He is the Way out of no way. So when you feel you have nothing lef don't despair. Remember what Jesus did for the widow and her son.

What do you need Jesus to be for you today? Do you need Him to be you comforter, healer, or shelter? Seek Him now and allow Him to be all you need.

Knock

What do you know for sure, dear friend? You can add this to the list: *God' people can always find comfort and encouragement in Him when times are hard.* Fo some, the times have never been leaner. Others may be one or two paycheck from hard times. No matter what the situation is, God will always find a way.

Look and listen for encouragement from God today. Sometimes we mis God's voice because we forget to listen. On a separate piece of paper or in journal, write a letter to yourself from God. Let Him tell you how He loves you and cares for you.

> *O Father,*
>
> *We are so grateful that You are mindful of us, that You hear us when we call, that You know our need for healing even before we ask. We praise You for having a plan for healing in our lives even now. We know that You can do more than we can ask or imagine. We pray in the name of Jesus that healing will come to the broken places in our lives. And Lord, we cannot wait to tell everyone we know that You are the great God who heals, saves, restores, redeems, and loves us completely. This I know for sure! In Jesus' name. Amen.*

Week 3

Video Viewer Guide

Storms don't come to _____; they come to _____.

"I will _____ leave you nor forsake you."
Hebrews 13:5b NKJV

Enkataleipō(*eng-kat-al-i'-po*)—to leave in _____ _____; to leave helpless; to totally abandon

Forsake—to quit _____, to _____ or desert

"Be strong and of good _____, do not fear nor be afraid of them; for the LORD your God, He is the One who goes with you. He will not leave you nor _____ you."
Deuteronomy 31:6 NKJV

We are hard-pressed on every side, yet not crushed; we are perplexed, but not _____; persecuted, but not _____; struck down, but not destroyed.
2 Corinthians 4:8-9 NKJV

Life may have dealt you a blow; it may have knocked you _____. But it does not have to knock you _____.

No longer will I take the position of _____ in there, but I will _____ and see the salvation of the Lord.

Week 4
My Life Is in God's Hands

Early in my ministry, I was invited to sing at one of the local women's jails in the Atlanta area. There was no meeting room at the facility, so my hosts and I improvised by setting up a stage area at the front of a small jail cell, large enough to hold only three wooden bleachers, welded to the floor. There, among the iron bars, I set up a portable sound system and prepared some music and an encouraging message from God's Word to share with the inmates. Since it was not possible to sing for a larger group of women all at once, the officers of the jail permitted smaller groups of women to come into the holding cell for fifteen to twenty minutes at a time for a series of mini-concerts.

In groups of five or six, women of every age and race, shackled and chained together at the hands and feet, were led into that cell where I could minister the hope and the love of Jesus to them for a few brief moments. I sang for about six different groups of women, and each time I sang and spoke before these women, I didn't hold anything back. I sang as if I were on stage at Madison Square Garden. I thought for a moment that prison bars might open up and set prisoners free just as they did when Paul and Silas sang praises to God at midnight in Acts 16.

During each mini-concert the women and I sang and worshiped together. We laughed and cried together, and each time I had the privilege of praying for the women, leading some to accept Jesus as Savior. By the time I had delivered the last mini-concert, I had sung for about thirty-five women. My prayer that day was that the hearts of the women who came to that sanctuary in a cell would be touched and changed. I know of one woman whose heart was forever changed— me! That was a very precious time of ministry for me, and I left the jail that day with a real sense of purpose, determined to do my part in leading women everywhere to Jesus. Some might consider those women hopeless cases, but I gave them every reason to believe that, with Jesus, there is no hopeless case.

Here is what I know for sure. When we place our lives in God's hands, we have a hope like nothing the world can offer. We have peace like nothing money

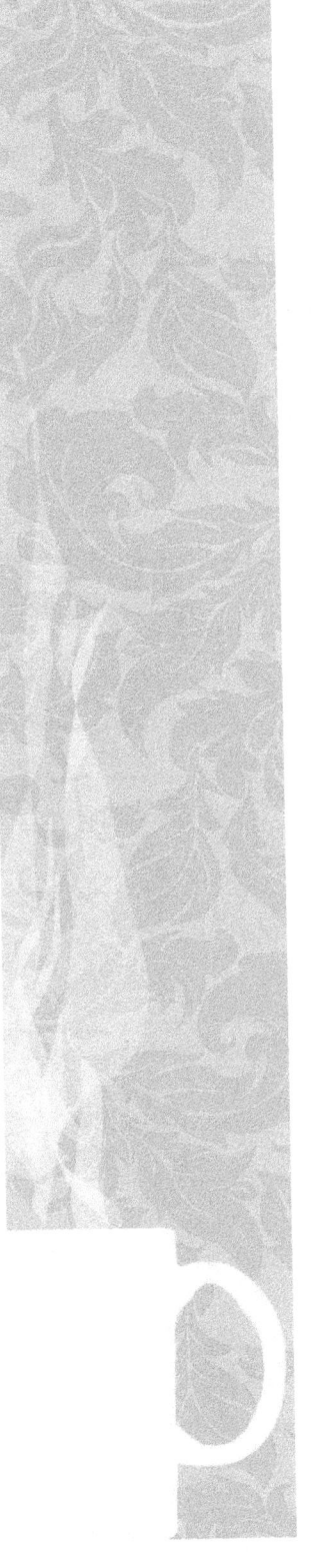

can buy. We have joy overflowing, even in sorrow. Friend, I hope you have placed your life in God's hands. If you haven't, my prayer is that our study this week will lead you to choose to put your life into the hands of the One who loves you and knows you best.

This week we will be looking at people in the Bible who show us what it looks like to place our lives into God's hands. We will consider the role of prayer, determination, faith, obedience, and courage in becoming women of strong faith who boldly give our all—*everything*—for God's glory in our lives and in our world. When we know and believe beyond a shadow of a doubt that our lives are in God's hands, taking risks and exercising faith as God directs us, amazing things can happen!

Scripture Memorization

I hope that by now you are well on your way to memorizing our theme Scripture, 2 Timothy 1:12:

> *I know whom I have believed, and am persuaded that he is able to keep that which I have committed unto him against that day.* (KJV)

Are you fully persuaded that God is able to hold your life in His hands? As you continue to rehearse this wonderful verse through recitation or song, go beyond just committing it to memory; claim it for your life!

Day 1: Begin with Prayer

Read God's Word

¹The words of Nehemiah the son of Hachaliah.

It came to pass in the month of Chislev, in the twentieth year, as I was in Shushan the citadel, ²that Hanani one of my brethren came with men from Judah; and I asked them concerning the Jews who had escaped, who had survived the captivity, and concerning Jerusalem. ³And they said to me, "The survivors who are left from the captivity in the province are there in great distress and reproach. The wall of Jerusalem is also broken down, and its gates are burned with fire."

⁴So it was, when I heard these words, that I sat down and wept, and mourned for many days; I was fasting and praying before the God of heaven.

⁵And I said: "I pray, Lᴏʀᴅ God of heaven, O great and awesome God, You who keep Your covenant and mercy with those who love You and observe Your commandments, ⁶please let Your ear be attentive and Your eyes open, that You may hear the prayer of Your servant which I pray before You now, day and night, for the children of Israel Your servants, and confess the sins of the children of Israel which we have sinned against You. Both my father's house and I have sinned. ⁷We have acted very corruptly against You, and have not kept the commandments, the statutes, nor the ordinances which You commanded Your servant Moses. ⁸Remember, I pray, the word that You commanded Your servant Moses, saying, 'If you are unfaithful, I will scatter you among the nations; ⁹but if you return to Me, and keep My commandments and do them, though some of you were cast out to the farthest part of the heavens, yet I will gather them from there, and bring them to the place which I have chosen as a dwelling for My name.' ¹⁰Now these are Your servants and Your people, whom You have redeemed by Your great power, and by Your strong hand. ¹¹O Lord, I pray, please let Your ear be attentive to the prayer of Your servant, and to the prayer of Your servants who desire to fear Your name; and let Your servant prosper this day, I pray, and grant him mercy in the sight of this man."

Nehemiah 1:1-11

Reflect and Respond

If you want to know what it looks like when someone places *everything* in God's hands, Nehemiah is one to examine. As the royal cupbearer to King Artaxerxes, king of Persia, Nehemiah was found to be a very dedicated and trustworthy man who had gained tremendous favor and the friendship of the king. He was a man of great resolve—a man devoted to God and the people he loved.

Although Nehemiah enjoyed a comfortable lifestyle under the king's authority, he was still a Hebrew servant, a slave in the king's palace. He lived far away from Jerusalem, but his heart longed for the land of his heritage. While many Jews who lived in Persia during the Babylonian captivity assimilated and became like the culture around them, Nehemiah chose to serve God rather than people. Nehemiah shows us that when we live a life that pleases God, it may not be comfortable, popular, or convenient. But he cared only about doing what was right and remaining faithful to God and the mission assigned to him from on high.

Review Nehemiah 1:1-11 and answer the following questions:

What news did Nehemiah discover about Jerusalem? (v. 3)

What was Nehemiah's response to the news? (v. 4)

How would you summarize Nehemiah's prayer? (vv. 5-11)

When Nehemiah received word that far-off Jerusalem's walls were in dilapidated condition and its city gates burned, his heart was broken. In those days, a city with a great wall system was fortified; on the other hand, a city without walls was at great risk and exposed to its enemies.

When we read the Book of Nehemiah, it's as if we are peering over his shoulder to read an entry from his journal. Nehemiah was so grieved by the condition of his people that he took his burden immediately to God in prayer. He knew that he needed God's help. He loved his homeland, but what could he do for his people who were so far away? His heart was broken but moved to do *something*.

Have you ever been so burdened by something that it broke your heart? When have you been grieved to the point of prayer and action?

When you feel that kind of burden, the Lord is moving upon your heart to become involved, to be a conduit or a catalyst for change. Take your cue from Nehemiah and see how your misery may open the door to your ministry.

What is your usual response to a heart burden? Circle one:

I become angry or frustrated.

I throw up my hands and walk away.

I worry and complain that somebody ought to do something about the problem.

I immediately go to God in prayer to ask how I can do my part.

Other:

Sometimes when we are burdened by something, we can feel paralyzed or overcome with fear. Nehemiah shows us how to act. He didn't get mad and throw a tantrum. He didn't say, "Too bad for them; I'm glad I'm doing so well." He didn't sit around worrying and wondering when someone would do something. No, he immediately went to God. Let's look more closely at his prayer.

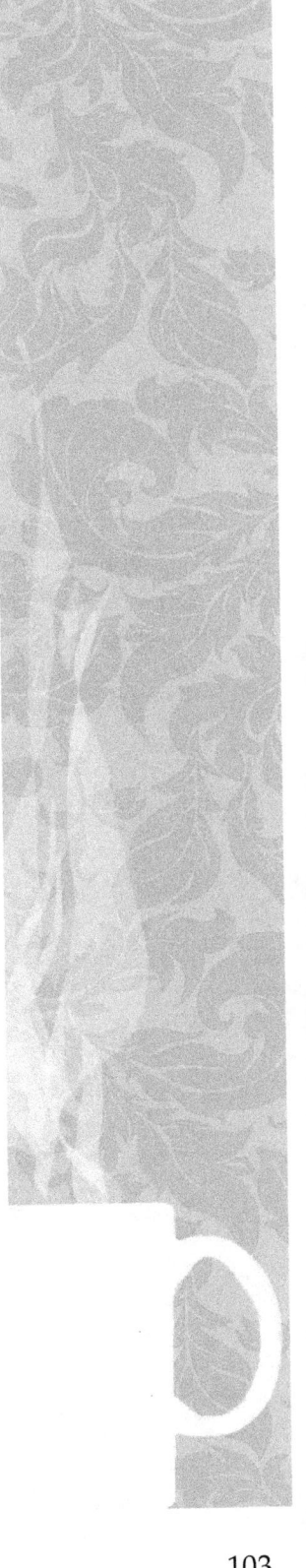

Nehemiah's prayer has a definite pattern: worship, confess, request. Reread verses 5-11 and determine which verses fit in each section.

Which verse is the "worship" section of the prayer?

How does Nehemiah express worship? What characteristics of God does he praise?

Which verses make up the "confess" section of the prayer? What sins does Nehemiah confess—for himself and for his people?

Which verses make up the "request" section of the prayer? What does Nehemiah request from God?

> Nehemiah shows us that prayer is the first step in exercising faith and making our lives count.

After Nehemiah worshiped and confessed the sins of his people, he gave God an open invitation to use him to save his people and rebuild Jerusalem. The Lord heard Nehemiah's prayer and moved upon the heart of King Artaxerxes, who not only gave his blessing for Nehemiah to go but also donated all the supplies to be used in the building project *and* provided the proper letters of authority that permitted Nehemiah to pass through other lands on his way to Judah. We'll continue his story in tomorrow's reading.

For now, consider this: have you ever looked back over the course of your life and wondered how you arrived where you are now? When we look at Nehemiah's life, we can see how one thought set the course for the rest of his life. Believing that his life truly was in God's hands, Nehemiah had the faith to take the risk of making a bold request of the king. He allowed that one thought—concern for his people and homeland—to direct the course of the rest of his life, trusting everything to God.

Nehemiah shows us that prayer is the first step in exercising faith and making our lives count. By observing Nehemiah's life, we learn how to rebuild and restore the things that are broken down in our lives. The qualities that Nehemiah possessed are not reserved for a special brand or breed of people. The same qualities are meant for you and me! You see, there is a special mission assigned to each one of us. There is a specific work God desires each of us to "build up."

If you had told me when I was in college that God would allow me the privilege of composing and recording original songs, writing books and Bible studies, nd standing before women to teach the Bible, I'd say, "I don't think so! You've ot me confused with someone else!" Now I *know* personally that God always oes exceedingly more than we could ever ask or imagine! That's what I love bout Him—one thing always leads to another. God will develop gifts and talnts that you may not know you have. I know this for sure!

There's no doubt that writing *This I Know for Sure*—both this Bible study and he book—and recording a music project by the same title was God's idea. You ee, I would never make such demands of myself on my own. It would scare me alf to death! I don't have the courage or the confidence to do all of this on my wn. God always requires more of us than we require of ourselves. That way, we re totally dependent on Him to complete the task.

I had to say, even with my knees knocking together, "Okay, God. I'm not sure how You will do this, but if You will equip me, if You will help me, I'll make myself available to You." Some days I have to take a giant leap of faith; other days it's like jumping off a cliff and not knowing where I'll land. But I really do believe that as I place my life in God's hands, He will either strap on the parachute in mid-flight or give me wings! What an adventure this faith walk is.

What is God's mission for *you*? Does it seem bigger than you can handle? This is your opportunity to trust God with everything you've got. Remember, you don't have to help everybody. Just help somebody. You don't have to do everything. Just do one thing. You'll find that once you give God something to work with, God will bless and multiply your efforts.

The journey begins with prayer. In God's divine presence, you will be empowered to carry out your mission until it is completed—because your life and destiny *are* in God's hands!

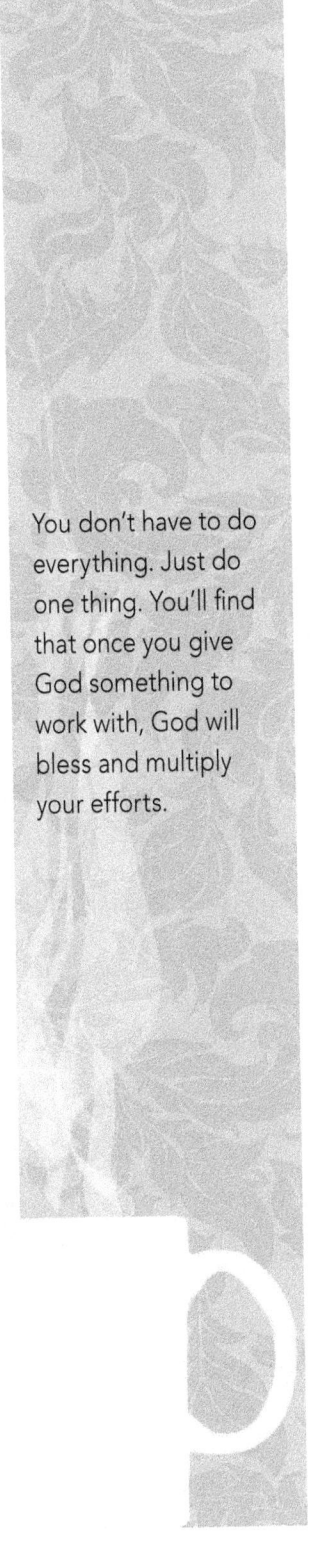

You don't have to do everything. Just do one thing. You'll find that once you give God something to work with, God will bless and multiply your efforts.

Go to God

Ask

God promises to equip and empower us to do whatever He calls us to do. Jesus isn't looking for more church folk to warm a pew; He's looking for ambassadors to spread His love throughout the earth. If God is prompting you to do something, don't delay another moment, dear friend.

What burdens are on your heart today? List them here and go to God in prayer, using Nehemiah's model of worship, confess, and request.

Seek

Talk more with God about His plan for your specific assignment. Is someor around you in need? Is there a mission or a ministry that needs your suppor Could a friend or neighbor use a personal visit or a phone call of encouragemen Follow Nehemiah's lead. By faith he took his burden to God. By faith he receive a plan from the Lord. And by faith he carried out the plan.

What is God saying to you about the plan for your assignment?

Knock

You can do the work of Jesus as you put your faith into action. When you d this, an amazing thing will happen: you will find that faith is not just believin; that the power of God can change the world; faith is believing that the power o God can change the world through *you!*

What specific action will you take today, this week, or this month to pu your faith into action and do the work of Jesus?

Dear heavenly Father,

Nehemiah was burdened by a torn-down wall around his city. I am burdened by the torn-down places in our world. Have I been complacent or neglectful, avoiding areas that need attention? God, give me a passion to help others. Then, Lord, I give you permission to take that passion and turn it into a burden. Maybe I could help single moms, senior citizens, or those who are incarcerated. Maybe I could mentor kids on the street or spend more time with my own family. Maybe I need to fortify the walls of my marriage, get out of debt, or complete my education. Whatever it is, Lord, open my eyes to see the places in my own life that have been torn down and left in ruins. Help me to see the relationships that need repair or the situations concerning my health that need to change. So, here I am, Lord, turning my life over to You. Thank You that my life is in Your hands! In Jesus' name. Amen.

Day 2: Be Determined

Read God's Word

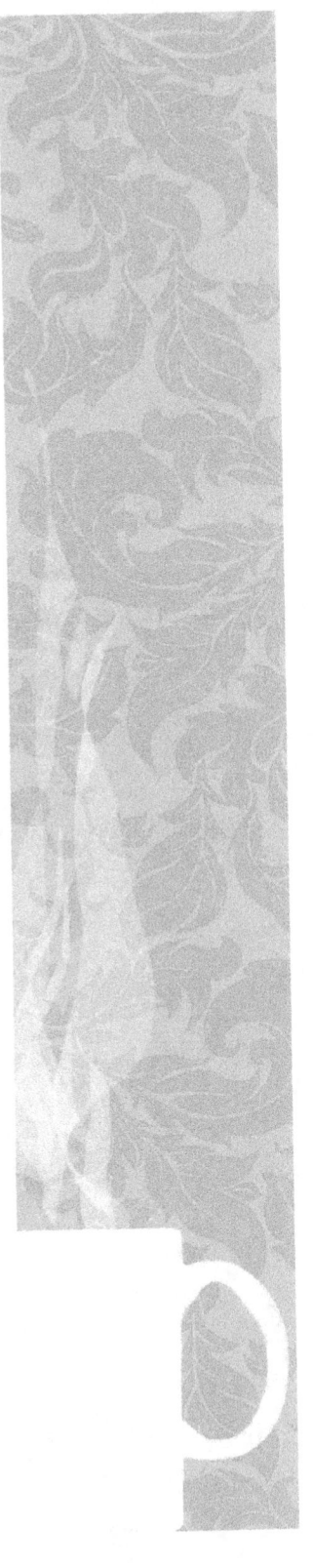

¹*And it came to pass in the month of Nisan, in the twentieth year of King Artaxerxes, when wine was before him, that I took the wine and gave it to the king. Now I had never been sad in his presence before.* ²*Therefore the king said to me, "Why is your face sad, since you are not sick? This is nothing but sorrow of heart."*

So I became dreadfully afraid, ³*and said to the king, "May the king live forever! Why should my face not be sad, when the city, the place of my fathers' tombs, lies waste, and its gates are burned with fire?"*

⁴*Then the king said to me, "What do you request?"*

So I prayed to the God of heaven. ⁵*And I said to the king, "If it pleases the king, and if your servant has found favor in your sight, I ask that you send me to Judah, to the city of my fathers' tombs, that I may rebuild it."*

⁶*Then the king said to me (the queen also sitting beside him), "How long will your journey be? And when will you return?" So it pleased the king to send me; and I set him a time.*

⁷*Furthermore I said to the king, "If it pleases the king, let letters be given to me for the governors of the region beyond the River, that they must permit me to pass through till I come to Judah,* ⁸*and a letter to Asaph the keeper of the king's forest, that he must give me timber to make beams for the gates of the citadel which pertains to the temple, for the city wall, and for the house that I will occupy." And the king granted them to me according to the good hand of my God upon me.*

⁹*Then I went to the governors in the region beyond the River, and gave them the king's letters. Now the king had sent captains of the army and horsemen with me.* ¹⁰*When Sanballat the Horonite and Tobiah the Ammonite official heard of it, they were deeply disturbed that a man had come to seek the well-being of the children of Israel.*

¹¹*So I came to Jerusalem and was there three days.* ¹²*Then I arose in the night, I and a few men with me; I told no one what my God had put in my heart to do at Jerusalem; nor was there any animal with me, except the one on which I rode.* ¹³*And I went out by night through the Valley Gate to the Serpent Well and the Refuse Gate, and viewed the walls of Jerusalem which were broken down and its gates which were burned with fire.* ¹⁴*Then I went on to the Fountain Gate and to the King's Pool, but there was no room for the animal under me to pass.* ¹⁵*So I went up in the night by the valley, and viewed the wall; then I turned back and entered by the Valley Gate, and so returned.* ¹⁶*And the officials did not know where I had gone or what I had done; I had not yet told the Jews, the priests, the nobles, the officials, or the others who did the work.*

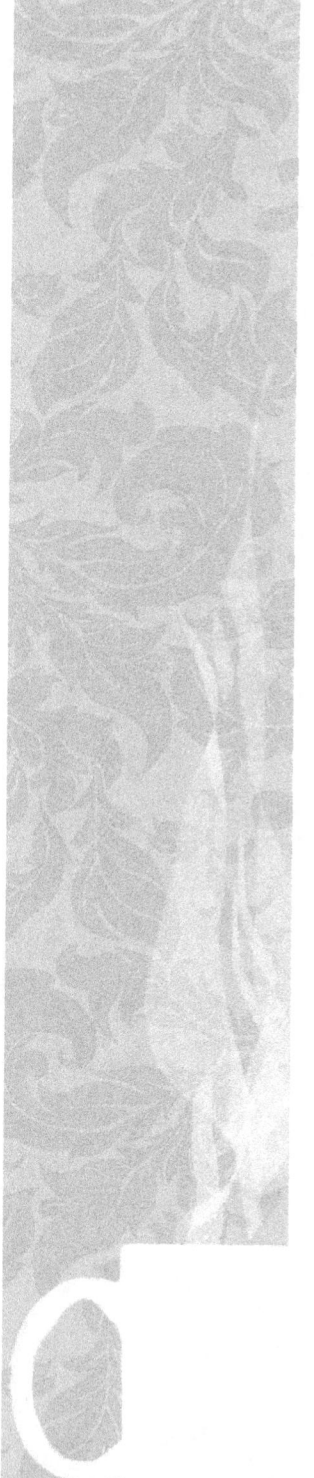

¹⁷*Then I said to them, "You see the distress that we are in, how Jerusalem lies waste, and its gates are burned with fire. Come and let us build the wall of Jerusalem, that we may no longer be a reproach."* ¹⁸*And I told them of the hand of my God which had been good upon me, and also of the king's words that he had spoken to me.*

So they said, "Let us rise up and build." Then they set their hands to this good work.

¹⁹*But when Sanballat the Horonite, Tobiah the Ammonite official, and Geshem the Arab heard of it, they laughed at us and despised us, and said, "What is this thing that you are doing? Will you rebel against the king?"*

²⁰*So I answered them, and said to them, "The God of heaven Himself will prosper us; therefore we His servants will arise and build, but you have no heritage or right or memorial in Jerusalem."*

Nehemiah 2:1-20

Reflect and Respond

Yesterday we saw that in order to put your life into God's hands, you must begin with prayer. We eavesdropped on Nehemiah as he pleaded with God to forgive his people and to be used to rebuild the city wall in Jerusalem. Nehemiah gave God an open invitation to use him to save his people and rebuild Jerusalem. The Lord heard Nehemiah's prayer and moved upon the heart of King Artaxerxes.

Today we continue exploring Nehemiah's story, focusing on his determination to carry out the work God gave him to do. As we will see from his example, knowing with confidence that your life is in God's hands produces incredible determination and amazing results!

Review Nehemiah 2:1-20 and answer the following questions:

What did Nehemiah do immediately before making his requests of the king? (v. 4)

What did Nehemiah ask for from the king? (vv. 5-8)

Why did the king give Nehemiah what he asked for? (v. 8)

The king not only gave his blessing for Nehemiah to go; he even donated all the supplies to be used in the building project and provided the proper letters of authority to permit Nehemiah to pass through other lands on his way to Judah. But that's not all. The king also provided something Nehemiah didn't even ask for.

What did the king send with Nehemiah? (v. 9)

Think about it: the Babylonian king sent army officers and soldiers along with a *Hebrew slave* to validate the king's authority and ensure safe passage. I love it when God shows off!

Once Nehemiah arrived in Jerusalem, he wasted no time before he set about the work he had come to do. Clearly he had a sense of urgency and determination.

How soon after arriving did Nehemiah set to work? (v. 11)

When did Nehemiah set out, and what did he do? (vv. 12-15)

What did he *not* do? (vv. 12, 16)

After carefully assessing the excessive damages that had been done to his beloved city, Nehemiah devised a plan and shared it with the people.

How did Nehemiah make a case for the rebuilding of the wall of Jerusalem? (vv. 17-18)

What was the people's response? (v. 18)

Did you notice that they not only agreed to start the work but they did so *eagerly*? Nehemiah's challenging project was off to a good start.

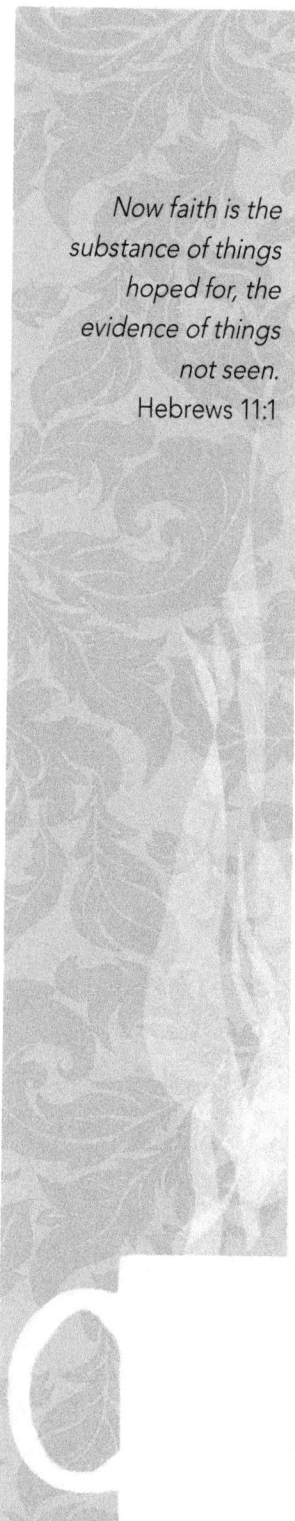

Have you ever been faced with a huge challenge? Your answer is probabl yes. Going into that challenge, did you know how things were going to wor out? Your answer is probably no. There is no way to know the outcome of ever problem; that is where your faith in Jesus Christ comes in.

Read Hebrews 11:1 in the margin. This is a landmark passage that can giv you great strength when facing challenges. Rewrite this verse in your ow words below.

Now faith is the substance of things hoped for, the evidence of things not seen.
Hebrews 11:1

Faith is much more than just believing *in* God; faith is *believing* God— believing He will do just as He promised, even though you might not see any evidence. Faith isn't passive. Faith is a verb; it's an action word. It's a demonstra tion of your trust in the Lord. It requires a response on your part.

I grew up hearing the saints in my father's church say, "If you make one step He'll make two." Sure, there are times when you are too weak to fight and you couldn't take another step if your life depended on it. God knows that, and He is there for you in those times. But there comes a time when you must do as Nehemiah did. You must get up, get dressed, get a plan, and get to work. You must take off your Sunday best and put on your coveralls and work boots.

James 2:20 tells us that *"faith without works is _____."* (NKJV)

Of course, whenever you step out in faith, you can be sure that at some point along the way you will encounter a foe. There will always be opposition when- ever it's time to do anything for the kingdom of God. Nehemiah encountered his share of foes, for sure.

Reread Nehemiah 2:19. Who were Nehemiah's foes?

Which of these foes is mentioned again in Nehemiah 4:1?

According to Nehemiah 4:1-2, what was this foe's attitude toward the rebuilding of the wall? What are some possible reasons for his anger?

Sanballat was from Samaria (Nehemiah 4:2), and the Samaritans and Jews despised one another. It has been suggested that perhaps he was an officer in the Samaritan army since he later organized forces to fight against Jerusalem. Clearly he did not want the welfare of the Jews to be improved.

Nehemiah's enemies, people with power and influence, banded together to try to stop his progress. His challengers even resorted to mockery, mudslinging, and name calling.

Read Nehemiah 4:2-3. List the insults hurled against Nehemiah and the Jews:

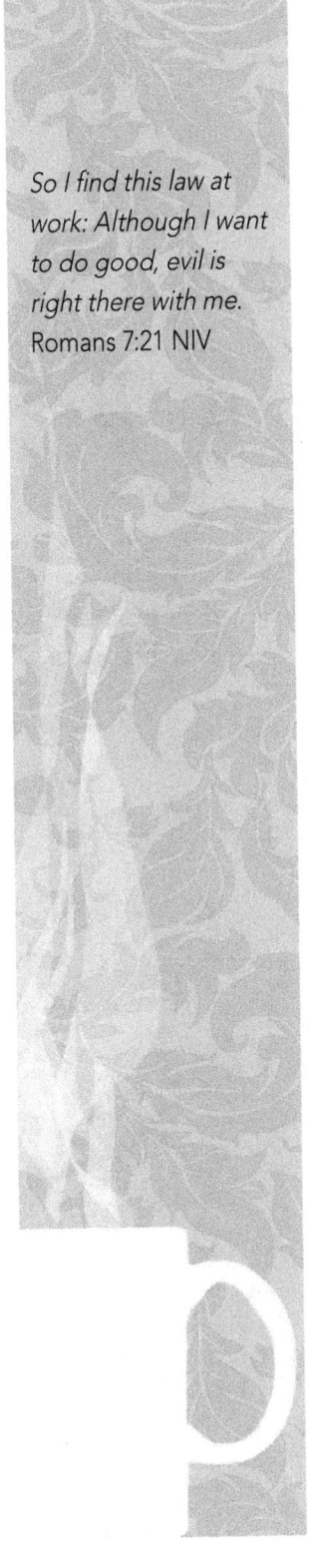

So I find this law at work: Although I want to do good, evil is right there with me. Romans 7:21 NIV

This is what I've found to be true: whenever I've attempted to do anything at all for Jesus, I've encountered some sort of difficulty. I've been in ministry for thirty years as a full-time vocation—longer than that if you count the years that I was bi-vocational, singing while teaching school. At every turn I have encountered some sort of challenge or opposition. I've experienced challenges in my marriage. At times, it was difficult maintaining a family and a growing ministry. My husband has had challenges with his health. There have been times I've been very discouraged. Yes, difficulties are a given. As a matter of fact, I've come to expect difficulty. I take it as a compliment that I must be doing something right.

I'm not alone in this. The apostle Paul spoke to this as well.

Read Romans 7:21 in the margin and write it in your own words below:

I like the way the New Revised Standard Version puts it: "So I find it to be a law that when I want to do what is good, evil lies close at hand." But here is the good news: Jesus is the great Deliverer. Whenever you bring your faith in Jesus and the truth of His Word into your circumstances, your enemy's plot is exposed and destroyed.

The kingdom of evil is darkness while God's kingdom is light. So the very moment darkness poses a threat to you, bring the light of Jesus into the situation, and darkness will have to flee.

What does James 4:7 tell us happens when the light of Jesus comes into a situation?

It's just like walking into a darkened room and flipping on the light switch. The second you do that, the darkness is overcome—gone! When light fills the room, anything that lives in the dark runs for cover. Don't be afraid; move closer to Jesus and the light of His promises. If you are discouraged, bring the presence of Jesus into your situation by encouraging yourself in the Lord. Let me explain what I mean.

Whenever you are tempted to doubt what God has said, use the authority Jesus gave you by opening up your mouth to speak the truth of His Word. All authority in heaven and on earth has been given to Jesus (Matthew 28:18), so call on His name and speak His Word. With Jesus on your side, your enemy is already a defeated foe. This is why it is so important that you know the Word of God.

What did Jesus say in John 8:32?

"You will know the _____ and the _____ will set you _____." **(NIV)**

Owning a Bible won't set you free. But knowing the truth and standing on what you know will empower you not only to wage war against the enemy's assaults, but also to be victorious!

Nehemiah and God's people could have thrown in the towel and quit building. Mocked, cheated, laughed at, mistreated—it didn't matter. The naysayers' threats didn't deter the people of God from their mission. The opposition only empowered them and gave them even more determination to complete the work.

Read Nehemiah 6:1-3 and describe the situation below.

How did Nehemiah handle the scheming of his adversaries? Write the response he gave the messengers to deliver. (v. 3)

Do you hear Nehemiah's dogged determination and tenacity? He was not about to allow anything to keep him from rebuilding that wall.

According to Nehemiah 6:15, how many days did it take to complete the wall?

> Whenever you are tempted to doubt what God has said, use the authority Jesus gave you by opening up your mouth to speak the truth of His Word.

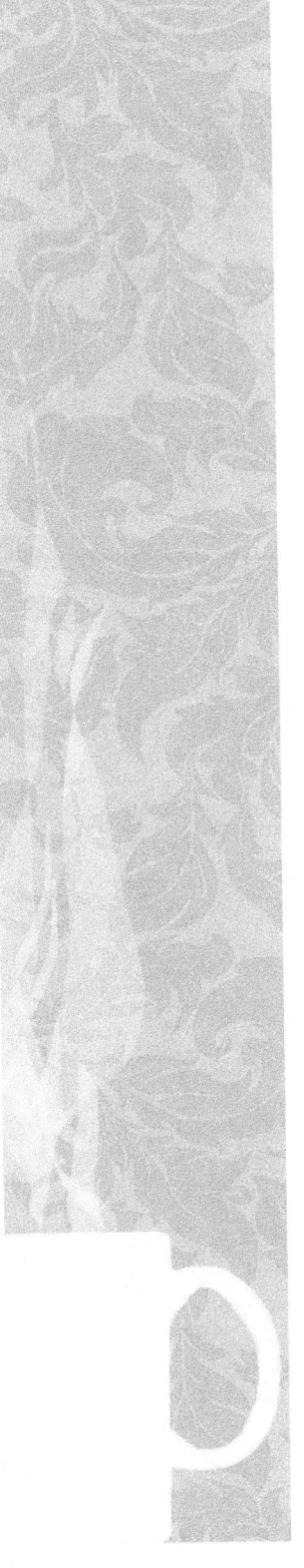

In just a little less than two months, they were able to complete a wall around the entire city of Jerusalem. That's what I call determination! And when you combine determination with the plan and favor of God, nothing is impossible.

Oh, dear friend, what is the wall God has assigned *you* to build? Are there influences in our culture that are trying to dissuade you from building your marriage and family? Your response must be, "I am doing a great work, so that I cannot come down" (Nehemiah 6:3). Are you trying to get a business off the ground or pursue a creative endeavor using your God-given gifts? No matter what you come up against, you must say, "I am doing a great work, so that I cannot come down." Are you working on your finances, trying to lose weight, getting free from an addiction? Speak to anything and everything that is standing in your way: "I am doing a great work, so that I cannot come down."

There's something powerful about setting God's Word to music. When Scripture is set to music, the message not only adheres to your memory; it gets in your spirit, too. Then as you hear yourself singing it, it brings strength to your inner being. That's why I love to set the Word of God to music. I was inspired to write a song about Nehemiah, so I got together with my dear friend and songwriting buddy Turner Lawton. She and I wrote a song about this great man of God who rebuilt the wall around the city of Jerusalem. It's called "Stay Up on the Wall." Let me share the chorus with you.

Stay up on the wall
And don't come down
You've got too much work to do
No time to turn around
With a hammer in one hand
And a weapon in the other
My sister, my brother
Stay up on the wall[1]

Stay up on the wall, my friend. Be determined to accomplish whatever God has put before you, remembering with confidence that you are in your Father's hands.

Go to God

Ask

Spend more time today praying about the assignment God has given you. What are the obstacles that threaten to distract or discourage you? Fall on your knees before God and talk to Him about it now.

Seek

Continue to seek God's guidance as you step out into the work of your mission. Surrender completely before God and invite Him to use you as He will, committing to be determined regardless of the obstacles that come your way.

Knock

Ask God for the wisdom to think strategically about the opposition you have encountered or anticipate encountering as you begin your work.

What can you do now to be ready when opposition comes?

Dear heavenly Father,

We come humbly before You today knowing that in Your hands our lives are so much more than we can ever imagine. Thank You for helping us to see that we can accomplish so much more with You than we could ever do on our own. What an honor it is to be used to accomplish Your purposes. Reveal to us the places You call us to act. Show us what needs to be done and how to do the work. Help us to stand firm against our foes and rely on Your wisdom and strength to get us through. You are the light that blots out any darkness around us. Shine your light in and through our lives, and hold us firmly in the palm of Your hand. In Jesus' name. Amen.

Day 3: Be Strong in Faith

Read God's Word

⁸By faith Abraham obeyed when he was called to go out to the place which he would receive as an inheritance. And he went out, not knowing where he was going. ⁹By faith he dwelt in the land of promise as in a foreign country, dwelling in tents with Isaac and Jacob, the heirs with him of the same promise; ¹⁰for he waited for the city which has foundations, whose builder and maker is God.

Hebrews 11:8-10

Reflect and Respond

You can't entrust your life to God, believing that He holds all that concerns you in His hands, unless you are strong in your faith. It's simply not possible. So today we will consider what it looks like to be a person who has a strong faith.

When I think of someone with a strong faith, I think of my grandfather, Pastor John Wade. Born in the Deep South at the close of the nineteenth century, he grew up the son of a preacher and served God from his youth. One of nine children, his family progressed as farmers, educators, and entrepreneurs. They married, raised families, and thrived in spite of tremendous racial prejudice and indifference, and the economic hardships they endured because of their race. No stranger to hard work, my grandfather was extremely ambitious, exercising tremendous resilience during those early days of the industrial revolution. But tough times didn't make him a bitter man; tough times made him a better man. He possessed a deep, vibrant faith in Christ, along with strength of character and a resolve of steel.

When God called him to preach, he became a powerful minister of the gospel with a voracious hunger for the things of God. His recall of the Scriptures was remarkable, as he was able to recite entire chapters from the Bible. His understanding of the Scriptures, his ability to interpret the truths of the Word of God, and his fiery preaching were something to behold. When my grandfather would visit us from time to time at our home in Jackson, Michigan, people would come from far and wide to hear him preach revivals at my father's church. Papa Wade, as we called him, was a pastor for many years in Mississippi, where he lived with my grandmother until she passed away. After that, he lived as a single man until a dear lady caught his eye. He took her as his bride when he was close to eighty years of age.

My grandfather continued to preach well into his eighties, pastoring four different congregations in neighboring towns, which he visited on the same Sunday once a month. One fifth Sunday morning, he was the guest preacher at a nearby church. When it came time to deliver the sermon, he stirred every heart as he preached with power and conviction concerning faith in Christ. After delivering that soul-stirring sermon, Papa Wade sat down behind the pulpit, drew his last breath, and went home to be with the Lord. He was a remarkable man, one who preached his own eulogy while he lived. I will always remember him and his deep love for Christ, his family, and the church. He lived as a man of faith and died in the same manner—a man of great faith.

We need examples of faithful followers in our lives today. They show us that we can practice radical faith and that God will always be faithful, holding us securely in His hands.

When we look for people of faith in the Bible, Abraham stands out as one of the greatest persons of faith the world has ever known. He is included in the

"Hall of Faith" in the Book of Hebrews for good reason: he had a deep and abiding faith in God and placed His life completely in God's hands.

Read Genesis 12:1-9 and answer the following questions.

What was Abraham's name at the beginning of the story? (v. 1)

What did God ask Abram to do? (v. 1)

What did God promise Abram? (vv. 2-3)

What did Abram do when he reached his destination? (v. 8)

Abram, as he was called before God changed his name, left the country he loved and the people he deeply cared for to venture out into the unknown—to a place he had never seen and from which he would never return. Can you imagine your spouse (or boss, if you are not married) rushing in to tell you to start packing—that for reasons untold you'll immediately be relocating to an unknown destination and won't be coming back? Basically, that's what happened with Abram and his wife Sarai, later renamed Sarah. They packed up and moved with no idea of where they were headed. They didn't know how long they would be gone and had no idea who they would meet along the way. There was no way to know what was waiting for them around the next bend. God called and, without question, Abram obeyed. Talk about faith!

Look now to Genesis 17:1-9 to witness Abram's name change.

How old was Abram at this time? (v. 1)

What was God's instruction to Abram? (v. 1)

Why did God change Abram's name to Abraham? (v. 5)

Abraham means "father of many nations." God promised to make Abraham fruitful so that nations would come from him, and Abraham's name change was a constant reminder of God's promise.

The apostle Paul gave Abraham another title.

Read Romans 4:11*b* in the margin. What did the apostle Paul call Abraham?

Abraham believed God before seeing any visible evidence of what was promised, and it was credited to him as righteousness (Genesis 15:6). You might say that Abraham is the poster child of faith! His name is loved and highly esteemed by Christians and Jews alike.

A great pastor once said, "When you came to Jesus Christ, God enrolled you in the school of faith. Life is the classroom, the Bible is the textbook, the apostles and the prophets are the professors and Abraham would have to be the dean in this school of faith."[2] If you are a Christian, then you are considered a student of faith. So pull up your assigned seat, lean in, and listen. I believe God wants to speak to your heart. If you desire to live a life of faith, taking God at His Word without wavering and entrusting your life into His hands, then you must *believe* God's Word.

Let's turn to Hebrews 11:8, a verse from our focus Scripture for today.

Write everything we know about Abraham's call from this verse:

How did Abraham respond?

Based on this verse, what kind of faith did Abraham have in the promises of God?

> *So then, he is the father of all who believe but have not been circumcised, in order that righteousness might be credited to them.*
> Romans 4:11*b* NIV

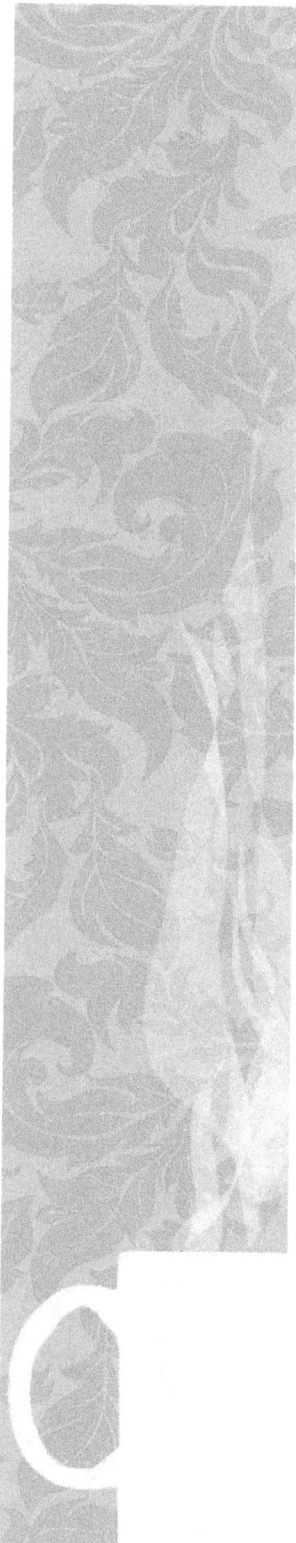

When was the last time you heard God's call, and what was God calling you to do?

How did you respond?

Abraham was not a perfect man, but he shows us that a life of faith is not only noble; it is necessary. Hebrews 11:8 shows us that Abraham was *attentive* to God's voice. There is an important dynamic here. God called, and Abraham answered the call. This means that Abraham was in a position to hear God's voice.

What a great lesson for us in this noisy age of reality television, Internet streaming, infomercials, and twenty-four-hour news channels. Look around you at this moment. How many potential distractions are just within an arm's reach? A cell phone? A television? An electronic listening device of some kind? How many times have you heard the annoying ringtone of a cell phone right in the middle of a Sunday morning worship service? It often seems to happen at the precise moment the congregation pauses to pray.

Not long ago Charles and I were out having dinner. Just across the aisle from us was a family of four. Instead of enjoying the company of family and engaging in conversation concerning the day's activities, this family totally ignored one another, their food growing cold while they buried their faces in their cell phones.

Is it any wonder we have trouble hearing God's voice? We are too preoccupied with so many things. I'm not saying we should do away with cell phones, TV, music, and the like. Not at all. It's okay to enjoy these things. Just be careful that you are not consumed by them. There's no harm in owning this stuff. But be careful that your stuff doesn't own you.

Underline the words in Hebrews 11:8 below that point to Abraham's faith.

By faith Abraham obeyed when he was called to go out to a place that he was going to receive as an inheritance. He went out without knowing where he was going. **(CEB)**

The story goes that a mother called her child to come in from the yard and prepare for dinner. The child failed to obey his mother's voice, so she called a second time. Again the child continued to play, disobeying his mother's instruction. A third time, his mother called, but that time, she raised her voice, counted to

three, and called the child by his first, middle, and last names in a very authoritative manner! If you're a parent, you probably have a good picture of what that looks like.

Is that the way it is with you and your relationship with God, dear one? Are you slow to answer when the Lord speaks? Must He poke and prod and command your attention before you obey His directives?

We have many opportunities to hear the voice of God today. We don't need a supernatural revelation from God to knock us off our feet as happened to Saul on the road to Damascus. We don't need to hear an audible voice as Samuel did when he was a young boy. Instead, God has given us His written Word. All we have to do is read it!

Read Romans 10:17 in the margin. Where does faith come from?

So then faith comes by hearing, and hearing by the word of God.
Romans 10:17

Read 2 Timothy 3:16 and fill in the blanks:

All Scripture is _____ and is useful for _____, rebuking, _____ and _____ in righteousness. **(NIV)**

First Corinthians 2:16 says that we have the mind of Christ. This is possible because the Holy Spirit dwells in us. As we've seen earlier in our study, the Holy Spirit leads us into truth and gives us the wisdom we need. So, with the help of the Holy Spirit, we can put what we learn from God's Word into practice.

Dear friend, when God speaks, it may not make sense to you. You may not understand all the details. But know this: when He speaks, don't hesitate to step out in obedience. Delayed obedience is still disobedience. Follow Abraham's example and obey. The voice of God spoke to Abraham, and the voice of God will speak to you, too. Answer the Lord the moment He calls.

This is my heart's desire: to be a person of great faith and conviction who will not be swayed, no matter what challenges come my way! My purpose for writing this study is that you would know God intimately through a personal relationship with Jesus Christ and take Him at His Word without wavering. Is that your desire? You see, faith is a most vital ingredient to your Christian growth. Not only must you have faith; faith must have you!

In this crazy, mixed-up world we're living in, the only thing that will keep you grounded is your faith and belief in Christ Jesus. It's like a fishing boat that is able to withstand the wind and rains on the open waters. How? Because it has an anchor that holds it steady.

Did you know that your greatest responsibility and calling is to believe God? If you are unsure about that, consider what Jesus had to say about it.

Read John 6:29 in the margin. What is the "work of God"—the work that God wants from us?

Believing on Jesus is the only way to realize eternal life—which begins right now, in this life. John 20:31 says, "But these are written that you may believe that Jesus is the Messiah, the Son of God, and that by believing you may have life in his name" (NIV). My prayer for you is that you will possess great faith—faith like that of father Abraham—which will enable you to release your life into God's hands. When you do, you will discover the joy, freedom, and power that come from knowing that, come what may, you are safe in God's hands.

Go to God

Ask

You can know how to live a life that is well pleasing to God, and it begins with faith. As I said at the beginning of today's reading, faith is necessary in order to entrust your life into God's hands. Following Abraham's example will help you not only to better understand God's purpose for your life but also to fulfill His plan. Talk to God about where you are on your faith journey. Are you ready to give your life to Him completely without reservation, just as Abraham did?

Seek

Dear friend, God desires to speak to you concerning His will and His ways. In fact, He is speaking to you right now. If you want to hear what God is saying to your heart, turn off the noise. Rid yourself of the distractions. He is always speaking, but His voice doesn't always sound like rolling thunder or crashing seas. Sometimes, as Abraham learned, He speaks in the whisper of a still, small voice. Seek His voice even now.

What is the voice of the Lord whispering to you today regarding your faith and your future?

Knock

At nearly every turn, Abraham demonstrated a life of faithfulness. He submitted to God's vision although he didn't understand all the details of God's

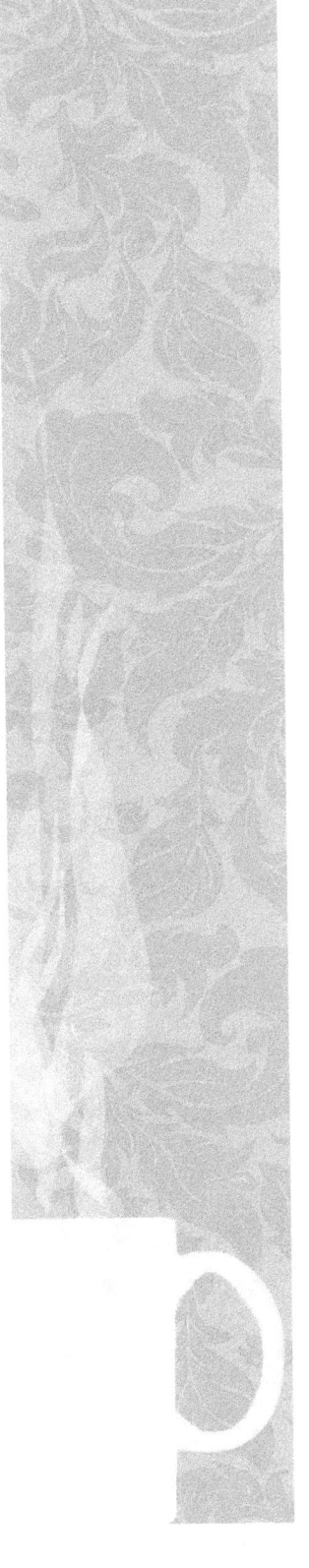

instructions. Submit yourself to the will of God right now. Give yourself over to His great plan for you. Listen closely, trust easily, and obey immediately.

Dear loving Father,

Thank You for the example of Abraham and the promises in Your Word that show us great men and women of faith—and Your great faithfulness to them. You are so very good to us. Give us the courage to step out in faith, even when we can't see where You're leading us. Lead us every step of the way, and we will follow faithfully. In Jesus' name. Amen.

Day 4: Obey God

Read God's Word

[1]Now faith is the substance of things hoped for, the evidence of things not seen. [2]For by it the elders obtained a good testimony.

[3]By faith we understand that the worlds were framed by the word of God, so that the things which are seen were not made of things which are visible.

[11]By faith Sarah herself also received strength to conceive seed, and she bore a child when she was past the age, because she judged Him faithful who had promised. [12]Therefore from one man, and him as good as dead, were born as many as the stars of the sky in multitude—innumerable as the sand which is by the seashore.

[13]These all died in faith, not having received the promises, but having seen them afar off were assured of them, embraced them and confessed that they were strangers and pilgrims on the earth. [14]For those who say such things declare plainly that they seek a homeland. [15]And truly if they had called to mind that country from which they had come out, they would have had opportunity to return. [16]But now they desire a better, that is, a heavenly country. Therefore God is not ashamed to be called their God, for He has prepared a city for them.

Hebrews 11:1-3, 11-16

Reflect and Respond

When Abraham and Sarah ventured into the land of the unknown, they left family members, work, and even their friends behind. Striking out into the land of promise must have seemed like a rather huge and frightening move. But

> No matter how daunting the task God gives us, He will help us do it. All He asks of us is to obey and step out in faith.

Abraham obeyed God. Obedience enabled Abraham to release his life into God's hands, and releasing his life into God's hands resulted in obedience. You might say that obedience is both cause and effect when it comes to living a life that is fully surrendered to God.

Abraham obeyed because he trusted God to go with him wherever he went. He was committed to a faith-filled adventure with God. He would rather venture into an unfamiliar land with God than stay in a familiar place without God.

We learn a valuable lesson from Abraham. No matter how daunting the task God gives us, He will help us do it. All He asks of us is to obey and step out in faith. You may be facing a task that seem daunting, like paying your monthly bills, parenting a toddler or teen, or beginning a new ministry in your church or community. Be assured that when you step out in faith to do what God is asking you to do, He will reward you for your obedience—and your persistence.

I have often found that as I pray and ask God to help me complete tasks that I'm not looking forward to—like cleaning out a closet or mopping the kitchen floor—or tasks that I find challenging—like preparing our taxes or handling a difficult situation—He is more than willing to help me. Most of the time, I find that the task doesn't get any easier, but my attitude toward completing it changes as I offer the work as an act of obedience to the Lord. Some of the sweetest ventures I've had with Jesus have been while I was doing something that I had not been particularly eager to do.

Sometimes we make excuses when it comes time to obey God. "Lord, I would do what you're asking if it weren't for (fill in the blank)." The Bible says that Abraham was seventy-five years old when God called him. We know that with God, things such as age, race, marital status, income bracket, or even ability don't matter. Don't let anyone tell you that you're too old or too young. Don't allow anyone to declare that you're the wrong color or the wrong size, or that you're unqualified. Don't let anybody put limits on you. You just continue to obey God. He promises to bless anyone who will obey Him.

In spite of the fact that Abraham and Sarah were what we would call senior citizens, the Lord blessed Abraham and made a covenant with him.

Circle the blessing that God described in Genesis 15:5-6:

Then God led Abram outside and said, "Look at the sky. There are so many stars you cannot count them. Your descendants also will be too many to count."

*Abram believed the L*ORD*. And the L*ORD *accepted Abram's faith, and that faith made him right with God.* **(NCV)**

Now read Genesis 21:1-2. What promise was fulfilled?

Look at God! Though they were well past their childbearing years, God fulfilled His promise. He allowed a one-hundred-year-old man to father a child and a ninety-year-old woman to have a baby. This goes to show that sometimes the miraculous may appear to be just plain ridiculous.

When God is at work, it may not make sense to your natural way of thinking, but God is at His best when He is parting seas and slaying giants. He is at His best when He is bringing the dead back to life again. He is at His best when He adds His super to your natural to do the supernatural. You see, that's how God works. He wants to do the impossible in your life. Your part is to believe and obey.

By their faith and obedience, Abraham and Sarah created a legacy that generations after them would witness. The apostle Paul wrote about their legacy, the author of Hebrews wrote about their legacy, and countless scholars, preachers, and authors have lifted up their witness as a prime example for us to follow. So let's consider how we can leave a legacy of faithful obedience to God for future generations. I want us to see how placing our lives in God's hands can open up doors of blessing not only for us but also for our descendants.

Take a look at Hebrews 11:1-31 and note the acts of faith carried out by the litany of faith heroes and heroines in these verses.

<u>**Hero or Heroine of Faith**</u>　　　<u>**Act of Faith**</u>

Abel

Enoch

Noah

Abraham

Sarah

Isaac

Jacob

> When God is at work, it may not make sense to your natural way of thinking, but God is at His best when He is parting seas and slaying giants....He wants to do the impossible in your life. Your part is to believe and obey.

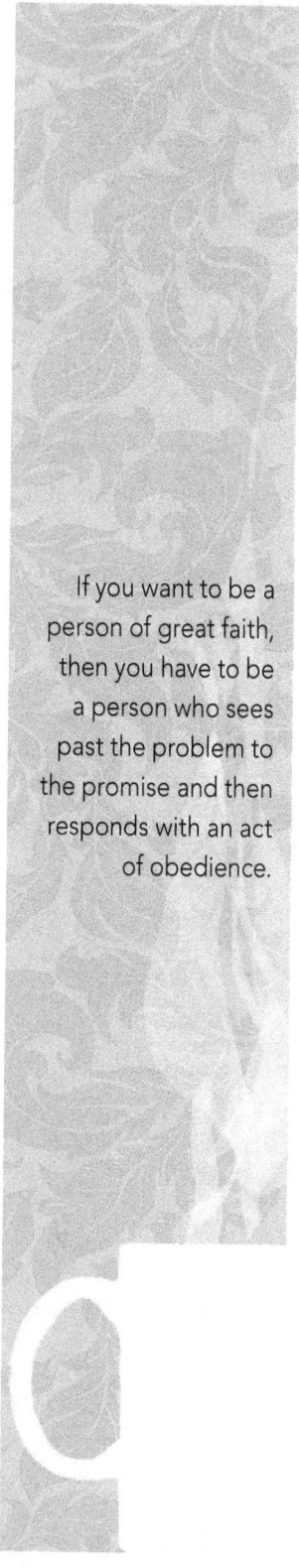

Hero or Heroine of Faith	Act of Faith
Joseph	
Moses	
Rahab	

I love what verse 32 says: "What more can I say? I would run out of time if I told you about…." (CEB). There are so many heroes and heroines of the faith that the author of Hebrews can't get to them all. Their legacy is a witness to us of their faith in God's promises and also of God's faithfulness to them. They were living a legacy in the making as they took each step of obedience to God.

In my song "This I Know for Sure," the bridge says,

> *Eyes grow dim then knees get weak*
> *How quickly seasons change*
> *But this one thing is constant*
> *God's love remains the same*

You see, years may go by, situations may change, feelings may change, people may change, the odds may seem stacked against you, but when our loving God makes a promise, He doesn't forget. And you and I are heirs of that same promise. Like Abraham, we can believe God for the impossible and trust God for the invisible. Then, in God's own time, He will do the incredible.

Are you standing on a promise from the Lord that is yet to be realized? Are you waiting for a husband or a child to come to faith in Christ? Are you waiting for healing—whether physical or emotional? Do you trust God to carry you through a difficult season in your life or family? God did not promise that the way would be easy. Oftentimes God's ways are harder than the ways of the world. But He did promise that He would be with you always and that His plans for you would be fulfilled. Your life is in His trustworthy hands!

Don't give up on God, my sister. He certainly has not given up on you! He will never turn his back on you or walk away from you. God will fulfill His promises no matter how challenging a situation or problem may be. As a matter of fact, problems and promises go hand in hand. If you want to be a person of great faith, then you have to be a person who sees past the problem to the promise and then responds with an act of obedience.

I encourage you to stop talking to God about your problems and start talking to your problems about God! Then start praising God for the answer. I think of my grandfather, Papa Wade, who was pastor of so many churches long ago. Although he could only see "down the road a piece," as the saying goes, in his spirit he envisioned generations of people who would worship God in those churches and serve God in the world. Because of his example, we have a family full of people who passionately love, worship, and serve God.

I want it to go on record that I believe God. So I am standing on 2 Timothy 1:12. Will you go on record with me?

Write our theme verse below (by memory if you can):

Are there generations of believers in your family, just like there are in mine? Then we have the joy of knowing that we are continuing a great spiritual heritage of faith for those who will follow us. Does your family's spiritual heritage begin with you or your generation? Then you are to be commended for laying the groundwork for a godly legacy in your family that will continue for generations to come.

As you believe God today, remember that faith without works—without action—is not really faith at all. When James wrote about this, he used Abraham as an example.

Read James 2:14-24. What example did James give to show that Abraham demonstrated his faith with action? (v. 21)

Like Abraham, we must not only believe but also put our belief into action. This is obedience. If God says, "Go," then step out in faith and trust Him to do a wonderful work in and through you. God has never, ever turned His back on people who believe and obey, and He's not going to start now! This you can know for sure: your life is in God's hands.

Go to God

Ask

What kind of legacy are you leaving by the way you live your life? Will generations after you remember your faithful witness? Talk to God about what you can do to begin living a legacy of faith and obedience.

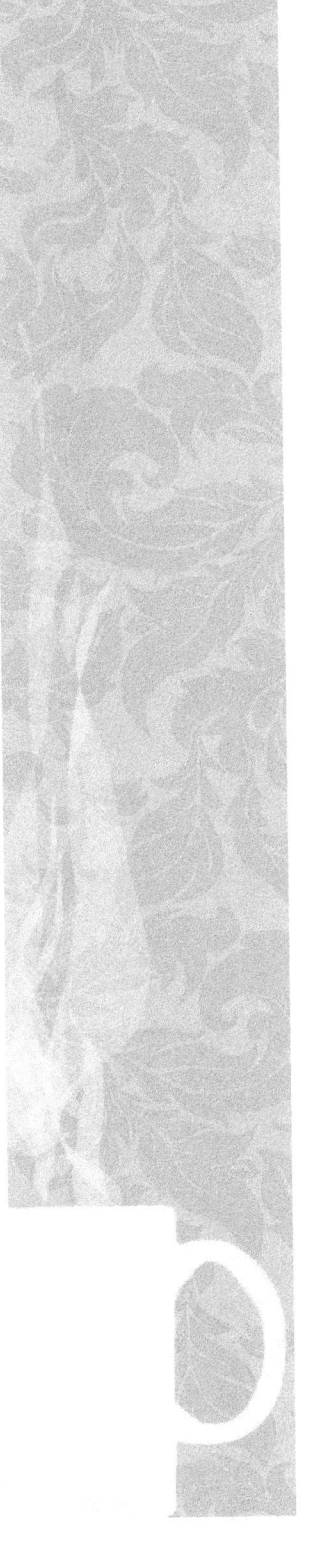

Seek

One thing the faith heroes and heroines in Hebrews have in common is that they were attentive to God's voice. Each of them sought God's wisdom, counsel, direction, and will.

How are you attentive to God's voice? What can you do to create more space to listen?

Knock

Who is a living faith hero or heroine to you? Write a letter of appreciation, thanking this person for his or her faithful witness in your life.

Faithful God,

Thank You for the "Hall of Faith" that we read about in the Book of Hebrews. It's such an amazing witness to Your faithfulness and the great faith of Your people. Help us to be counted in that list of people who risked everything to obey You. Give us hearts that are attentive to Your leading, and give us courage to obey. In Jesus' name. Amen.

Day 5: Be Courageous

Read God's Word

¹*Now Joshua the son of Nun sent out two men from Acacia Grove to spy secretly, saying, "Go, view the land, especially Jericho." So they went, and came to the house of a harlot named Rahab, and lodged there. ²And it was told the king of Jericho, saying, "Behold, men have come here tonight from the children of Israel to search out the country."*

³*So the king of Jericho sent to Rahab, saying, "Bring out the men who have come to you, who have entered your house, for they have come to search out all the country."*

⁴*Then the woman took the two men and hid them. So she said, "Yes, the men came to me, but I did not know where they were from. ⁵And it happened as the gate was being shut, when it was dark, that the men went out. Where the men went I do not know; pursue them quickly, for you may overtake them." ⁶(But she had brought them up to the roof and hidden them with the stalks of flax, which she had laid in order on the roof.) ⁷Then the men pursued them by the road to the Jordan, to the fords. And as soon as those who pursued them had gone out, they shut the gate.*

8Now before they lay down, she came up to them on the roof, 9and said to the men: "I know that the LORD has given you the land, that the terror of you has fallen on us, and that all the inhabitants of the land are fainthearted because of you. 10For we have heard how the LORD dried up the water of the Red Sea for you when you came out of Egypt, and what you did to the two kings of the Amorites who were on the other side of the Jordan, Sihon and Og, whom you utterly destroyed. 11And as soon as we heard these things, our hearts melted; neither did there remain any more courage in anyone because of you, for the LORD your God, He is God in heaven above and on earth beneath. 12Now therefore, I beg you, swear to me by the LORD, since I have shown you kindness, that you also will show kindness to my father's house, and give me a true token, 13and spare my father, my mother, my brothers, my sisters, and all that they have, and deliver our lives from death."

14So the men answered her, "Our lives for yours, if none of you tell this business of ours. And it shall be, when the LORD has given us the land, that we will deal kindly and truly with you."

Joshua 2:1-14

Reflect and Respond

This week we've been focusing on our fourth landmark: *My life is in God's hands.* We've been looking at people in the Bible who show us what it looks like to place our lives into God's hands, and we've been considering what this requires. We've talked about the role of prayer, determination, faith, and obedience.

Today our focus is *courage.* Courage is both a requirement for faithful living and an outcome of faithful living. When we know who holds our lives, we find ourselves stepping out in faith and taking risks for the sake of God's kingdom.

I like to think of God's kingdom as a family—the family of faith. You know, there's nothing more central to God's plan for humanity than the concept of family. There is real joy and strength to be found when you know there are people there for you who truly care about you.

After more than thirty-three years of marriage and ministry, my greatest support is still my husband, Charles. We have traveled all over the world together—from the Windy City to the City of Lights; from the concrete jungles in urban centers of America to the dusty roads and lush jungles of Africa. Charles is the quintessential roadie and residential song critic. Bless his heart, he has heard some of the songs in my repertoire over and over again for almost as long as we have been married, and he often responds to those same songs as if he is hearing them for the first time. He assures me that of all the singers he enjoys, he considers me his favorite.

My life is also richly blessed by my two sons, who are great musicians in their own right. They are singers, composers, performers, music producers, and audio engineers. Now that they are adults with careers of their own, I'm no longer their teacher but their student. We've had the privilege to work together on stage and in the studio, on music projects and recordings, and nothing thrills my heart more than for one of them to pat me on the back and say, "You did a great job, Mom!"

What about your family? How do they give you both joy and strength?

In what ways has your family challenged you to be creative with the resources you have?

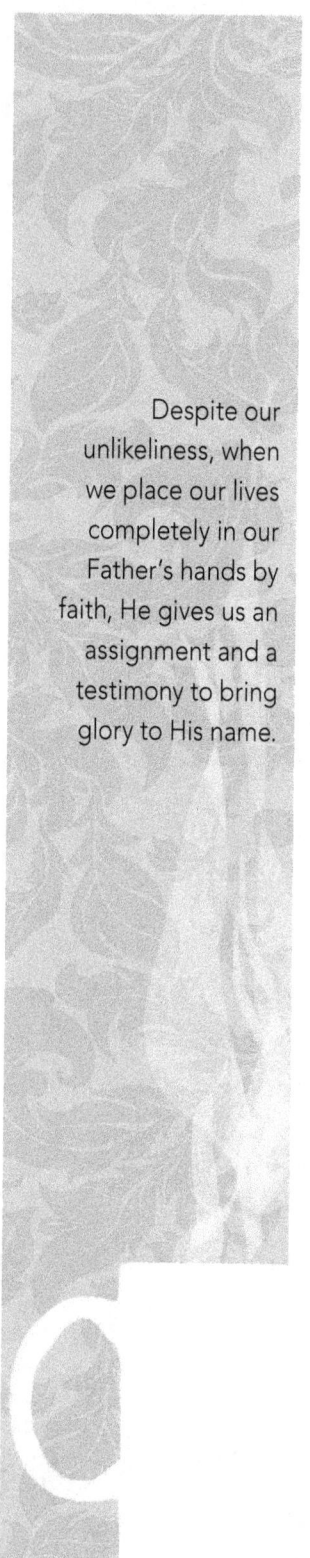

Despite our unlikeliness, when we place our lives completely in our Father's hands by faith, He gives us an assignment and a testimony to bring glory to His name.

Yes, there is great joy and strength to be found in family. Though imperfect, our families are meant to nurture and encourage us, giving us the courage to be all that we were created to be so that our lives bring glory to our heavenly Father. A similar thing happens within the family of faith.

I don't know about you, but I am awed by the realization that Almighty God wants us to be part of His family—the family of faith. It is mind-boggling to think that a holy God would adopt unholy children and allow us to call Him *Father*, but that is exactly what He has done! What's more, He is the initiator in this relationship, loving us first, pursuing us relentlessly, drawing us to Himself, and giving us His name.

As members of the family of God, we are part of a diverse collection of unlikely characters from all walks of life, each with a story of being dead in sin and brought to life through God's grace and mercy in Christ. And despite our unlikeliness, when we place our lives completely in our Father's hands by faith, He gives us an assignment and a testimony to bring glory to His name. You and I are evidence that God can do so much with so little.

After years of studying the Bible and observing the lives of believers, I've concluded that regardless of our assignment, courage is sure to be required somewhere along the way. An unlikely member of the family of faith who lived many centuries before Christ is a beautiful example of this. She was a woman of questionable moral character in a questionable occupation. Known as Rahab the Harlot, she shows us what God can do when a person places her heart and her life in God's hands. God is so good at taking the worst in us and using it to bring out the best in us. Let me give you the context for the story.

For forty long and tedious years, the Israelite nation had wandered through the wilderness. Moses, their leader, had died, and they were under the capable leadership of Joshua, a very faithful and courageous man. Joshua knew that in order for God's people to occupy the Promised Land, they had to take the city of Jericho, so he sent his spies to get the lay of the land.

Read Joshua 2:1-24 and answer the following questions:

Why did Joshua send spies to Jericho, and where did the spies wind up spending the night? (v. 1)

How did the king find out about the spies? (v. 2)

What did Rahab tell the king's men? (vv. 4-5)

Where did she hide the spies? (v. 6)

What did Rahab tell the spies that she knew? (vv. 9-10)

How did she describe her reaction and that of her people? (vv. 9, 11)

What did she request of the spies? (vv. 12-13)

What did the spies promise Rahab? (v. 14)

How did she help the spies escape? (vv. 15-16)

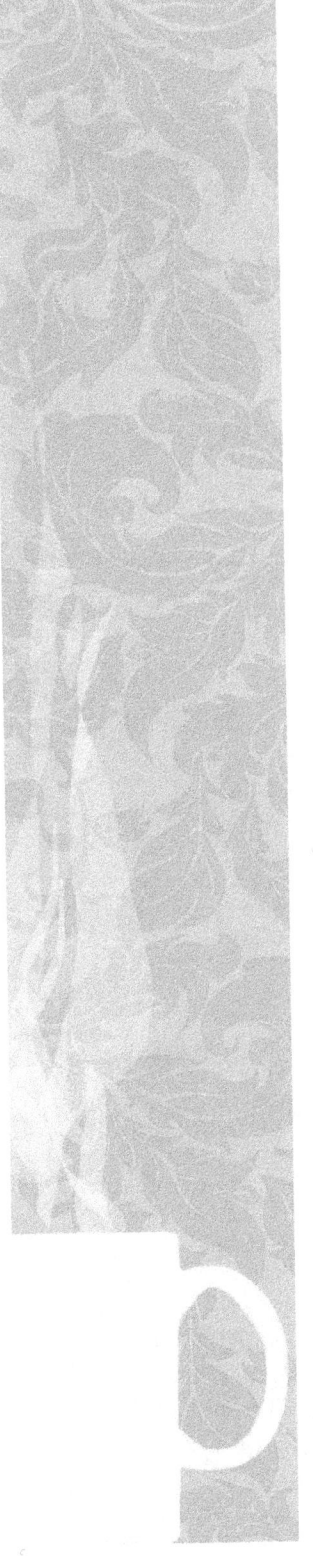

What sign did the spies tell Rahab to hang in the window? (vv. 17-18)

Rahab's home, which she also used as her place of business, was a part of the city wall of Jericho. Some scholars describe her as a savvy businesswoman who seized an opportunity to make a decent living. No matter how acceptable to the culture of the day her occupation may have been, the Bible still refers to her as harlot, a common prostitute. The two men that Joshua sent to scope out the land most likely did not seek Rahab for her occupation but for her location—her home was built right into the city wall. This was significant because many men who traveled through the city found accommodations in Rahab's home, and wherever men gather, they talk. Even today it's commonplace to see men gathered in the barbershop or around the lunch table at the local town restaurant, discussing politics, sports, religion, and the state of the economy. Over the years, Rahab had heard the stories of the God of the Israelites—of His power to deliver His people, slay their enemies, and conquer kings and kingdoms on behalf of His chosen people. She also knew that all of Jericho was terrified of the Israelites. God strategically used Rahab the Harlot—an unlikely heroine—to save the lives of two Israelite spies and help the Israelites return to the Promised Land.

Now Rahab was a very insightful woman. She had heard all the things that were being said about the God of Israel. This Canaanite woman, who lived among a pagan people, was not only a good listener; she had understanding. She understood that the God of Israel was like no other god in history. Although she had only heard about the great exploits God had performed on behalf of His people, she did what every believer must do—she accepted what she heard by faith, believing not only that the God of the Israelites existed but also that what she had heard about His power and greatness was true. So she decided to help the two enemy spies. She believed Jericho would inevitably be conquered by the Israelites, and she made up in her mind that when the walls came tumblin' down, she would be on the Lord's side.

How did Rahab demonstrate faith?

How did this require courage?

Rahab courageously put everything on the line for God and God's people. She possessed the kind of courage and conviction that could only come from God. She was able to look impending doom, even death, squarely in the eye and decide not to be a victim of certain disaster but to be used as a vital key to certain victory for God's people.

No matter how noble and courageous Rahab's response was, all of her actions were not perfect. She did lie to protect the two Israelite spies who came to check out the city of Jericho. Some scholars say Rahab had developed a heart for God but was not yet acquainted with His laws. Perhaps she did not understand all the implications of the immoral life she had led, but she knew one thing for sure: the God of Israel was the God she would serve for the rest of her life. And it's just like God to use her life, and even her lifestyle, to bring her into the family of God.

Read Romans 2:4 in the margin. What does this verse tell us about the kindness of God?

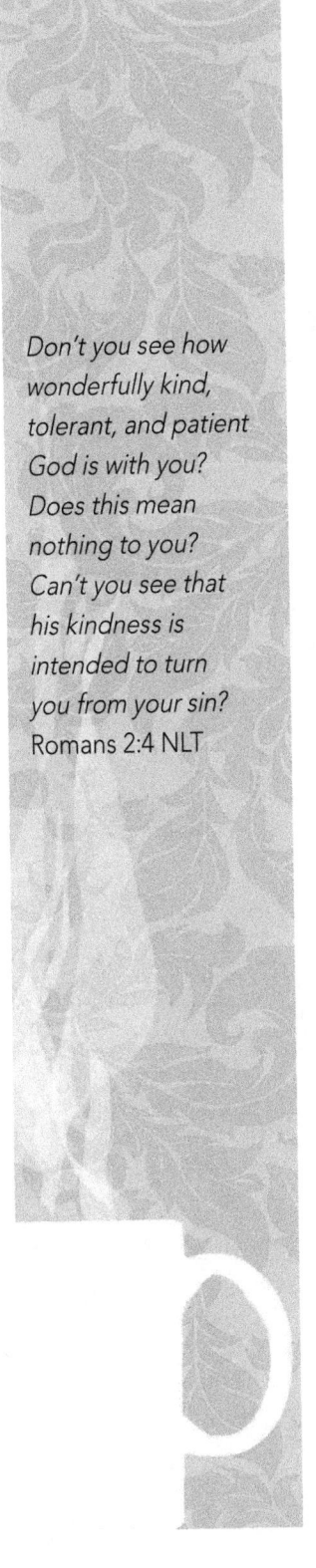

Don't you see how wonderfully kind, tolerant, and patient God is with you? Does this mean nothing to you? Can't you see that his kindness is intended to turn you from your sin?
Romans 2:4 NLT

How has God shown patience and kindness to you?

In her heart, Rahab had sensed the Lord drawing her, and she responded. And the end of Rahab's story in Joshua 6 shows us the grace and mercy of our God. Here we find powerful evidence of what God can do when we courageously place our lives in His hands and take risks for the sake of God's kingdom—even if we have a sordid past.

Read Joshua 6:22-25. What happened to Rahab and her family?

Because of Rahab's actions, the Israelites defeated the people of Jericho and received Rahab and her family into the nation of Israel. She went on to marry an Israelite and likely learned the laws of God and matured in her faith, just as we all do. The transformation that came to this Canaanite prostitute is indicative of the fact that God can transform any life that is completely yielded to Him.

Take a look at Matthew 1:5-17. What is the significance of the family Rahab married into?

Rahab married Salmon, a great man and son of a prominent leader among the tribe. They had a son named Boaz, one of the most faithful men who ever lived. Boaz married Ruth, and they had a son named Obed, who was the father of Jesse, whose son was King David. And from the lineage of King David came Jesus Christ, the Savior of the world.

What's more, Rahab is included in the "Hall of Faith" in Hebrews 11, along with Abraham's wife, Sarah. Only God could take a woman from such a common beginning to a place of such high esteem. What a miracle. What a heritage. What a God!

God can use the most unlikely characters in the family of faith to do the most extraordinary things—things that require courage and conviction. When it comes to the most unlikely "family members" used by God, Charles and I are at the front of the line. We both know that if it had not been for the Lord, who was on our side, who knows where we would be. We'll be the first to tell you that apart from Jesus, everything about us is a disaster waiting to happen. But God, in all His grace, chooses to use us in spite of our shortcomings.

What is one way that God has used you in spite of your shortcomings?

Charles loves the nations of Africa, and on one of his missionary trips to Uganda, he was the only layperson in the group of six pastors. One Sunday morning each pastor was given a preaching assignment at a church throughout the city. Much to Charles's surprise, he was given a preaching assignment too. He rebutted, "I don't think so! I'm nobody's preacher. Don't expect me to get up before a congregation and deliver a sermon!" But the arrangements had already been made and there was no getting out of it.

That morning Charles courageously shared his testimony of how he came to know Jesus as Savior. Many hearts and lives were touched and changed as a result. Later that week, Charles and all of the pastors were meeting with the men in a nearby village for Bible study on the topic of marriage and family. During the lunch break, one of the African men approached Charles and asked if he could speak with him. The man said that he had accepted Christ the Sunday before and expressed his desire to live a life that was pleasing to Christ. Then he told Charles that he had seven wives. As a result, he had seven families and over twenty-five children to care for. He presented his dilemma to Charles, wondering what he should do. He asked, "Do I divorce six wives and choose only one? Do I divorce them all and start all over again? What do I do?" Charles swallowed hard, sending up a silent prayer before responding.

The answer Charles finally gave the man is simply amazing to me. Charles said this: "You can't undo what you've already done. You made the choice to marry those women, and what's done is done. You must continue to support and take care of them. You're going to have to live with the consequences of your choices. But from now on you must teach your children that God instructs men to have only one wife and women to have only one husband."

Only God could have imparted that kind of wisdom to Charles when he needed it most. God is faithful to give us both the courage and the wisdom we need every time we're called to complete an assignment. And it's all for His glory!

My friend, God has an assignment for you. There is a problem somewhere that needs to be addressed, and you have the skills that are needed. There is a dilemma that needs to be solved, and you hold the key. I hope you're not tempted to say, "Well, I'm not qualified to do anything for God." I pray that you're not thinking, "Why, God could never use me to accomplish anything." No, dear one, I hope by now you know for sure that God doesn't call the qualified; He qualifies the called. And that includes giving courage when courage is needed!

There are all kinds of people in the family of God, and each one has a story that testifies to the mercy, grace, and faithfulness of God. As He did with Rahab, God redeems the broken places in our lives and infuses us with faith and courage so that we are living witnesses of His transformational power.

Read 2 Corinthians 5:17 in the margin and rewrite it in your own words:

So if anyone is in Christ, there is a new creation: everything old has passed away; see, everything has become new!
2 Corinthians 5:17 NRSV

Take courage today, my friend, and put your life into God's hands, trusting Him to use every part of your story for His glory.

Here we are at the end of landmark number four. You're over halfway to the finish line! To strengthen your heart, I wrote these encouraging words so you could celebrate who Jesus is in you. I call it "Jesus Is Everything to Me."

Jesus is everything to me.
Miracle-worker
Peace-speaker
Way-maker
Water-walker
Life-giver
Death-slayer
Heart-mender
Mind-regulator
Great Emancipator
Promise-keeper
Soul-saver
Care-giver
Burden-bearer
Heavy load-sharer
Jesus is everything to me.

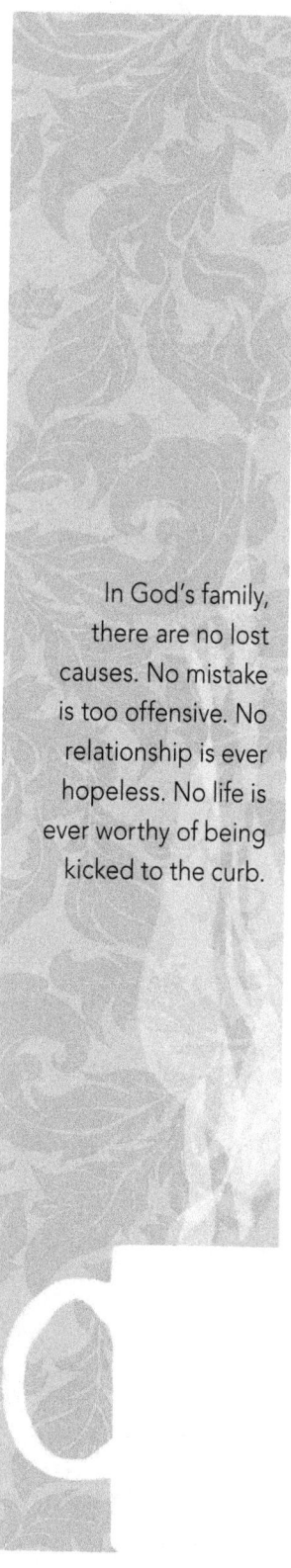

Go to God

Ask

How has God taken the broken places in your life and used them for good? How has God even used your mistakes and sins to make something good or beautiful of your life? Thank God for taking what is broken in your life and making it beautiful.

Seek

Rahab knew how to listen. She knew from hearsay that the God of Israel was the one true God. She courageously risked everything because of this belief, and she came to join the family of God.

How might others come to know God because of your openness about who God is in your life? How will this require courage on your part?

In God's family, there are no lost causes. No mistake is too offensive. No relationship is ever hopeless. No life is ever worthy of being kicked to the curb.

Knock

Do you know someone who needs to experience new life through God's grace? It's easy to give up and write that person off, thinking he or she is a lost cause. But in God's family, there are no lost causes. No mistake is too offensive. No relationship is ever hopeless. No life is ever worthy of being kicked to the curb. Rahab the Harlot is proof of that. And if we're honest, we can look at our own lives and thank God that He never gave up on us, either!

Say a prayer right now for this person. Ask God for the courage to write a letter or make a phone call to reach out with the love and kindness of our compassionate God.

> *Father God,*
>
> *You amaze us by taking our broken stories and making them beautiful. Thank You for the courage of Rahab, who risked her life to join Your family. Help us to remember that any life placed in Your hands can do amazing things! Help us to place our lives in Your faithful hands, even if it feels scary or risky. We know, Lord, that You will give us the courage we need at the precise moment we need it most, for You are always faithful. In Jesus' name. Amen.*

Week 4

Video Viewer Guide

When Abram was ninety-nine years old, the Lord *appeared to Abram and said to him, "I am Almighty God; walk before Me and be blameless. And I will make My _____ between Me and you, and will multiply you exceedingly." Then Abram fell on his face, and God talked with him, saying: "As for Me, behold, My covenant is with you, and you shall be a father of many _____. No longer shall your name be called Abram, but your name shall be _____; for I have made you a father of many nations.*

Genesis 17:1-5 NKJV

God asked a lot of things of Abram—some really difficult things. But they can all be summed up in one word: _____.

Abram _____ the Lord*.*

Genesis 15:6 CEB

Abram _____ the Lord*, and he _____ it to him as righteousness.*

Genesis 15:6 NIV

Abram believed the Lord*. And the* Lord *_____ Abram's faith, and that faith made him _____ with God.*

Genesis 15:6 NCV

If you're struggling to _____ God, ask yourself this question:
Do I really _____ God?

"By Myself I have sworn, says the LORD, because you have done this thing, and have not withheld your son, your only son—blessing I will bless you, and multiplying I will multiply your descendants as the _____ of the heaven and as the _____ which is on the seashore; and your descendants shall possess the gate of their enemies. In your seed all the nations of the earth shall be _____, because you have _____ My voice."

Genesis 22:16-18 NKJV

He who _____ in the secret place of the Most High
Shall abide under the shadow of the Almighty.
I will say of the LORD, "He is my _____ and my fortress;
My God, in Him I will _____."

Psalm 91:1-2 NKJV

Week 5

God's Boundless Love Will Lead Me
(As Long as Time Endures)

It was a landmark moment for me the day I realized how much God really loves me. I've heard the words "God loves you" all my life, but one morning a few years ago while reading John 17:23, the words seemed to leap off the page and into my heart.

In John 17, Jesus is praying for His disciples, as well as for those who would believe their message. In amazement, I realized that because I am a believer, Jesus was praying for me as He spoke to His Father—our Father—in heaven:

> *"I will be in them and you will be in me so that they will be completely one. Then the world will know that you sent me and that you loved them just as much as you loved me."*
>
> John 17:23 NCV

I had read those words in the past, but that day they impacted my heart like never before. The weight of Jesus' words came alive with new understanding for me. In fact, my first book and Bible study, both called *Embraced by God,* grew out of that very moment in my faith journey.

I thought, *God, You love me just as much as You love Jesus? That's incredible! That's way too much for my mind to take in. You, the God of the universe, love me like that? With all my faults? After everything I've done? You love me as much as You love Your holy, blameless Son? What kind of love goes to such an extent?*

That morning while sitting at the breakfast table with a cup of coffee and my Bible, the Word of God quickened my heart, and I haven't been the same since. Why? Because that day I discovered that God loves me as if I were the only one to love.

It's true for you as well! God loves you just as much as He loves His own Son. You see, He not only loves you; He is *in love* with you. The Lord says in

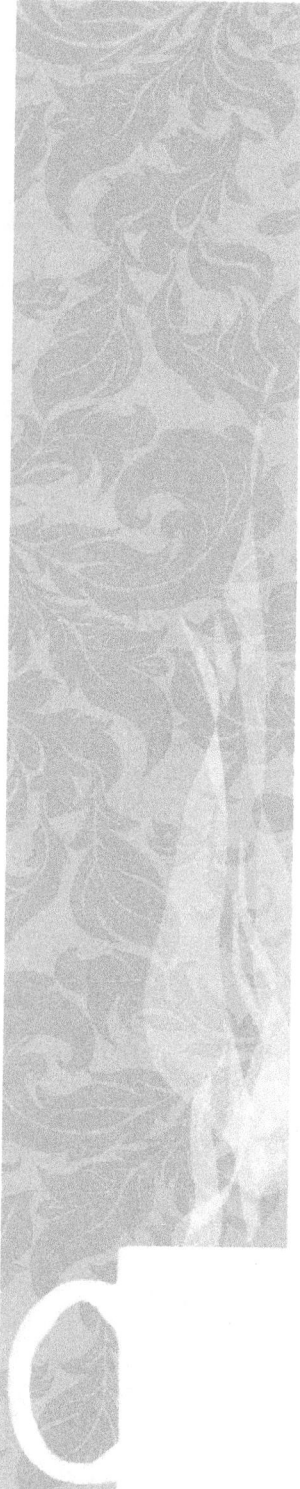

Jeremiah 31:3: "I have loved you with an everlasting love; I have drawn you with unfailing kindness" (NIV). Listen to how *THE MESSAGE* declares this promise: "I've never quit loving you and never will. Expect love, love, and more love!" God takes great pleasure in you and delights in finding ways to demonstrate His love toward you.

This week we are focusing on our fifth landmark: *God's boundless love will lead me (as long as time endures).* As we explore the nature and depth of God's amazing love, we will study some beautiful Scriptures about God's love, mercy, and grace as well as consider the stories of the prodigal son and the Samaritan woman at the well. By week's end, it is my prayer that you will have a richer and fuller understanding of just how much your heavenly Father loves you. Even if you have journeyed with me through *Embraced by God,* you will benefit greatly from revisiting this essential truth from God's Word. Living in a world that often devalues our worth and tells us we must "measure up" in order to earn love, we need to be reminded that God's love for us is *boundless.* And my friend, this we can know for sure!

Scripture Memorization

There are only a couple of weeks left in our study to work on our memory verse, 2 Timothy 1:12:

> *I know whom I have believed, and am persuaded that he is able to keep that which I have committed unto him against that day.* (KJV)

The One in whom you have believed is the One who loves you with boundless love. Continue rehearsing this powerful truth by reciting or singing the verse throughout the week.

Day 1: You Are Loved

Read God's Word

"I will be in them and you will be in me so that they will be completely one. Then the world will know that you sent me and that you loved them just as much as you loved me."

John 17:23 NCV

Reflect and Respond

One day a friend dropped by our home for a visit. Because she is a thoughtful person, she came bearing gifts—a jar of local honey from a beekeeper's farm right up the road to share with Charles and a beautiful bouquet of flowers for me. Surprised and grateful, I hugged her neck, thanked her, and went to put the bouquet in a pretty vase, placing it at the center of the kitchen table. We chatted while I put on the kettle for tea. Soon we were enjoying each other's company, sipping hot tea sweetened with the honey she had just brought.

I was able to enjoy the results of her visit for several days. The flowers brightened up the house and brought a smile to my face each time I went through the kitchen. The honey lasted for a long time after that. I thought about the generous spirit in which she shared her gifts and how a simple, heartfelt gesture could have such lasting impact.

Then I thought about the whole gift-giving process. That someone would think enough of me to take time and make the effort to bring me a gift was humbling. No matter how simple or elaborate a gift is, the process shows such sacrifice on behalf of the giver. In many instances, the act of giving far outshines the actual gift. How rude it would have been had I said to my friend on the day she visited, "Oh no. You shouldn't have. Please take these things back! I don't deserve them." I thought about how insulting it would have been for me to say, "Let me pay you for these things. Wait right here while I write you a check."

It's true. I didn't deserve the gifts. But gifts are never deserved. You can't earn a gift. A gift is bestowed. It's granted. She wanted to bless me. She knew her gift would make me happy. The moment I saw the gift bag leave her hands, I got excited. I love gifts! I anticipated what was inside the beautiful presentation of her gift bag, decked with colorful paper billowing out of the top and curly streamers cascading down the side. Words of thanks began coming out of my mouth before I could even reveal the contents. I was so happy to be a recipient, grateful that she thought of me in such a way. She was excited to give the gift, and I was excited to be on the receiving end of her generosity.

Dear friend, in the same way, God's love is a gift, demonstrated most powerfully through the sacrifice of His Son, Jesus Christ. Through Jesus we receive the incomparable gift of salvation and restoration with God.

Read Ephesians 2:8-9 in the margin. What does this verse say about the nature of God's gift of salvation? How do we receive it?

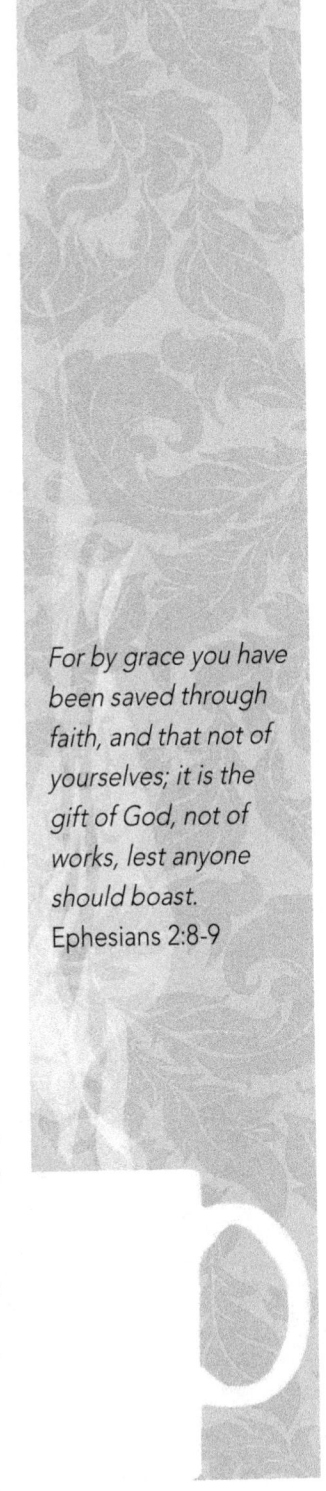

For by grace you have been saved through faith, and that not of yourselves; it is the gift of God, not of works, lest anyone should boast.
Ephesians 2:8-9

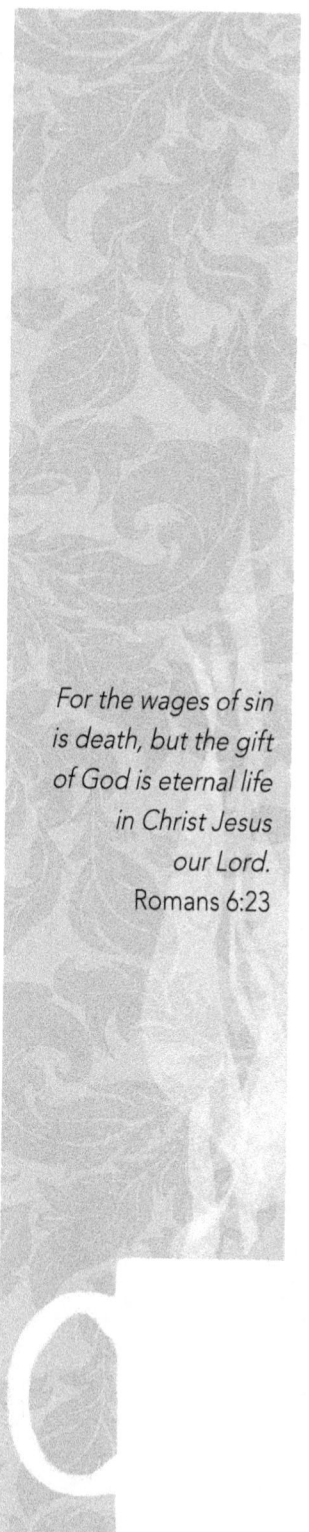

There is no way you could ever be good enough or do enough to earn God's love. No matter how hard you try, you could never repay Jesus for all He has done for you. You can never pray enough or go to church enough or do enough good deeds. You may as well stop trying. Hallelujah! *Jesus* has done enough!

Look up Romans 5:8 and write it below.

What does this verse tell you about God's love for you?

God granted you the Gift of all gifts, His Son. I love how THE MESSAGE paraphrases Romans 5:8:

> *We can understand someone dying for a person worth dying for, and we can understand how someone good and noble could inspire us to selfless sacrifice. But God put his love on the line for us by offering his Son in sacrificial death while we were of no use whatsoever to him.*

Your response is to receive the gift of salvation with a heart of gratitude and praise. The gift of God's love and favor is yours with no strings attached! Salvation is free, but it was not cheap. It cost Jesus His life through death on a cross.

Read Romans 6:23 in the margin. What does this verse remind us?

Take a moment to reflect on the gift of love that God poured out for you in Jesus Christ. What does Jesus' death on a cross mean to you?

What is your response to that gift?

The only appropriate response is to say, "Thank You, Jesus" in words and deeds, living a life that overflows with gratitude for all that Jesus has done. You see, God's grace means that you don't get what *you* deserve; instead, you get

For the wages of sin is death, but the gift of God is eternal life in Christ Jesus our Lord.
Romans 6:23

what *Jesus* deserves. You deserve death. But because you are loved with an ever-lasting love, you receive eternal life. You are not loved by God because of *who* you are. You are loved by God because of *whose* you are.

The renowned artist Paul Gustave Dore (1821-1883) lost his passport while on a tour in Europe. When he came to a border crossing, he explained his predicament to one of the guards. Giving his name to the official, Dore hoped that he would be recognized and allowed to pass. The guard explained that many people attempt to cross the border by claiming to be people they are not. Dore insisted that he was who he claimed to be.

"All right," the border guard replied. "We'll give you a test and if you pass it, we'll allow you to go through."

Handing him pencil and paper, he told the artist to sketch several peasants who were standing nearby. Dore did it so quickly and skillfully that the guard was convinced he was who he claimed to be. His work confirmed his word.[1]

Christ's work confirms His word. And His word is at work in you every day as you are being shaped and molded into His image. You are to walk (live) like Him, talk like Him, love like Him, and serve like Him. Your identity is not in who people say you are. Your identity is in who Jesus says you are.

Read Jesus' words in Matthew 5:48 from *THE MESSAGE*:

"You're kingdom subjects. Now live like it. Live out your God-created identity. Live generously and graciously toward others, the way God lives toward you. "

What does it mean to live like kingdom subjects?

What is your God-created identity, and how can you live it out?

Why are we called to live generously and graciously toward others? How easy or difficult is this?

Friend, you are a "kingdom subject"—a beloved citizen of God's heavenly and eternal kingdom! And what Jesus says about you in His Word is all that matters. Television, magazines, and Hollywood movies deliver the message that to be loved and accepted, to be considered beautiful, you have to look a certain

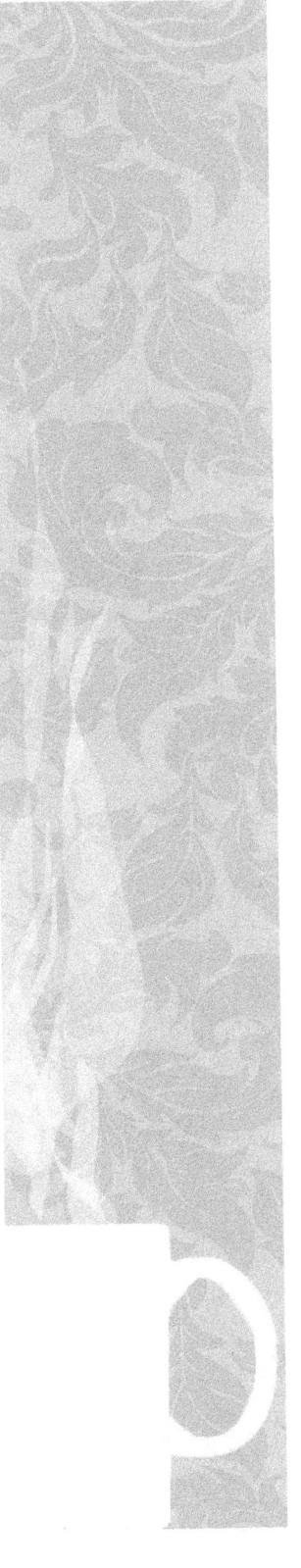

way, be a certain age, have a certain body size, or acquire certain possessions. But, you must not define yourself according to the world's standards.

The other day while standing in the grocery store checkout lane, I glanced at the magazine covers propped up in the stands. They displayed pictures of some of Hollywood's biggest sensations. The women were young, white, thin, and blonde. Let me say, I'm not mad at any of those women. They deserve accolades for their accomplishments and I applaud their efforts. In some cases, I can say that I appreciate their work. But if I were taking my cues from the messages delivered by the media, I'd never fit in! I'm an older, African American grandmother with hips! Sometimes I showcase my own naturally curly hair. Sometimes I put my hair on in the morning and take it off at night. No shame in my game. I'm happy just being me. And you have to be happy just being you! Don't fall for the subtle, alluring messages of our culture: *Blend in; conform to the latest trend; copy the crowd. If you want to be beautiful and successful, buy this product. Try this diet and be the perfect size. Wear this fashion accessory.*

Like a stained-glass window, your true beauty is best revealed by the light that is inside of you.

I'm not saying that outward appearances aren't important. Not at all. But like a stained-glass window, your true beauty is best revealed by the light that is inside of you. You were never meant to blend in. You are at your best when you stand out!

The apostle Paul speaks some very powerful words in Romans 12:1-2. Read the following passage from *THE MESSAGE* with intention, and underline the words that jump off the page at you:

So here's what I want you to do, God helping you: Take your everyday, ordinary life—your sleeping, eating, going-to-work, and walking-around life, and place it before God as an offering. Embracing what God does for you is the best thing you can do for him. Don't become so well-adjusted to your culture that you fit into it without even thinking. Instead, fix your attention on God. You'll be changed from the inside out. Readily recognize what he wants from you, and quickly respond to it. Unlike the culture around you, always dragging you down to its level of immaturity, God brings the best out of you, develops well-formed maturity in you.

You see, you're way beyond different; you're unique. You're one of a kind in your distinction. You're in a class all by yourself. There is nobody like you in the entire universe. Jesus celebrates *you*! Celebrate your own uniqueness by giving God glory for making you just the way He wanted. Don't waste your time trying to be someone else. If you are busy trying to be someone else, then you will leave a huge void in the world where the real you ought to be.

It all begins and ends with God's great love for you. Just how great is God's love for you?

Reread Jesus' words in John 17:23 and fill in the blanks:

"I will be in them and you will be in me so that they will be completely one. Then the world will know that you sent me and that you _____ them just as _____ as you loved _____." (NCV)

God loves you just as much as He loves His own Son, Jesus! Regardless of who you are or how far you have fallen, God's great love will reach to wherever you are. No matter how deeply you've been wounded or how badly it hurts, God's love is just the prescription you need for what ails you. No matter who has rejected you, God has already placed His stamp of approval on your life.

Consider what God's Word says about you.

Acceptance issues? Look up Ephesians 1:5-6. Write the verse below and underline what God calls you.

Don't think you're beautiful? Think again. If God says you're beautiful, that settles the matter. Read Psalm 45:11 in the margin. The "King" in this verse is God! Knowing this, what is this verse saying about your beauty?

So the King will greatly desire your beauty;
Because He is your Lord, worship Him.
Psalm 45:11

Need a really good friend? You've found one in Jesus. Read Proverbs 18:24. How close a friend is the Lord?

Been rejected? Not anymore! Read John 6:37b. What does Jesus promise you in this verse?

The one who comes to Me I will by no means cast out.
John 6:37b

Think you're too bad to be forgiven? Never! First John 1:9 makes this promise:

If we confess our _____, he is faithful and just and will _____ us our sins and _____ us from all _____. (NIV)

Never again do you have to wonder, *Does God love me? Does He even care about me? Do I matter to Him?* Decide once and for all to believe what God's Word says about you. Remember, God loves you just as much as He loves Jesus. From this moment on, begin seeing yourself as God sees you: accepted, beautiful, blessed, whole, righteous, forgiven, and free. You are a daughter of the Most High King! Before the day is over, look at yourself in the mirror and say these very words: *I am accepted, beautiful, blessed, whole, righteous, forgiven, and free. I am a daughter of the Most High King!*

Go to God

Ask

Do you know the absolutely wonderful love that God has for you? Ask God right now to speak His love deep into your heart. Take a minute to soak it in. Bask in the deep end of God's love, my sister!

Seek

What is keeping you from accepting that God loves you as much as He loves Jesus?

Behold what manner of love the Father has bestowed on us, that we should be called children of God.
1 John 3:1a

Don't let the voices of self-doubt or insecurity speak louder than God's loud and clear love for you. Seek the truth in God's Word by meditating on Scriptures that affirm God's love for you. (See John 3:16, Romans 8:37-39, 1 John 3:1a, and 1 John 4:9-12 for starters.)

Knock

Do you know someone who needs to know the immense love of God? Make a point to share God's love with her this week through a conversation, an act of service, or a gift of blessing.

> *Dear heavenly Father,*
> *We are just so grateful for Your awesome love for us. We can hardly believe that You love us as much as You love Jesus. Help us to believe it. Help us to share it. We love You, Lord. In Jesus' name. Amen.*

Day 2: God Loves Prodigals

Read God's Word

¹¹*Then He said: "A certain man had two sons. *¹²*And the younger of them said to his father, 'Father, give me the portion of goods that falls to me.' So he divided to them his livelihood. *¹³*And not many days after, the younger son gathered all together, journeyed to a far country, and there wasted his possessions with prodigal living. *¹⁴*But when he had spent all, there arose a severe famine in that land, and he began to be in want. *¹⁵*Then he went and joined himself to a citizen of that country, and he sent him into his fields to feed swine. *¹⁶*And he would gladly have filled his stomach with the pods that the swine ate, and no one gave him anything.*

¹⁷*"But when he came to himself, he said, 'How many of my father's hired servants have bread enough and to spare, and I perish with hunger! *¹⁸*I will arise and go to my father, and will say to him, "Father, I have sinned against heaven and before you, *¹⁹*and I am no longer worthy to be called your son. Make me like one of your hired servants."'*

²⁰*"And he arose and came to his father. But when he was still a great way off, his father saw him and had compassion, and ran and fell on his neck and kissed him. *²¹*And the son said to him, 'Father, I have sinned against heaven and in your sight, and am no longer worthy to be called your son.'*

²²*"But the father said to his servants, 'Bring out the best robe and put it on him, and put a ring on his hand and sandals on his feet. *²³*And bring the fatted calf here and kill it, and let us eat and be merry; *²⁴*for this my son was dead and is alive again; he was lost and is found.' And they began to be merry."*

Luke 15:11-24

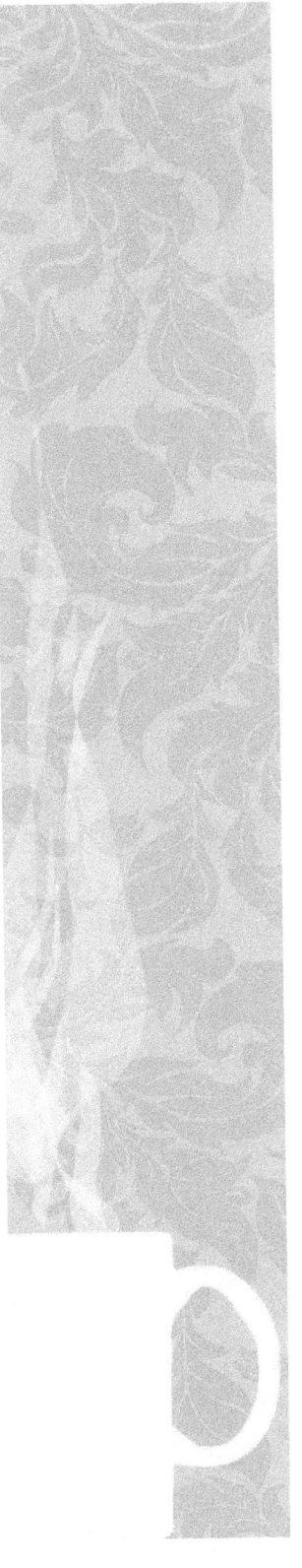

Reflect and Respond

God's boundless love is for *all*, regardless of past mistakes and sins. That's good news, my friend, because "all [of us] have sinned and fall short of the glory of God" (Romans 3:23 NIV).

I've heard it said that self is in the root, the shoot, and the fruit of our human existence. Isn't that how sin starts? A selfish act starts as the seed of a thought; then it rises up on the inside. Before long it stands to its feet, flails its arms, and says, "I want it my way. I want it all, and I want it now!"

Our story today is about the prodigal son, but there is a selfish prodigal daughter in each of us, my sister. Male or female—when we find ourselves unsatisfied with the way things are, we often do not stop until we get our way. It has been

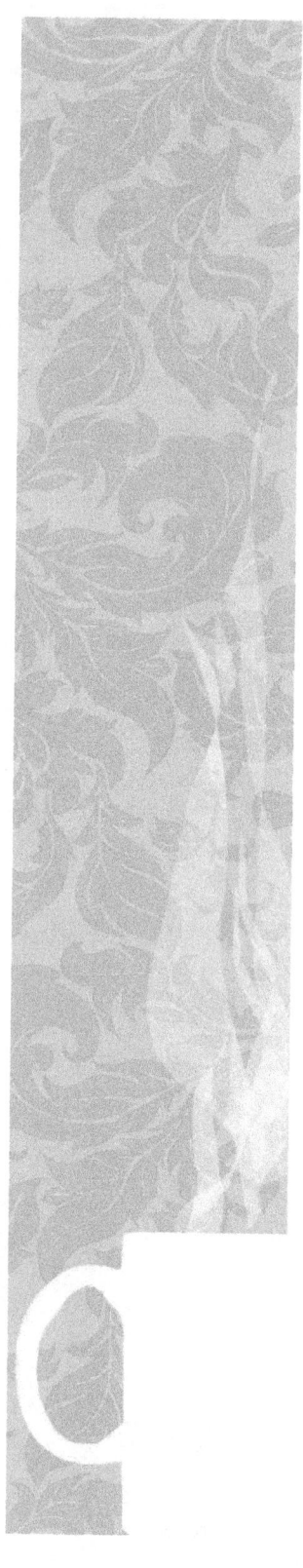

this way since the garden of Eden. When we look through the Bible, we see story after story of human beings taking what they wanted. Consider a few examples

1. Look at Genesis 3.
Who are the main characters?

What was the act of selfishness?

What were the results?

2. Look at 2 Samuel 11.
Who are the main characters?

What was the act of selfishness?

What were the results?

3. Look at Matthew 26:14-16, 47-56 and Matthew 27:3-10.
Who are the main characters?

What was the act of selfishness?

What were the results?

Do you see the pattern? Jesus told the story of the prodigal son, also known as the parable of the lost son, to reveal the nature of the human heart and, more important, to show the loving nature of our God.

Review Luke 15:11-24 and answer the following questions:

Who are the main characters?

What was the act of selfishness?

What were the results?

As I mentioned, the parable of the prodigal son is a story we all can relate to because in one way or another we've all had a prodigal's heart.

Let's review the story together. A father had two sons. One day the restless younger son asked his father to give him his share of his inheritance. Now, for a Jewish son to do this was an offense to his father, because a son never received his father's inheritance until after his father's death. In essence, the son was saying to his father, "I wish you were dead." But the son was insistent, and so his father granted his desire.

Once he had his money, the young man headed for a far off country where he wasted his wealth on what the Bible calls "prodigal living." In other words, he spent all his money on good wine, pretty women, and wild living. It wasn't long before his money began to run short and he could no longer afford the lifestyle to which he had grown accustomed. Then his money ran completely out just as a severe famine began to plague the land. When a person is desperate, he or she will do just about anything. And so it was that this nice Jewish boy got a job feeding pigs to earn a little bit of pocket change. He stooped so low that he not only touched unclean pigs; he was tempted to eat the food he was feeding them.

Sin will take you farther than you want to go, sin will make you pay more than you want to pay, and sin will make you stay longer than you want to stay.

On the following page is an excerpt from *Matthew Henry's Concise Commentary on the Bible*, which explains the nature of the prodigal heart. As you read the excerpt, look for four descriptions of a "sinful state," and underline each.

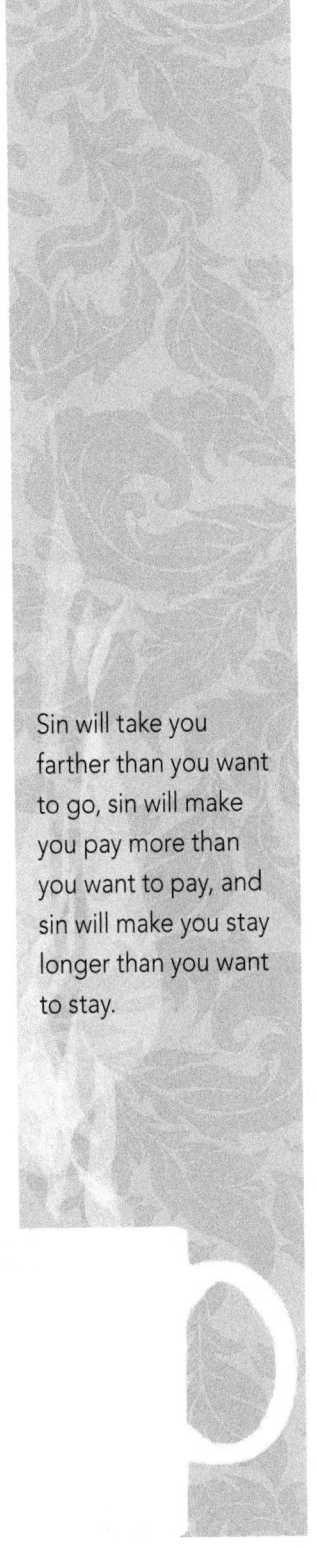

Sin will take you farther than you want to go, sin will make you pay more than you want to pay, and sin will make you stay longer than you want to stay.

A sinful state is of departure and distance from God. A sinful state is a spending state: willful sinners misemploy their thoughts and the powers of their souls, misspend their time and all their opportunities. A sinful state is a wanting state. Sinners want necessaries for their souls.... A sinful state is a vile, slavish state. The business of the devil's servant is to make provision for the flesh, to fulfill the lusts thereof, and that is no better than feeding swine.[2]

Put a check mark beside each "sinful state" that you have experienced:

__Departure and distance (living apart from God)
__Spending (wasting or misusing your thoughts, time, and opportunities)
__Wanting (yearning for satisfaction of the soul)
__Lusting (craving things of the flesh)

These sinful states describe each of us, don't they? Like the prodigal, who found himself in the pigpen with a hopeless heart, an empty belly, and nowhere to lay his head, each of us has experienced the despair and depravity of sin. Perhaps like the lost son, you have discovered that the road leading to the "big city"—or whatever it is that you have been seeking—is lined with bright lights and tempting sights. However, when you take that same road back home again, each step can be laden with regret. The lessons learned on the streets are usually learned the hard way.

Let me share my own prodigal story with you. If you've read my book or Bible study *Embraced by God,* this story will be familiar. But it bears repeating because it was the definitive turning point in my life—the moment when God got my attention and set me on the right path, and His boundless love has led me ever since.

When I was finishing high school, my dream was to go to a big state university near Detroit so that I would be closer to Motown and closer to realizing my dream as a Motown singer. But there was no money for me to attend the big university. Instead, I was accepted at Spring Arbor College, a small Christian school not even twenty miles from home. The deal was sealed when I was awarded a music scholarship to go to school there. I thought, "I'll just get my teaching degree, and that will give me something to fall back on." But while I was making my plans, God was activating His.

My heart was set on singing R&B music—the music of Aretha Franklin, Gladys Knight, Dianna Ross, and Roberta Flack. On Friday and Saturday nights, I tried my hand at singing in local bars and clubs around the state of Michigan, on college campuses, and in smoky hotel piano bars. Every Sunday morning, though, I'd show up to sing and play the piano at my father's church. I felt that I had one foot in the church and one foot in the world. Talk about a setup for a fall!

One afternoon in late autumn I decided to have lunch at the school snack bar. ordered a hot cup of beef vegetable soup and sat down at a nearby table. Snow vas already on the ground outside, and the hot soup felt good going down. A riend came by to chat, and in a few minutes she was on her way and I went back o my lunch. But since the soup had been sitting there for a few minutes, it had rown lukewarm. I noticed that the oil in the soup had formed an orange ring of rease around the rim of the white Styrofoam cup it was served in. I took another poonful, but the soup's lukewarm broth coagulated and rolled off the spoon. It ctually made my stomach feel a bit queasy.

At that moment, a passage of Scripture came to my mind. I remembered it vord for word since I had memorized it from my youth. Found in the Book of Revelation, the Scripture was written to the church at Laodicea. But that day, it vas like the letter said, "Dear Babbie." It was as if Jesus Himself sat down and iad lunch with me.

Look up Revelation 3:15-16 and fill in the blanks:

"I know your deeds, that you are neither _____ nor _____. I wish you were either one or the other! So, because you are _____—neither hot nor cold—I am about to _____ you out of my _____." **(NIV)**

God got my attention that day. I knew He was speaking directly to me, addressing my half-hearted commitment to Him and the compromising way I was living. Like the prodigal son, I came to myself. I surrendered my heart to the Lord right there at the lunch table. At that moment, I gave Jesus my desires, my dreams, my uncertainties, and my fears about the future. I realized at that moment that I didn't need a record contract, a full concert schedule, or a band to back me up. What I needed was a restored relationship with Jesus.

Have you ever compromised your testimony, dear one? Have you ever done less when you should have done more for the cause of Christ? Have you kept quiet when you should have spoken up? Have you ever put up a front and looked like a Christian with her act together on Sunday and lived a completely different way among your friends or coworkers during the week? I know firsthand that this is a miserable way to live.

We've been talking about driving a spiritual stake of faith in the firm foundation of God's Word all through this study. If there is compromise in any area of your life, confess it to Jesus now. He is ready to forgive you and make things right. You'll find that there is so much joy to be found when you commit your heart fully to Christ.

Remember, if Jesus is not Lord of all, then He is not Lord at all. Make Him Lord of every area of your life today.

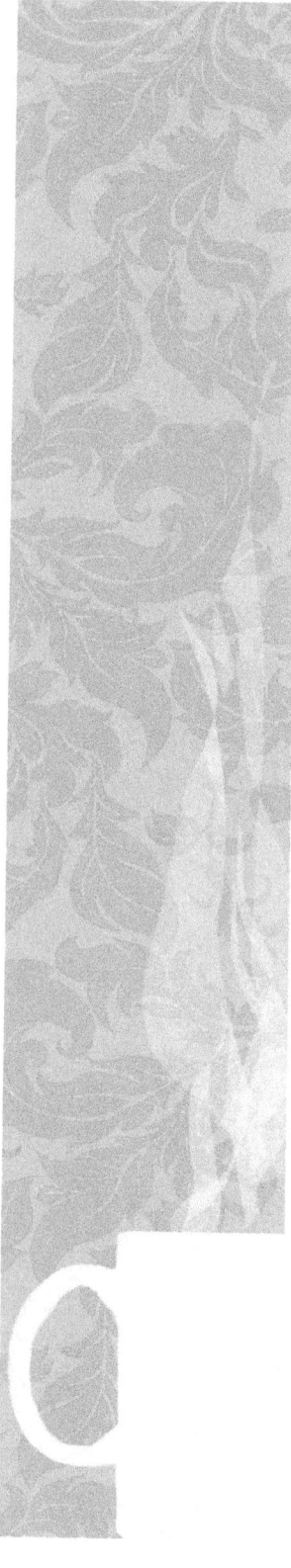

Go to God

Ask

Has sin ever left you feeling hopeless, empty, or out in the cold? You didn't plan for it to turn out that way, but most of the time sin isn't planned. Maybe that's why we use the phrase "fall into sin." You're walking along, minding your own business, when you lose your footing, and the next thing you know you're slip-sliding away. Your adversary is a strategist who sets you up to destroy you, catching you off guard and moving in when you're not looking.

Remember what we learned in Week 3: you have been given a powerful weapon with which to fight, the Word of God. Second Corinthians 10:4-5 says, "The weapons we fight with are not the weapons of the world. On the contrary, they have divine power to demolish strongholds. We demolish arguments and every pretension that sets itself up against the knowledge of God, and we take captive every thought to make it obedient to Christ" (NIV). Friend, pray the Word of God, sing the Word, and speak the Word—and watch the adversary flee.

Seek

Do not be misled by the lie that God cannot love you or forgive you because of what you have done. The parable of the prodigal son shows us that we are never outside God's boundless love. Meditate on and stand on this truth today:

> *Yet in all these things we are more than conquerors through Him who loved us. For I am persuaded that neither death nor life, nor angels nor principalities nor powers, nor things present nor things to come, nor height nor depth, nor any other created thing, shall be able to separate us from the love of God which is in Christ Jesus our Lord.*
>
> Romans 8:37-39

Knock

Do you have a prodigal in your life for whom you can offer grace and mercy—perhaps even a party? Pray now that God would take away all bitterness from the situation. Reach out with open arms and welcome the prodigal back into your life.

> *Dear heavenly Father,*
> *Thank You for loving prodigals like us. We can be so selfish. Thank You for proving to us time and time again that You are still faithful and full of grace when we turn from our sin and head home into Your arms. Forgive our sin and lead us on Your path. In Jesus' name I pray. Amen.*

Day 3: You Are Never Too Far from Grace

Read God's Word

¹¹*Then He said: "A certain man had two sons. ¹²And the younger of them said to his father, 'Father, give me the portion of goods that falls to me.' So he divided to them his livelihood. ¹³And not many days after, the younger son gathered all together, journeyed to a far country, and there wasted his possessions with prodigal living. ¹⁴But when he had spent all, there arose a severe famine in that land, and he began to be in want. ¹⁵Then he went and joined himself to a citizen of that country, and he sent him into his fields to feed swine. ¹⁶And he would gladly have filled his stomach with the pods that the swine ate, and no one gave him anything.*

¹⁷*"But when he came to himself, he said, 'How many of my father's hired servants have bread enough and to spare, and I perish with hunger! ¹⁸I will arise and go to my father, and will say to him, "Father, I have sinned against heaven and before you, ¹⁹and I am no longer worthy to be called your son. Make me like one of your hired servants."'*

²⁰*"And he arose and came to his father. But when he was still a great way off, his father saw him and had compassion, and ran and fell on his neck and kissed him. ²¹And the son said to him, 'Father, I have sinned against heaven and in your sight, and am no longer worthy to be called your son.'*

²²*"But the father said to his servants, 'Bring out the best robe and put it on him, and put a ring on his hand and sandals on his feet. ²³And bring the fatted calf here and kill it, and let us eat and be merry; ²⁴for this my son was dead and is alive again; he was lost and is found.' And they began to be merry."*

Luke 15:11-24

If we confess our sins, He is faithful and just to forgive us our sins and to cleanse us from all unrighteousness.

1 John 1:9

God's love and grace are inextricably connected. Because of God's love for us, He showers us with His grace—His undeserved favor and kindness.

Reflect and Respond

Today we are mining more treasure from the parable of the prodigal son. This beautiful story illustrates not only God's boundless love but also God's amazing grace. God's love and grace are inextricably connected. Because of God's love for us, He showers us with His grace—His undeserved favor and kindness.

It was a landmark moment in the prodigal's life when he realized what he had left at his father's house was better than what he faced on the streets.

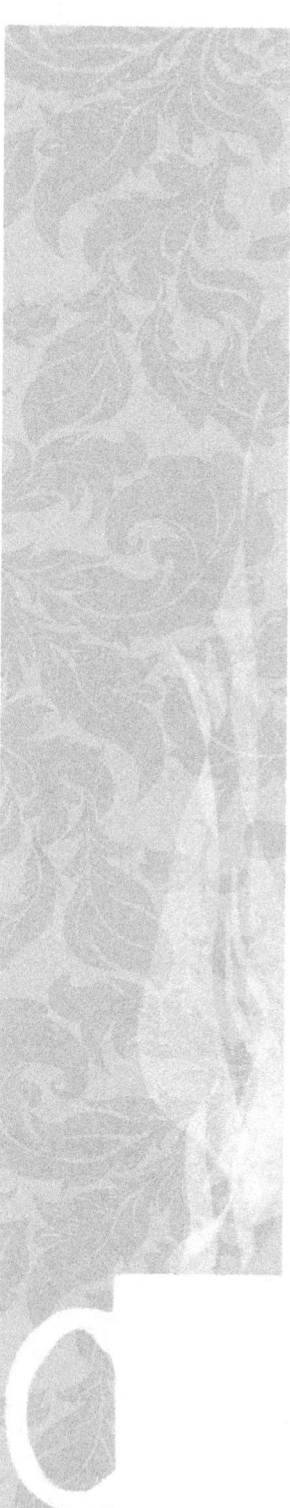

What realization did the son come to in Luke 15:17?

What does verse 20 say he decided to do?

We learn in verse 17 that the prodigal "came to himself." Have you ever come to yourself? You see, until you come to yourself, you'll keep on getting what you've always gotten; you'll continue to do what you always done. When you come to yourself, you'll have one of those soul-searching conversations with yourself that may go something like this. "I'm sick and tired of having too much month and not enough money." That's when you start getting out of debt. "I can't take this anymore." That's when you decide to get help for your addiction. "I can do bad all by myself." That's when you change the circumstances concerning the relationship that's gone south. "I know I can do it." That's the moment you decide to take the first step toward furthering your education or pursuing your God-given dream.

The son came to himself. He got up from the pigpen and made the decision to go home. As the wayward son rounded the bend near home, he saw the familiar sites he had only dreamed of for so long. At first, reluctance and regret surely caused his gait to be slow and deliberate. His mind may have played tricks on him. Perhaps he wondered, *What will my father say? What will he do? Turn his back on me? Make me like one of his hired servants? Serves me right if my father never speaks to me again. Anything is better than where I've been.* Then who did he see coming up the road to meet him? Whose arms couldn't wait to embrace him?

With a heart full of love, overflowing with grace and mercy, his father sprinted to meet him. I can just imagine him running barefoot, leaving his sandals in the dust, with his robes hiked high and blowing in the breeze.

How would you describe the scene in verse 20?

I don't believe his father glanced up just in time to catch a glimpse of his son out of the corner of his eye. No, I believe his father had surveyed the horizon day after painstaking day, hoping any moment to see his son coming down the road. I believe he sat by the window each night keeping vigil until well after bedtime, and then leaving a light on just in case his son came home in the middle of the night. Then the day finally came.

When the son was still down the road—road-weary, thin, gaunt, and smelling like the hog pen—his father recognized even the slightest form of his son's silhouette and ran to meet him. It's likely that the son collapsed into his father's arms in a state of disbelief, kissed by grace and mercy. No I-told-you-so's. No sermon. Only a ring, a robe, and a party.

The prodigal's story is our story. Every one of us has defied our Father's wishes. We've all broken His heart. We've all wandered far from home and found ourselves in a faraway place, wallowing in the mire of sin. But no matter how far we roam, we are never beyond the reaches of God's grace. His grace is not only abundant and vast; it is continual, never ceasing, flowing without interruption into our lives.

God extended His grace and forgiveness to me over thirty-five years ago, and he has continued to shower me with His grace ever since.

Read 1 John 1:9 in the margin. What does this verse promise us?

Read Hebrews 4:16. What does this verse assure us about God's grace?

Read Romans 5:1-2. How do we receive God's grace? What is required of us?

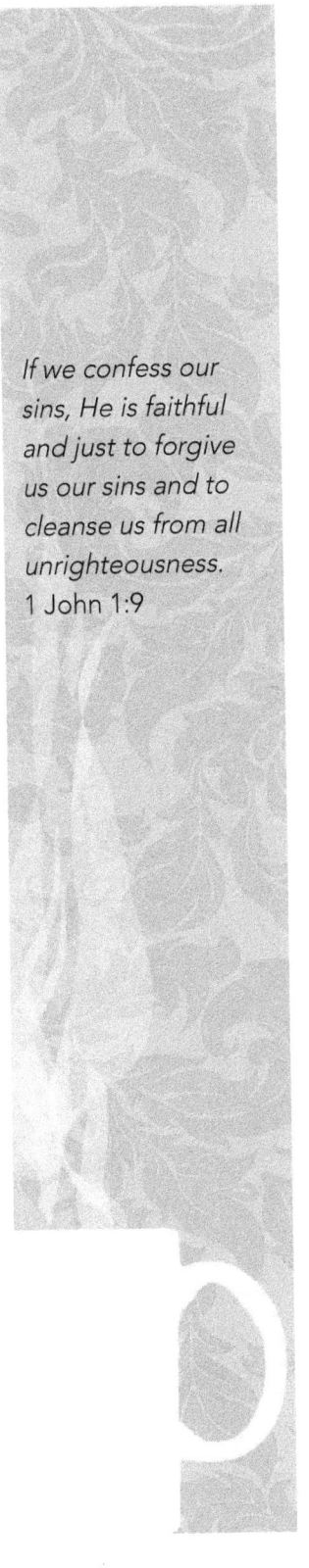

If we confess our sins, He is faithful and just to forgive us our sins and to cleanse us from all unrighteousness.
1 John 1:9

The very moment you confess your sin and turn to Him, He is right there—ready, willing, and able to forgive. That's grace. We can turn to God confident that we *will* receive grace. It is a gift we receive by faith, with no strings attached.

Luke chapter 15 is not only the story of the prodigal son; it is the story of our Father, the Father of prodigals, who continues to astonish us with His extravagant display of boundless love and grace. Don't deny yourself for another moment the joy of knowing you are forgiven and restored. You see, the Father withholds from you the very things you deserve: judgment and condemnation. And He extends to you the very things you don't deserve: grace and mercy.

Have you been running in the wrong direction? Do you think it's time that you turn around and look toward home? When you do, you will find that God has been there all along, waiting to receive you and lovingly restore you to your rightful place in His eternal family. Your loving Father has a royal robe and a signet ring that have been designed with you in mind, and He is waiting to clothe you with His choicest blessings. This I know for sure: the best is yet to come.

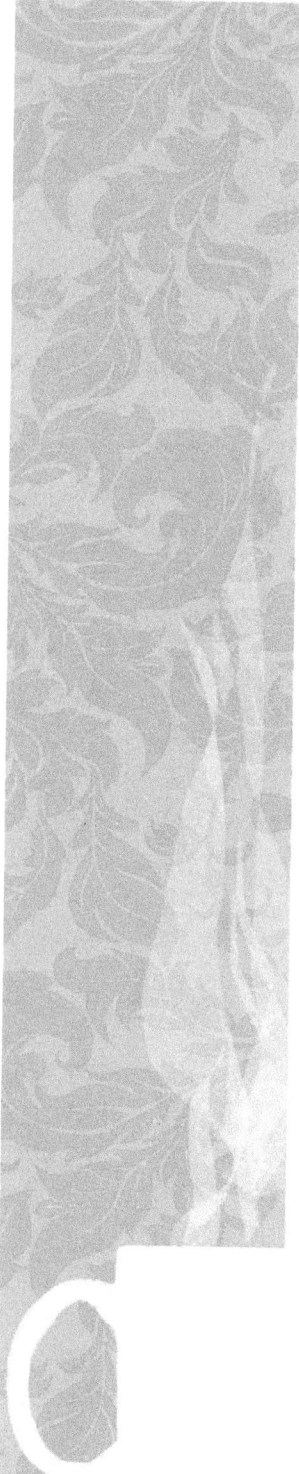

God has thrown a party in your honor. What are you waiting for? Don't let the celebration begin without you!

Go to God

Ask

Take some time now to ask God to hear your confession. Acknowledge the ways you have neglected or disobeyed His Word, acted selfishly, or chosen your own way. Ask Him to forgive you. When we ask for forgiveness, God throws our sins into the deep sea of forgetfulness, and we are set free.

Seek

Take some time each day to reflect on the ways that you might be clinging to selfishness. Invite the light of God's grace to shine into the deep, dark, secret places, blotting out the darkness of sin that may be hiding there.

Knock

Do you have a prodigal story that someone else needs to hear? I challenge you to tell someone the story of how you ran away from God and how He ran to meet you when you returned home to His arms. That is a story of grace we all need to hear!

> *Dear loving Father,*
> *We praise You for Your amazing grace. When we confess our sins, You are so very faithful to forgive us and cleanse us from our past. Help us to receive Your grace so that we do not dwell on our sin anymore. Give us courage to walk in Your freedom. In Jesus' name. Amen.*

Day 4: Jesus—The Ultimate Expression of God's Love

Read God's Word

For God so loved the world that He gave His only begotten Son, that whoever believes in Him should not perish but have everlasting life.

John 3:16

Reflect and Respond

It was an exciting day. My friend, who had just produced her first motion picture, had planned a big premiere at her home church, and Charles and I were invited to come. On the way to the church, I glanced at my watch and surmised that I still had just enough time to dash into a store to buy my friend a gift— maybe a bouquet of flowers to celebrate her accomplishments. Unfamiliar with the area, the only store we could find was one of those warehouse-type super-stores. It was the only choice we had at the moment, so Charles parked the car in the lot and waited while I dashed into the huge warehouse.

I was a bit overwhelmed at the expansive size of the store. It seemed to stretch as far as it was wide. A nice store clerk pointed me in the direction of their fresh flowers. I thanked her, found a nice gift to go with the flowers, and was back at the front of the store in no time. I stepped into the checkout line, filing in behind two other people already in line. The clerk told me I'd have to pay a bit extra because I didn't have a membership card. I'd never shopped at one of those warehouse superstores before, so I didn't know that a membership card was required. But I was willing to pay a little extra for the gifts rather than spend time, effort, and gas looking for another store.

Just then, a very kind middle-aged lady behind me said, "No problem, I'll be glad to let you use my card so you can get the discount."

I replied with gratitude to her offer, "Oh, thank you so much! God bless you for that!"

"Oh, honey," she said, "I really do need God to bless me. I've had a tough go of it these last few months. My grandkids have come to live with me, and I'm not as young as I used to be. It's a challenge to raise kids nowadays."

In an effort to offer a simple word of encouragement, I smiled and said, rather conversationally, "Well, may the Lord give you the strength you need to raise your grandkids. I pray He will open up the windows of His heaven and shower down so many blessings upon you and your grandchildren that you won't have room to receive them all."

That lady was catching the vision before I could get the words out of my mouth! The next thing I knew, she was lifting her hands, and shouting praises to God, right there in the check-out line. "Praise You, God! Hallelujah! I receive that blessing right now, Jesus. Thank You, Lord, for blessing me!" she said.

Now, I've been privileged to worship Jesus in a lot of different places, but that was the first time I'd ever had church in the check-out line of a warehouse superstore. Then, before I could turn around, a young lady standing behind us in line said, "Will you bless me, too?"

While the first lady was yet praising God, I smiled, took the young lady by the hand, and said to her, "Well, my sweet friend, God loves you so much! May

155

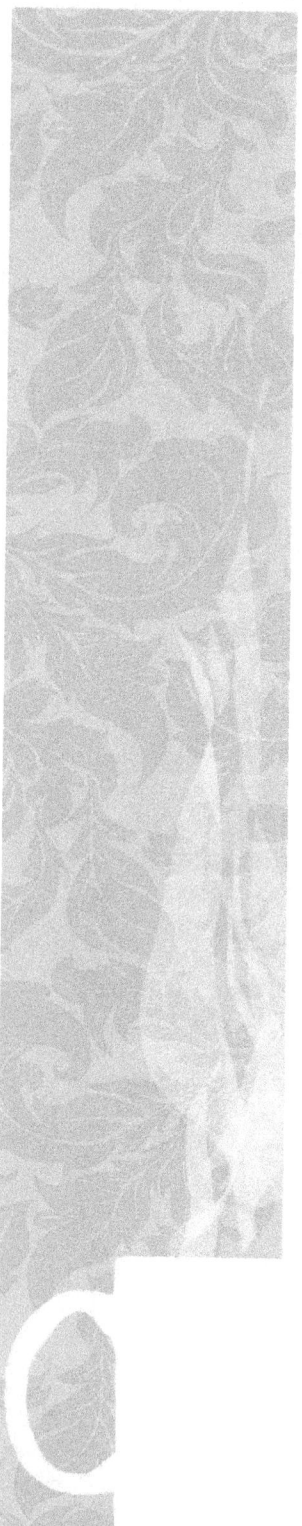

you always live for the Lord. As you do, I pray that He will supply all your needs according to His riches in glory by Christ Jesus."

The next thing I knew, tears came rolling down her face as she savored those words that were spoken into her life. I paid for my items and was heading out the front door when the security guard standing at his post of duty greeted me on the way out and said, "If you don't mind, would you bless me, too?"

The words I spoke to those I met that day at the store weren't exceptional. I only did what I was led to do—to encourage weary hearts through the power of the Word of God. I marveled at how persuasive the spoken word of God is. I went into that store that day for one reason, but it was evident God sent me out of my way on a greater mission—to share His love with those who needed it.

How has someone gone out of her or his way to share God's love with you?

Jesus is the ultimate expression of God's love. Today I want us to reflect on the ways He spent His entire life and ministry going out of His way to draw others to Himself so that they might receive the Father's love and grace. As a matter of fact, that's what Jesus did best. Leaving the beautiful splendor of heaven, He consented to come all the way to earth so He could show us what love looks like in flesh and blood. The King of kings, He deserved a royal entourage to announce His arrival to earth. Instead, He chose to come into the world just like the rest of us—as a baby. And He was placed in a humble manger, a feeding trough for the animals. Instead of the wonderful fragrance of heaven, the first aroma He inhaled was the pungent odors of a stable filled with dirty, smelly farm animals.

That's what Jesus did—and what He still does today. Because of God's boundless love, Jesus came to be the bridge between a holy God and a hopeless humanity so we could cross over from death to life.

In Luke 4:18-19, Jesus spoke the words that the prophet Isaiah had said about Him. What did Jesus come to do?

Jesus said "the Spirit of the Lord is upon me. . . . He has sent me to preach good news" (Luke 4:18 CEB). That good news can be summed up in three words: God's boundless love. My father, Pastor Willie G. Wade, preached this good news every Sunday for almost forty years to a mighty band of saints at Lily Missionary Baptist Church. It didn't matter what the subject of the sermon was, Dad always losed every sermon with the message of God's love expressed through Jesus Christ. And in that message, I can see clearly how far Jesus had to come, how long Jesus had to reach, how wide His arms had to stretch, and how deep His love had to go to rescue us from the clutches of sin.

As you read the following words from one of my father's sermons, I invite you to imagine him preaching with that fiery, fervent passion black preachers of his generation are known for. Use your holy imagination and picture him decked in his black robe, proclaiming the message of the gospel with every impassioned inflection of his voice:

> Jesus came down from heaven to earth, through forty and two generations. He caught Mary's nine-month train, He got off somewhere in Bethlehem, and there was no room for Him in the inn. The Word became flesh and dwelt among us. And we have seen His glory—the glory of the only begotten of the Father, full of grace and truth. Then they arrested Jesus and placed upon Him the sins of the whole world. They whipped Him. They pierced Him in the side, gambled for His robe, nailed Him to an old rugged cross, and laid Him in a borrowed tomb. But He didn't stay there. He went down in the grave on Friday. He stayed down in the grave on Saturday. But early . . . early . . . early one Sunday morning, the grave could no longer hold Him down. All power of heaven and earth is in His hands.

That's the message of God's boundless love in a nutshell!

Jesus began his earthly ministry at the age of thirty. I can imagine Him taking one last look around His earthly father's carpenter shop—perhaps shaking the sawdust from His work apron and running his calloused hands across the wooden worktable—kissing His mother good-bye, and then leaving to go about His heavenly Father's business. He walked the distance from Nazareth to the Jordan River where John the Baptist was ministering to the crowds of people who had come to be baptized. And that day He showed the people the vastness of God's love as He, the Savior of the whole world, went out of His way to get in line with sinners to be baptized.

Read Luke 3:21-22 in the margin. When did Jesus go to be baptized? What was His heavenly Father's response?

When all the people were baptized, it came to pass that Jesus also was baptized; and while He prayed, the heaven was opened. And the Holy Spirit descended in bodily form like a dove upon Him, and a voice came from heaven which said, "You are My beloved Son; in You I am well pleased."
Luke 3:21-22

Jesus humbled Himself, identifying Himself with sinful human beings even though He was sinless, and received the anointing of the Holy Spirit for the work he had come to do—work that would take Him all the way to the cross, the grave, and the right hand of the throne of God in heaven.

My friend, Jesus' ministry of demonstrating God's boundless love is not over simply because he lived, died, and rose again. No, He is alive and active in you and me. I've shared with you how moved I was to consider that God loves me as much as He loves Jesus. Well, it gets even better!

Read John 14:12-14 in the margin What did Jesus assure His followers?

What do you think Jesus meant by this promise?

"Very truly I tell you, whoever believes in me will do the works I have been doing, and they will do even greater things than these, because I am going to the Father. And I will do whatever you ask in my name, so that the Father may be glorified in the Son. You may ask me for anything in my name, and I will do it."
John 14:12-14 NIV

By the power of Jesus Christ in your life, you will do "even greater things" than Jesus did. Now, Jesus did some pretty great things. He healed bodies and hearts. He forgave sinners. He performed miracles. He trusted God in unimaginable ways. And He said that we—you and I—will do even greater things! As we carry on Jesus' work in this world, others will come to know the boundless love of God.

As the host of a television show called *Babbie's House,* I have the opportunity to meet so many wonderful people who have beautiful testimonies of what Jesus has done in their lives. I get to see the joy on their faces as they tell how Jesus has delivered them, healed them, and restored them in so many ways. I've heard some of them say that they are counting the days since they have been "clean" from an addiction. I've heard them say that they are still excited about what Jesus has done in their lives and are pressing on in the name of Jesus one day at a time.

If you have received Jesus as your Lord and Savior, then you, too, have been made "clean"! You have been delivered from something that had the power to destroy your life: sin.

At the time this study is published, I will have been "clean" for fifty years! Now I know why they call that fifty-year time span the year of Jubilee. It's the year to celebrate every sin forgiven, every debt cancelled, and every hope restored! I can look back and see how far God's boundless love has brought me. And I know that, come what may, His limitless love will take me the distance I have yet to go.

The Gospel of John contains one of the most famous Bible verses in all of history and probably one of the most memorized among believers. When you forget the depth of God's love for you, when you believe the lie that you have nothing to offer, when you forget that you can do all things through the power of Christ, remember the words of John 3:16.

Read John 3:16 in the translations below. Circle the words or phrases that indicate the depth or extent of God's love.

"God so loved the world that he gave his only Son, so that everyone who believes in him won't perish but will have eternal life." **(CEB)**

"This is how much God loved the world: He gave his Son, his one and only Son. And this is why: so that no one need be destroyed; by believing in him, anyone can have a whole and lasting life." **(THE MESSAGE)**

"For God so loved the world that he gave his one and only Son, that whoever believes in him shall not perish but have eternal life." **(NIV)**

"God loved the world so much that he gave his one and only Son so that whoever believes in him may not be lost, but have eternal life." **(NCV)**

I hope you circled the words *so, how much,* and *so much.* God loved you so much that He sent His Son, Jesus, to set you free from sin and bless you with His boundless love and grace. Will you join me in following Jesus wherever He leads and carrying on His work, no matter the cost? Let's look to Paul's letter to the Philippian church to see exactly what this means.

Read Philippians 2:1-18 and answer the following questions:

What advice does Paul give (vv. 1-4)?

What is the attitude of Christ that we are called to adopt? (vv. 6-8)

What happened when Christ humbled himself on earth? (vv. 9-11)

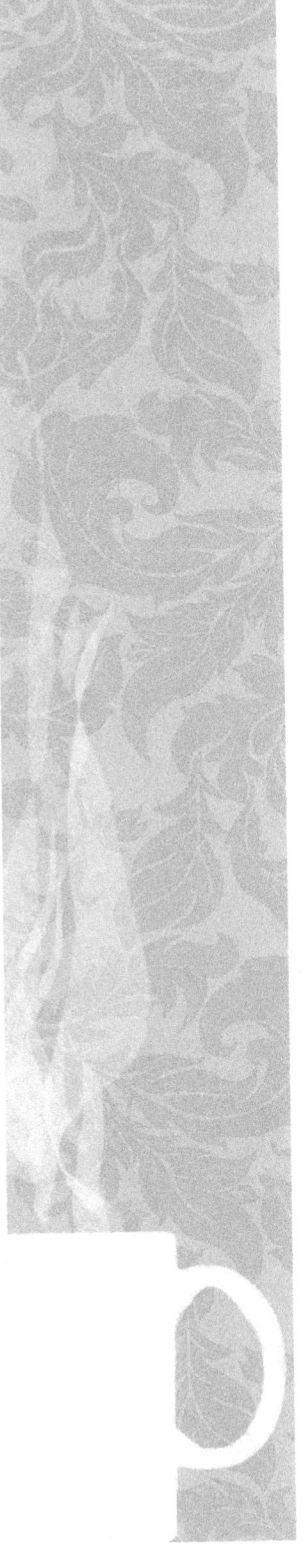

How are we instructed to carry out our salvation? (vv. 13-18)

Want to know how you can join Jesus in His work? Shine like the stars. Let your life shine like the stars so that everyone around you can see the light of God's love and grace. Live so that people who encounter you in public places will ask for blessings. Live so that you sing God's praise regardless of what trials you face because you know for sure that God's boundless love will lead you. Live so that the whole world will know that God *so* loved them—and still does!

Go to God

Ask

Being in a hurry can impede us from following God's plan for us. Sometimes God interrupts our hurriedness with opportunities to be a blessing. Ask God to give you spiritual eyes to see the needs of others and spiritual ears to hear His promptings concerning others who need a word of encouragement or an act of service. Then, ask for courage and wisdom to *be* a blessing.

Seek

When you read John 3:16, do you believe with all your heart that God loved you so much that He sent His Son to die for your sins? Believing that God loves you just as much as He loves His Son, Jesus, may be a lot to take in. But it's absolutely true. Seek the Lord today and ask Him to fill your heart with even greater knowledge of His deep love for you.

Knock

Is there a mission, a person, or a need that has been heavy on your heart? What has the Lord been speaking to you about? Offer yourself to join in Jesus' work right here and now. Lay yourself, your time, your gifts, your attitude, your abilities—all you are—before Jesus and invite Him to use you for His purposes.

Loving God,
Thank You for Your great love. Thank You for sending Jesus to save us from our sin and to make a way for us to live forever with You. Forgive us for shying away from Your love. Help us to accept it or return to it. In Jesus' name. Amen.

Day 5: God's Love Has No Boundaries

Read God's Word

³⁹*Many Samaritans in that city believed in Jesus because of the woman's word when he testified, "He told me everything I've ever done." ⁴⁰So when the Samaritans came to Jesus, they asked him to stay with them, and he stayed there two days. ⁴¹Many more believed because of his word, ⁴²and they said to the woman, "We no longer believe because of what you said, for we have heard for ourselves and know that this one is truly the Savior of the world."*

John 4:39-42 CEB

Reflect and Respond

God's love has no boundaries, and the story of the woman at the well illustrates this so beautifully.

Wherever Jesus went, He went out of His way to minister to the lost, the lonely, the sick, and the broken. Jesus went out of His way one day when He traveled through Samaria, because Samaria was not a place Jews wanted to go. You see, the Jews and Samaritans despised one another. Yet Jesus stopped to rest at Jacob's well that lazy, hazy day.

Read the full account of Jesus' encounter with the woman at the well, found in John 4:1-42. Keep a placeholder there so that you can answer the questions throughout today's reading.

What time was it when Jesus came to the well? (v. 4)

Most of the women went to draw water in the early morning, avoiding the heat of the day. But this woman was at the well alone in the hottest part of the day.

Based on the details you find in the story, why do you think this woman might have chosen to go to the well alone at midday?

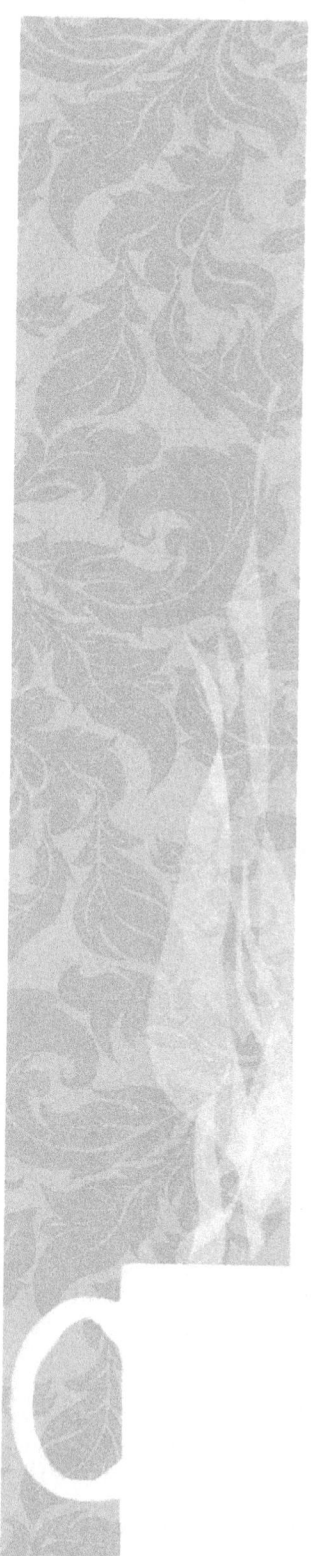

No doubt this woman had been shunned by the other women of the community. Perhaps she was tired of being ridiculed, stared at, or gossiped about. imagine her furrowed brow and sullen eyes told the painful story of her life. victim of her own circumstances, it was obvious that the burden the woman ca ried in her soul weighed more heavily upon her than the water pot she struggle to hoist upon her aching shoulders.

After five failed attempts at marriage, she had all but given up on love an had given in to living with a man who was not her husband, resigning to th fallacy that if you can't find what you need, you must hold on to what you've go whether you want it or not. Relationships had stolen her dignity and self-wort one disappointment at a time until there was nothing left but a shell of a woma with little to show for her life but empty hopes and broken dreams.

What did Jesus ask of the woman, and what did she say? (vv. 7-9)

Why do you think she responded in this manner?

She must have been astonished that Jesus would speak to her, a woman and a Samaritan. Yet Jesus was not bothered at all by her gender or race—or even he checkered past.

How did Jesus reveal that he knew about her past? (vv. 16-19)

No doubt she could see something different about this man she met at the well. Surely there was real love in His eyes, real hope in His voice, real truth in His words.

What are some of the boundaries that should have kept Jesus from loving this woman? (vv. 9, 18, 29)

What are some reasons we often assume that Jesus can't possibly love us?

What did Jesus say to the Samaritan woman in verse 10?

What can keep us from recognizing God's voice and God's gift?

This is what I love about Jesus. It doesn't matter who you are, where you've been, or how long you have stayed there. His love will draw you back from the brink of hopelessness and despair. He spoke into every parched place of this woman's heart—into every longing she'd had in her heart for years.

Friend, Jesus did not let any societal, cultural, or political boundary keep him from loving this woman. And you can be sure that there is nothing that can keep Him from loving you! His boundless love will lead you—as long as time endures!

Realizing that He was indeed the long-awaited Messiah, the Samaritan woman dropped her water pot and went running back to the town to spread the news.

What did the woman say as she ran to tell the people in her village about Jesus? (v. 29)

What was the result of her witness? (vv. 39-42)

How can our witness to the wonderful love of God bring others to believe?

That's what Jesus did best. He went out of His way to speak life into those places in people's lives where death had already won. He did that when he encountered this woman at the well, and He did that when He heard that His dear friend Lazarus had died.

Jesus was delayed in getting back to Bethany, the very place where earlier the Jews had tried to stone Him. But He was compelled to travel the distance and brave the indifference of His adversaries to go back and offer comfort to Lazarus's sisters, Mary and Martha, after the death of their brother.

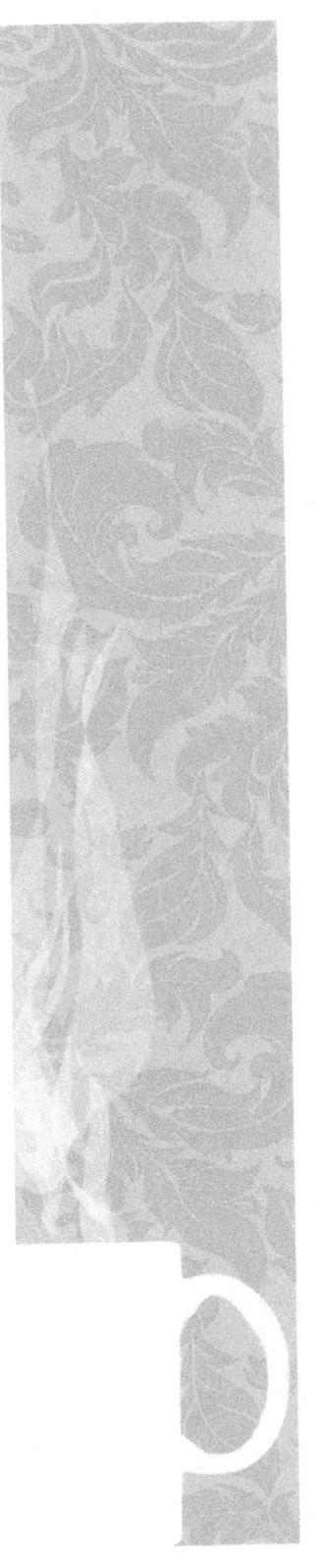

This I Know for Sure

> Now when He had said these things, He cried with a loud voice, "Lazarus, come forth!"
> John 11:43

Everything changed when Jesus came on the scene. He found Mary and Martha grieving and distraught over their loss. Jesus wiped His own tears and spoke to Lazarus who was already decomposing in his grave.

Look at John 11:43 in the margin. What three words did Jesus speak?

_____ _____ _____.

Only three words. Life conquers death. Let faith arise. Tears are dried. Death is defeated. Family is united. Sinners would believe.

Jesus went from big cities to small villages, healing the lame, feeding the multitudes, giving sight to the blind, teaching in the temple, raising the dead. He journeyed up the mountains, down by the river, to the garden, to the cross, to the grave—and back to prepare a place for us with Him in heaven.

James Whittaker was a member of the World War II crew that flew the famed B-17 Flying Fortress. The plane was reported lost at sea in October 1944. Captained by Eddie Rickenbacker, the plane ran into trouble after it ran out of radio range, and soon after that ran out of gas somewhere over the Pacific and crashed into the ocean. The nine-man crew spent the next month adrift in the ocean on three rafts. They fought the heat of day, storms, and ocean waves. Gigantic sharks rammed their nine-foot rafts, waiting for a meal. In eight days, their rations had been eaten or ruined by seawater. Their only hope for survival would be a miracle.

One morning, following their daily devotions, Rickenbacker leaned his head back against the side of the raft and pulled his hat down over his eyes, when he felt something land on his head. Peering out from under his hat, with every eager eye glued on him, he caught the seagull perched on his head and the crew ate it. They used the bird's intestines for fish bait, and that provision allowed the crew to survive the thirty-day ordeal to tell their story.

God went to an unbelievable extent to provide for the crew until they were rescued. But that's not the real miracle. One of the crew members, James Whittaker, was not a believer. The plane crash didn't persuade him to give his life to Christ. All those days facing death on the open seas didn't cause him to think about eternity. In fact, Whittaker grew more and more irritated with John Bartak, another crew member who continually read his Bible audibly and privately. But Bartak didn't stop reading, and the Holy Spirit didn't stop turning over the fallow ground of Whittaker's heart. Then came the moment the seagull landed on Captain Rickenbacker's head just after that morning's Bible reading. And that was the moment James Whittaker became a believer.[3]

Only God would go to such extremes to capture one man's heart, sending a winged missionary into the middle of nowhere to deliver a personal message of love and hope. Hearing that story brings to mind a verse we looked at yesterday.

164

Review yesterday's reading. What did we highlight about John 3:16?

Affirm again today that God doesn't just love you; He *so* loves you. He loves you to the greatest degree—to an immeasurable extent. His love is *boundless*. And no matter how hard you try, you can't count that high or go that far.

Wherever you are at this very moment, whatever condition your heart is in, whatever your story is, remember that Jesus wants you to be certain that He is at work in your life. His boundless love is leading you wherever you are. By a well, by a tomb, on the open seas—the situation doesn't matter. The God of the universe wants you to always know for sure, beyond any shadow of doubt, that He will move heaven and earth for you. That's how much He loves you!

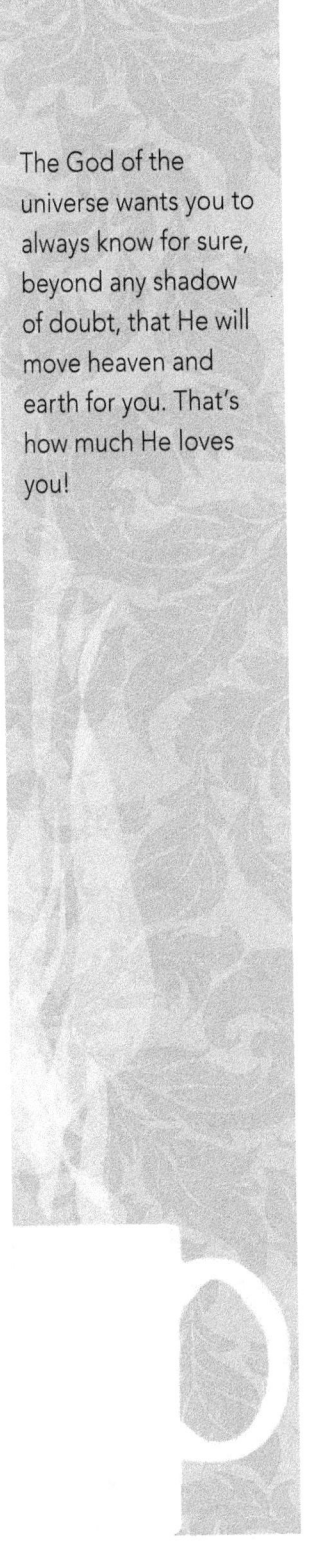

The God of the universe wants you to always know for sure, beyond any shadow of doubt, that He will move heaven and earth for you. That's how much He loves you!

Go to God

Ask

What walls of resistance do you put up that prevent you from giving your heart fully to Jesus? Examine your heart right now. Is there any part of your life that you need to surrender to the boundless love of God?

Seek

The Samaritan woman was quick to believe once Jesus revealed who He was. She felt seen and known for probably the first time in her life. Do you sometimes feel invisible? Unlovable? Out of reach? Off the map? Seek the Lord right now. I promise you, you are never too far away from the reach of God's love.

Knock

Do you know someone who, like the Samaritan woman, is feeling washed up and overspent? Someone who needs a fresh start and knowledge of a different kind of love? Reach out to her this week with a word of hope.

Father God,
We are so grateful that Your love knows no end. Your love stretches across the heavens and reaches down into the deepest parts of us. We are just so very grateful that You are mindful of us. Help us to receive Your love, to share Your love, and to be led by Your love. In Jesus' name. Amen.

Week 5

Video Viewer Guide

"I've never_____ loving you and _____ _____.
Expect love, love, and more love!"

Jeremiah 31:3 *THE MESSAGE*

"And he arose and came to his father. But when he was still a great way off, his father saw him and had compassion, and _____ and fell on his neck and kissed him. And the son said to him, 'Father, I have sinned against heaven and in your sight, and am no longer worthy to be called your son.'

"But the father said to his servants, 'Bring out the best _____ and put it on him, and put a _____ on his hand and sandals on his feet. And bring the fatted _____ here and kill it, and let us eat and be merry; for this my son was dead and is alive again; he was lost and is _____.' And they began to be merry."

Luke 15:20-24 NKJV

No matter how far you _____, no matter how long you stay, you cannot _____ the love of God

For God so loved the world that he gave his only begotten Son, that whoever believes in Him should not perish but have everlasting life.

John 3:16 NKJV

God doesn't just love you; He _____ loves you.

Week 6
This I Know for Sure

My faithful sister, here we are at the final week of our study. It wasn't long ago that we laced up our walking shoes and embarked upon this journey called *This I Know for Sure*. We're coming around the last few bends in the road, and soon we'll cross the finish line together.

Without a doubt, journeying with sisters in the faith builds me up like few things can. Sharing my heart with you has been one of the greatest joys of my life. My own faith in Christ has grown tremendously on this journey. Oh, sweet sister, stay the course. Our reward is guaranteed to be sweet! God's Word tells us in Galatians 6:9, "And let us not be weary in well doing: for in due season we shall reap, if we faint not" (KJV).

This I know for sure: as you yield your heart and life to God's purposes, His Word will continue to accomplish His will in your life in the coming days. Remember Isaiah 55:11: "So shall my word be that goeth forth out of my mouth: it shall not return unto me void, but it shall accomplish that which I please, and it shall prosper in the thing whereto I sent it" (KJV). That's what I want for each of us—to see the Word of God accomplishing the will of God in our lives. As you trust in the Lord Jesus Christ and stand on what you know to be true, you will see your life bearing much fruit for the kingdom of God.

Up to this moment, we've determined some powerful truths that we can know and affirm beyond a shadow of doubt:

> There is a God in heaven.
> I am in God's plan.
> God will never forsake me.
> My life is in God's hands.
> God's boundless love will lead me (as long as time endures).

Now, this is where the rubber meets the road. How do we take what we know for sure and walk it out on a daily basis? How do we put what we know into practice to the point that it changes the way we live? This week we will prepare

our hearts for the days ahead. With God's great help, we will be equipped to stand firm. Some days will be harder than others. That is a given. But this is what will make your relationship with Jesus so strong. Time after time, you will see Jesus become real to you in every situation. Remember, we're not moved by what we see or feel. We're not even "hanging in there" anymore. Because of what Jesus has done for us, we can stand confidently on His powerful Word.

This week, my prayer is that we will catch the vision of what victorious living really is. You are assured the victorious life not because of how you feel or the people you associate with or your own accomplishments, but because of *Who* you know. We will explore how knowing God—and putting into practice what we know for sure about God—leads to faith, confidence, a changed life, peace, and hope. These are characteristics of a victorious life. I hope that this week will help to solidify and reinforce all that we have studied as you prepare to put the five landmarks of faith into practice, taking God at His Word every step of the way!

Scripture Memorization

By now you have likely memorized our theme verse, 2 Timothy 1:12:

> *I know whom I have believed, and am persuaded that he is able to keep that which I have committed unto him against that day.* (KJV)

Continue rehearsing the truth of this verse as you begin to put into practice the foundations of faith we have studied together. You can be confident that the One whom you have believed is able to keep all that you have committed unto Him now and forever!

Day 1: Knowing God Leads to Faith

Read God's Word

> *And those who **know** Your name will put their trust in You;*
> *For You, LORD, have not forsaken those who seek you.*
>
> Psalm 9:10 (emphasis added)

Reflect and Respond

Have you found that when you place your faith in something, your trust level rises each time it proves faithful? Perhaps you turned on a light switch as you began your day. The moment you flipped the switch, the lights came on because there is a connection between the light switch and the power source. The same applies to your faith walk. The moment you activate your faith, Christ's power comes alive in you through the Holy Spirit. Faith is the connection point—the light switch, so to speak—between you and the power of God. As a child of God, that power is accessible to you every moment of every day. By faith, you must activate God's Word by putting it into practice. Remember this acronym for Faith:

> Forsaking
> All
> I
> Trust
> Him

Let's consider four steps to putting our faith into practice. I call them the four R's: rehearse, relate, repeat, and remind.

Rehearse

The details of life will always be uncertain, but you have a reliable recourse against the uncertainties of life. Out of the trusted relationship that you have established with Jesus, you have the privilege of knowing His promises and drawing the comfort and strength you need any time of night or day. He will bring His promises to your remembrance to strengthen you. How do you deepen your level of trust in the Lord and follow Him more closely? The Bible tells us to meditate on God's Word. Let me give you a great example of meditating on God's Word.

As a child, I often observed my father, a great preacher and pastor, as he came and went in and out of the house during the day. I noticed that he often talked to himself, muttering words to himself under his breath. I wondered whom Dad was talking to as I heard the inflection of his voice rise and fall. Although he was going about his daily routine, he seemed rather purposeful about this activity. Now that I look back on those times, I realize Dad was meditating on God's Word. He was pondering and rehearsing the promises of God, rolling them over in his mind.

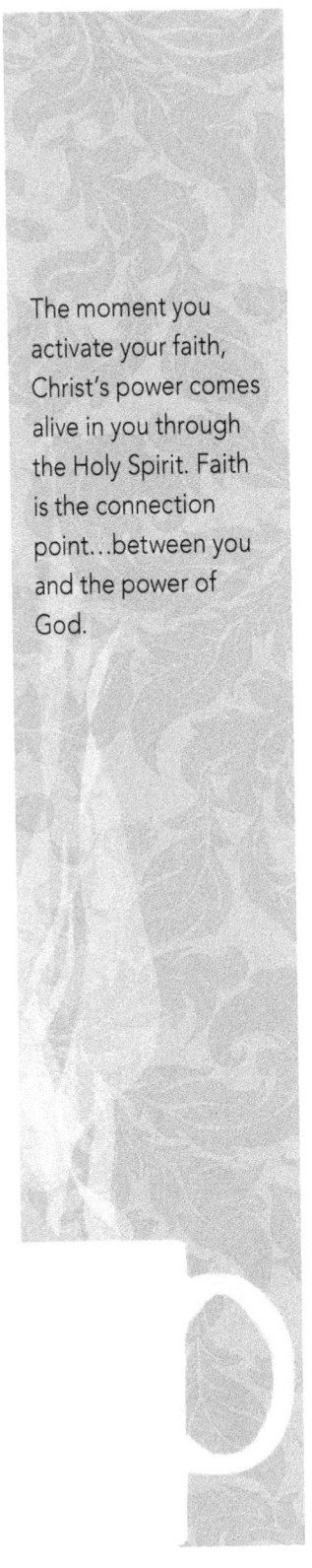

The moment you activate your faith, Christ's power comes alive in you through the Holy Spirit. Faith is the connection point...between you and the power of God.

Read Joshua 1:8 in the margin. When are we to meditate on God's Word? What is the result of meditating on God's Word?

"This Book of the Law shall not depart from your mouth, but you shall meditate in it day and night, that you may observe to do according to all that is written in it. For then you will make your way prosperous, and then you will have good success."
Joshua 1:8

The Hebrew word for meditate in this verse is *hagah*, which means to moan, utter, muse, mutter, or meditate.[1] In the same way, you must take the initiative to hide the promises of God in your heart. Recite the Scriptures. Sing them. Memorize them. Speak them to yourself all through the day. Meditating on God's Word is not just a way to test your memory but a means to store the precious treasure of God's Word in the secret places of your heart, incorporating them into your very being. Only then will you be able to keep your mind on Jesus and your life free of sin.

When you were a child, did you take piano, tennis, or dance lessons or learn some other skill? If so, what application did you use to learn that skill?

When did you go from rehearsing that skill to becoming so familiar with it that it became second nature?

What skill do you possess now that you know so well it has become a part of you?

How might you apply that same method to hiding God's Word in your heart?

You will reap great rewards by hiding God's Word in your heart—by meditating on it and memorizing it. When you memorize Scripture, the Holy Spirit can bring that passage to your remembrance at the precise moment you need it.

Look up Psalm 119:11 and write it below. Repeat the verse several times until you have it memorized.

Rehearse the passage several times today. Then ask the Lord to bring it to your remembrance each time you need it, day or night.

Another great passage to meditate upon is Proverbs 3:5-6: "Trust in the LORD with all thine heart; and lean not unto thine own understanding. In all thy ways acknowledge him, and he shall direct thy paths" (KJV).

As I've emphasized throughout our study, we must spend time with God in the Word and prayer every day, quietly meditating on God's Word and contemplating what the Lord is teaching us. God desires that we keep His Word on our minds and in our hearts, allowing the Lord to speak to us at all times.

Consider these promises:

> *But his delight is in the law of the LORD,*
> *And in His law he meditates day and night.* (Psalm 1:2)

> *I will also meditate on all Your work,*
> *And talk of Your deeds.* (Psalm 77:12)

> *I will meditate on Your precepts,*
> *And contemplate Your ways.* (Psalm 119:15)

> *Finally, brethren, whatever things are true, whatever things are noble, whatever things are just, whatever things are pure, whatsoever things are lovely, whatever things are of good report, if there is any virtue and if there is anything praiseworthy—meditate on these things. The things which you learned and received and heard and saw in me, these do, and the God of peace will be with you.* (Philippians 4:8-9)

How often do you meditate on God's Word? What benefits have you experienced as a result?

What Scriptures can you recall that bring encouragement to your heart? List some of them here.

> The key to your peace of mind, your strength of character, your ability to love those who are difficult, and your wherewithal to face daily challenges is God's Word living in you.

The key to your peace of mind, your strength of character, your ability to love those who are difficult, and your wherewithal to face daily challenges is God's Word living in you. Of course, you will encounter interruptions and distractions. But don't let them deter you. Don't look back to the mistakes of your past. Don't look around or take your eyes off the course you are on. Look up to the Lord Jesus, my friend! That is where your help comes from. Without a doubt, whether it feels like it or not, God's Word works; it is working in you and for you.

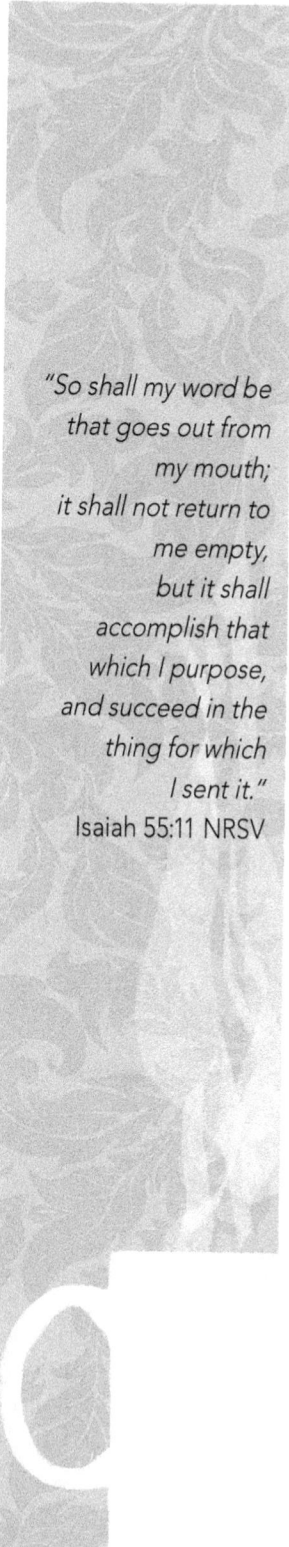

"So shall my word be that goes out from my mouth; it shall not return to me empty, but it shall accomplish that which I purpose, and succeed in the thing for which I sent it."
Isaiah 55:11 NRSV

Relate

When I was growing up, I played the piano for my father's church. During those years I'd learn a new song during the week at choir rehearsal. Then I'd have to apply what I'd learned by playing that song in an actual worship service the following Sunday. We rarely used printed sheet music, so I had to learn to play all the music by ear. At first I could only play in one key. But as I practiced more and more, I could easily apply what I was learning, transposing to other keys. The same is true of your relationship with Jesus and His Word. As you learn to hide God's Word in your heart, you will quickly find that God's Word is applicable and relevant, relating to every area of living. The Word of God will always accomplish its mission in your life. I shared Isaiah 55:11 in the introduction to this week, and it bears repeating. This is such a powerful truth.

Read aloud Isaiah 55:11 from the margin. Now write it below in your own words. How can you apply these words to your situation today?

Repeat

The more you know about Christ, the greater your capacity will be to love Him. The more you love Him, the more you trust Him. The more you trust Him, the more you want to follow Him. As you follow Him more closely, the more you will learn of Him. And then you repeat the process. It's like a never-ending circle of love. It all starts with knowing Him.

Think about those things you *know* for sure. The truth is that the only things we can know for sure are those things that are related to God and His Word. Everything else in life changes. Your circumstances change. The times change. People change. Seasons change. But God's Word will never change. It is always firm, always faithful, and always true.

Consider the definition for the verb *to know*. In the Greek, "to know" is *ginosko*. It means *to know, understand, perceive,* and *have knowledge of.*[2] Can you know everything there is to know about life? No way! This side of heaven our capacity for knowledge is very limited. But can you know, perceive, and recognize with certainty the promises of God concerning you? Absolutely, you can! Because of Jesus, we can know what matters most. As you seek the Lord, He will increase your capacity to know and understand His will and His ways.

The list of things we don't know can be mind-boggling. But the list of things we *do* know is the very list that we need to keep coming back to, repeating them again and again. At the top of that list is the profound truth that God is overeign—He is in control. The second part of that profound truth is that we re not. No matter how much you try to control your life or your circumstances, t's a futile endeavor. But that's not a reason to throw in the towel. You have an nchor for the soul that keeps you grounded and stable when everything around ou is reeling out of control. There is a landmark that is always just ahead when ou need a signpost at the fork in the road.

Read aloud Psalm 135:5 from the margin. In what ways has the Lord demonstrated to you that He is above all gods? Answer that question by making a list of the things you know for sure about God. Continue this faith-building exercise in your journal. I'll help you get started here.

I know <u>God is sovereign.</u>

I know <u>God loves me unconditionally</u>.

I know <u>God is greater than all my sin</u>.

I know_____.

I know_____.

I know _____.

I know_____.

I know_____.

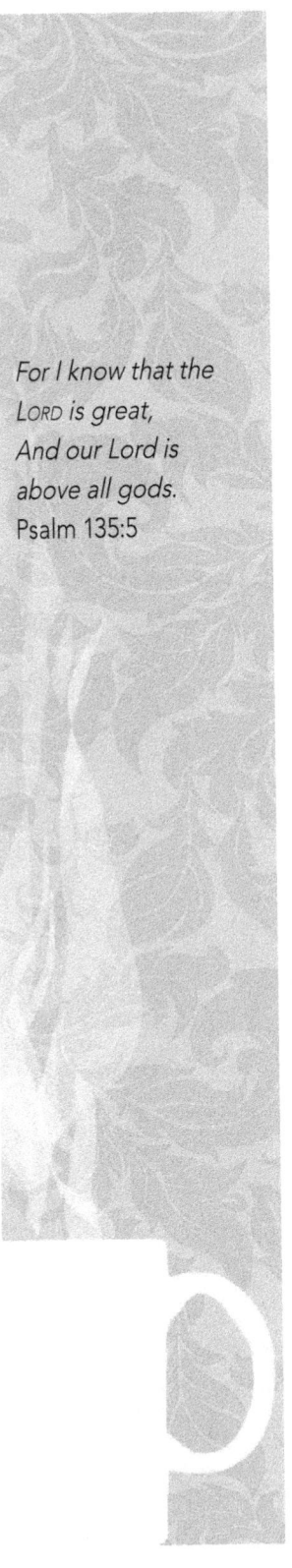

*For I know that the L*ORD *is great, And our Lord is above all gods.*
Psalm 135:5

Remind

Just as there are positive things you can be sure of, there will always be forces that come against you as well. You must remind yourself of the truth in order to stand firm. I'd like us to practice this right now. Some may call this self-talk. I call it encouraging myself in the Lord. Either way, it's a very good thing to do.

Write your name in the blank before each of the following statements, and read each one aloud:

_____, know that there will always be scary moments and close calls. You'll never go through them alone.

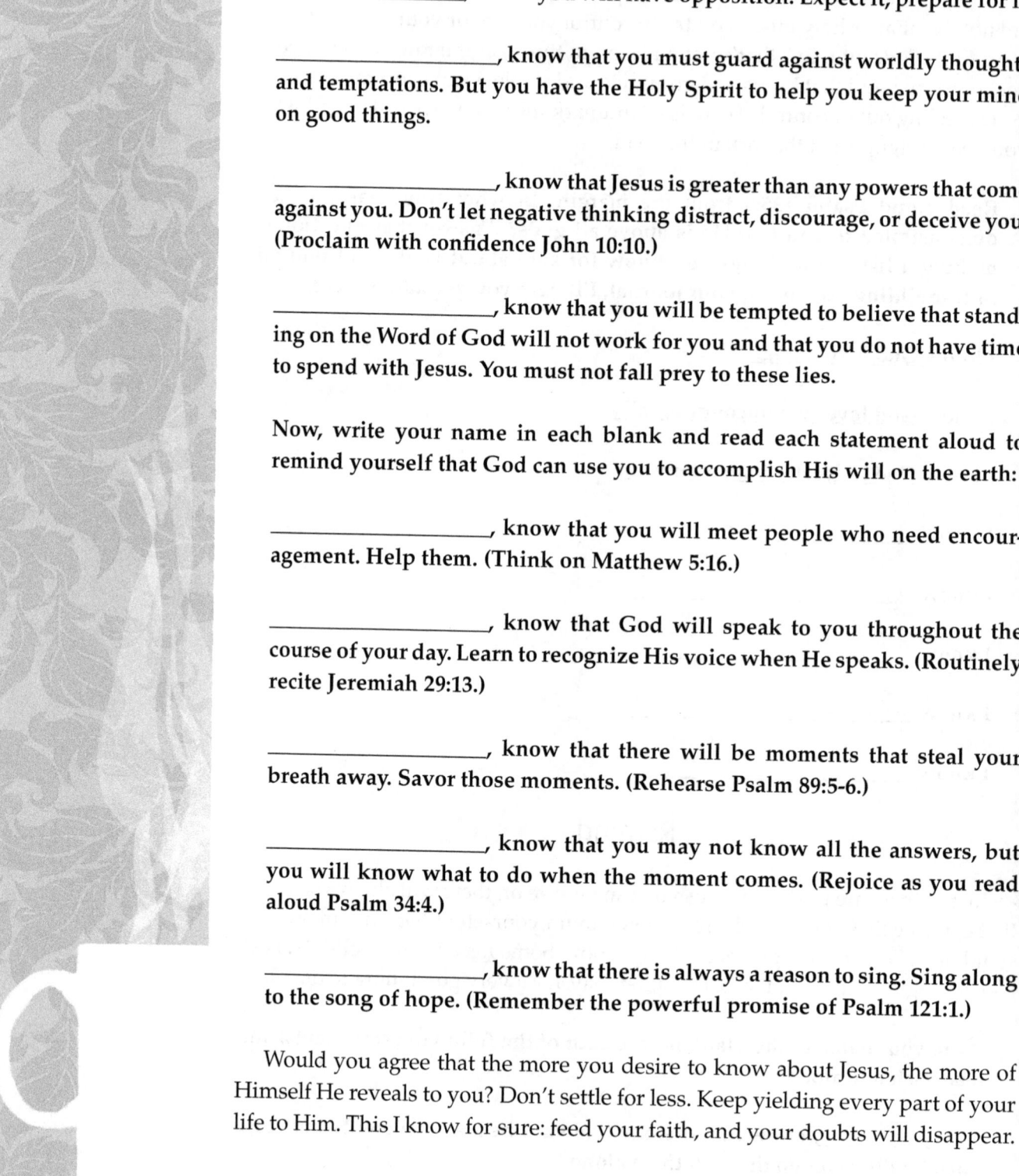

_____, know you will have opposition. Expect it; prepare for i

_____, know that you must guard against worldly thought and temptations. But you have the Holy Spirit to help you keep your mind on good things.

_____, know that Jesus is greater than any powers that come against you. Don't let negative thinking distract, discourage, or deceive you (Proclaim with confidence John 10:10.)

_____, know that you will be tempted to believe that stand ing on the Word of God will not work for you and that you do not have time to spend with Jesus. You must not fall prey to these lies.

Now, write your name in each blank and read each statement aloud to remind yourself that God can use you to accomplish His will on the earth:

_____, know that you will meet people who need encouragement. Help them. (Think on Matthew 5:16.)

_____, know that God will speak to you throughout the course of your day. Learn to recognize His voice when He speaks. (Routinely recite Jeremiah 29:13.)

_____, know that there will be moments that steal your breath away. Savor those moments. (Rehearse Psalm 89:5-6.)

_____, know that you may not know all the answers, but you will know what to do when the moment comes. (Rejoice as you read aloud Psalm 34:4.)

_____, know that there is always a reason to sing. Sing along to the song of hope. (Remember the powerful promise of Psalm 121:1.)

Would you agree that the more you desire to know about Jesus, the more of Himself He reveals to you? Don't settle for less. Keep yielding every part of your life to Him. This I know for sure: feed your faith, and your doubts will disappear.

Go to God

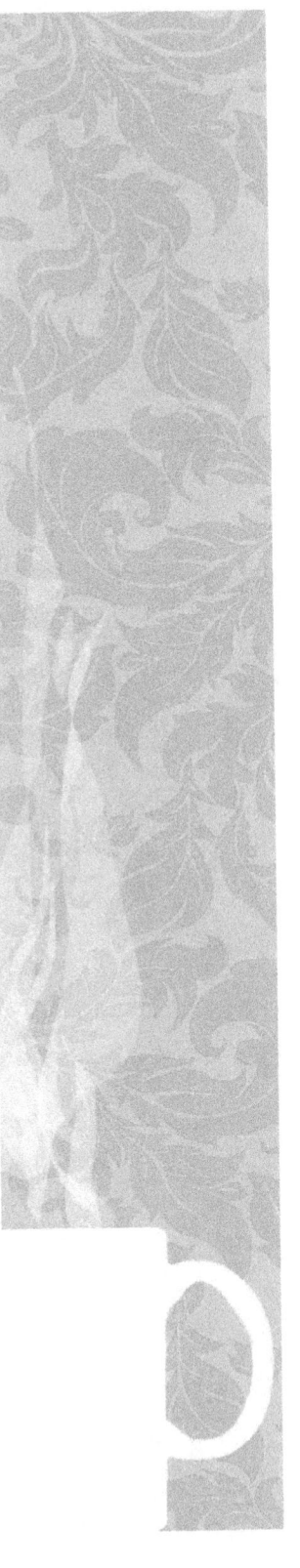

Ask

Do you find yourself concerned about the things you cannot change or control? In your mind's eye, place your need for control in your hands and lift the need up to the Lord. Then picture God taking it from you and placing in your empty hands just what you need. Do you need faith to trust Him, steadfast determination to stand your ground, or peace to rest in Him? Whatever it is, ask the Lord for it now, and then trust that He will give you just what you need.

Seek

Ask yourself these questions: How often do I meditate on God's Word? If this is a challenge, what stands in the way of this faith-building practice? Do I find time for other things that are less import? Do I consider the Word of God the highest priority? Do I believe it is a precious treasure worthy of hiding in my heart? Be honest and transparent before the Lord, seeking His help to overcome any roadblocks, whatever they may be. He is patient and able to help you.

Knock

What weighs heavy on your heart today? This is the time to relentlessly press into Jesus. Express the greatness of your need for Him. Rap on the door of heaven by spending time in prayer. Bang on the door of God's heart by reading His Word. Turn the Word of God over and over in your heart as you meditate on His goodness.

Let's pray together.

> *Kind Father,*
> *This faith-walk is so daily. However, I know this is where I will get to know you best—in the daily-ness of life. I can find real joy because You are with me every step of the way. Thank You for giving me just what I need at the precise moment I need it. When my soul is hungry, You are my daily portion. You supply me with strength and wisdom to make daily decisions. Thank You for being all I need every day of my life. In Jesus' name. Amen.*

Day 2: Knowing God Leads to Confidence in Him

Read God's Word

¹Now Moses was tending the flock of Jethro his father-in-law, the priest of Midian. And he led the flock to the back of the desert, and came to Horeb, the mountain of God. ²And the Angel of the LORD appeared to him in a flame of fire from the midst of a bush. So he looked, and behold, the bush was burning with fire, but the bush was not consumed. ³Then Moses said, "I will now turn aside and see this great sight, why the bush does not burn."

⁴So when the LORD saw that he turned aside to look, God called to him from the midst of the bush and said, "Moses, Moses!"

And he said, "Here I am."

⁵Then He said, "Do not draw near this place. Take your sandals off your feet, for the place where you stand is holy ground." ⁶Moreover He said, "I am the God of your father—the God of Abraham, the God of Isaac, and the God of Jacob." And Moses hid his face, for he was afraid to look upon God.

⁷And the LORD said: "I have surely seen the oppression of My people who are in Egypt, and have heard their cry because of their taskmasters, for I know their sorrows. ⁸So I have come down to deliver them out of the hand of the Egyptians, and to bring them up from that land to a good and large land, to a land flowing with milk and honey, to the place of the Canaanites and the Hittites and the Amorites and the Perizzites and the Hivites and the Jebusites. ⁹Now therefore, behold, the cry of the children of Israel has come to Me, and I have also seen the oppression with which the Egyptians oppress them. ¹⁰Come now, therefore, and I will send you to Pharaoh that you may bring My people, the children of Israel, out of Egypt."

¹¹But Moses said to God, "Who am I that I should go to Pharaoh, and that I should bring the children of Israel out of Egypt?"

¹²So He said, "I will certainly be with you. And this shall be a sign to you that I have sent you: When you have brought the people out of Egypt, you shall serve God on this mountain."

Exodus 3:1-12

Reflect and Respond

It would be possible for me to know a lot about you without actually knowing you. I could gather a few facts about you—where you live, what you do for a living, your likes and dislikes. But to really *know* you, I'd need to spend time with you, one on one. I'd want to really get to know you as a dear friend, hearing your heart, understanding how you think. I'd spend time getting to know those closest to you such as family and friends. I'd long to know what makes you truly happy and what breaks your heart. And you'd want to tell me all about it! Then I'd want you to know me in the same way. Our relationship would be a reciprocation of time and intimate friendship. Over time, we would develop a strong confidence in one another, based on trust.

The same is true with God. As we've discussed throughout our study, there is a world of difference between knowing about God and knowing God in a real and personal way through His Son, Jesus Christ. While knowing about God is good, *knowing* God will change your life by building confidence in Him.

To really know God, you must spend time alone with God and take time to read His Word. As you open the Bible, it's as if God opens His mouth to speak to you. Then as you talk to God in prayer and see Him leading and guiding you, your faith grows just like a sapling that is planted in good soil, watered by heaven's rain, and nurtured by sunshine. You'll find that you will live differently and respond to the challenges of life much differently than if you were constantly tossed to and fro by doubt and uncertainty. Remember, it's not just about what you know that matters. It's about allowing what you know to lead you to a deeper level of confidence in Jesus Christ.

When I think of someone from the Bible whose confidence in the Lord grew as his relationship with the Lord grew, I think of Moses. He challenges me not only to know God in a real and personal way but also to respond to what I know with unwavering faith. This great Hebrew leader believed God and staked His life on God's promises. He has much to teach us about standing firm on what we know when everything we may see or feel tempts us to doubt God's promises. He shows us what it looks like to respond to God's Word with an unwavering faith and confidence—and the amazing ways God works in our lives when we do.

Moses had an encounter with God that changed his life forever. As we look at this amazing story today and tomorrow, I encourage you to think about your own faith journey. Are there specific times, places, or circumstances that opened your eyes to the reality of Christ and led you to committing your life fully to Him as Savior and Lord of your life? I call those encounters "God stories." Think about your own God story as we look at the powerful, life-changing encounter Moses had with God.

After fleeing from Egypt, Moses made a new life for himself in Midian where he married and started a family. His work was tending the flocks of his father-in-law's sheep. One day he was going about his work. That day was probably much like any other average day on the backside of the desert. Then Moses saw and heard something rather unusual. He was about to have a transformational encounter with almighty God—an encounter that would change his life.

Reread Exodus 3:2. How did God appear to Moses? What was unusual about what Moses saw?

Burning bushes in a desert were not an unusual sight. In the sweltering heat of day in unbearable temperatures, a burning bush would be a common occurrence. But imagine Moses' surprise when he saw this bush that burned *but was not consumed.*

Reread Exodus 3:3-5.

What did Moses do when he saw the burning bush?

How do you think Moses felt when he heard God calling his name from the burning bush? (Afraid? Confused? Astonished? Other?)

What did God say to Moses once He had his attention, and how did Moses respond?

Moses stopped to examine the bush when he saw this unusual occurrence. That burning bush got Moses' attention! Imagine if Moses had carelessly ignored the burning bush, dismissing it as something not worth his time or attention. It's possible that God's presence would have departed and Moses would have missed his opportunity to commune with God. Communing with God takes time. As Moses will show us, how we respond to God's presence can make all the difference in the world.

Have the cares of life or the distractions of the moment ever consumed your time and attention, finding you too busy to "turn aside" to answer God's call? If so, describe that time and situation.

Beyond a shadow of a doubt, Moses knew this encounter was like no other he had ever experienced before. The burning bush was quite a phenomenon.

What's more, the voice of God called to Moses from this bush that burned and kept burning. By hiding his face, Moses demonstrated that he recognized this was no ordinary moment but a holy moment. He knew he was in the very presence of God.

Think about your own relationship with God. When you've encountered God's presence, has it always been a sensational or dramatic experience? If not, describe how you have typically encountered God.

It would be great if God spoke to you from a "burning bush," wrote instructions for you on a billboard that you could see as you were driving by, or reminded you that He is with you by writing a message in white billows across a clear, blue sky. But the truth is that it is not necessary to have a sensational experience to hear God's voice. Phenomenal or unusual experiences are not a prerequisite to experiencing God's call or presence in your life.

God speaks to us in many ways. God always speaks through the pages of His Word. He may use a conversation with a godly friend or a sermon to speak into our lives. Sometimes God uses great books or beautiful music to speak to our hearts. Other times God uses personal circumstances or the experiences of others to teach us His ways. Sometimes God's voice is like rolling thunder, and other times He speaks with a gentle whisper. The important thing to understand is this: God still speaks in clear and unmistakable ways. And if you are listening when God speaks to you, one thing is sure: it will be an unforgettable and life-changing encounter. As God speaks and you lean in to listen, your heart will become attuned to His voice.

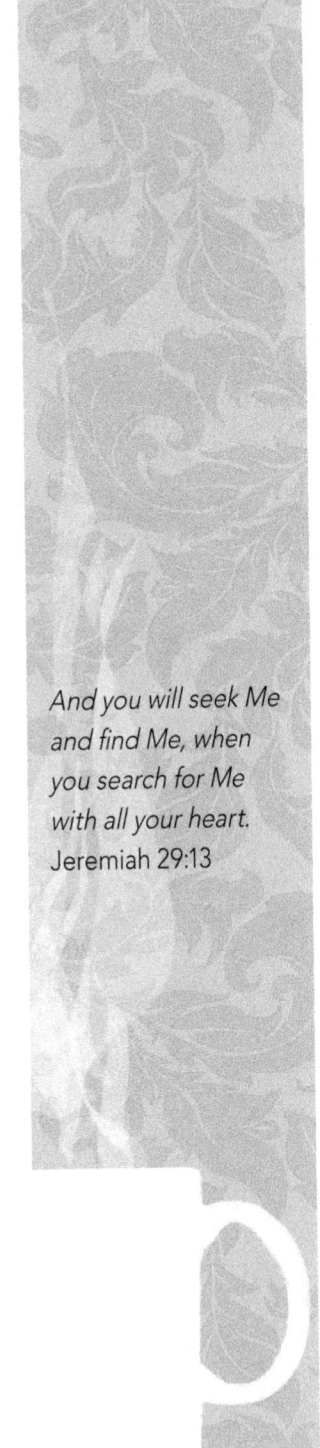

And you will seek Me and find Me, when you search for Me with all your heart.
Jeremiah 29:13

Read Jeremiah 29:13 in the margin. What does this verse promise? Is it a struggle for you to hear the voice of God? Why or why not?

As I've mentioned, Moses had come to Midian after fleeing from Egypt. Let's take a moment and read about what brought Moses to Midian, which will give us more understanding into the burning bush encounter.

Read Exodus 2:11-15. Why did Moses leave Egypt?

As a young man, Moses had been enraged when he witnessed how the Hebrew people were being treated unjustly by the Egyptian people. When he saw a Hebrew slave being beaten by an Egyptian, he became so angry that he killed the Egyptian and buried him in the sand. When the news of his crime got back to Pharaoh, Pharaoh sought to have Moses killed. Picture Moses running for his life. Running from the law. Running from God's call on his life.

What do you think might have been going through the mind of Moses while he was fleeing to Midian?

Think of a time when you tried to run from God. What were you running from? What were you running to? Write about it here.

What happens when we place confidence in ourselves instead of relying fully on God?

Moses thought he could outrun the law. Although he had yet to meet God, Moses was running from his spiritual destiny. It appeared he was in the middle of nowhere. But he could not outrun God.

My friend, no matter how fast you run, you cannot outrun God. When you get to wherever it is you are running, God is already there. Remember the saying "You can run but you can't hide." That old adage has never been truer than it is in this regard!

Moses may have run from God, but God was patiently waiting for him.

Read Exodus 2:16-25.

What happened to Moses in Midian? (vv. 16-22)

What happened to Pharaoh? (v. 23)

Read Acts 7:30. How long did Moses live in Midian before the burning bush encounter?

God was in no hurry to accomplish His purpose in the life of Moses, because Moses lived in Midian forty years before the burning bush experience. He had been in Midian long enough to stop his running, for the Egyptian pharaoh had died during this time. But the Hebrew people were still crying out to be delivered.

Never forget this, dear friend: no matter how long it takes, God is still working. Even though you can't see God or feel His presence all the time, He is still behind the scenes, working on your behalf. You can know this for sure: God is always working *on* your circumstances and working *in* your life. Like Moses, the moment you stop running from God will be the precise moment you begin to hear God's voice.

Take another look at Exodus 3:6 and fill in the blanks:

"I am the God of your father—the God of _____, the God of _____, and the God of _____." (NKJV)

When God revealed Himself as the God of Abraham, Isaac, and Jacob, He was making Himself known as a God of the covenant. A covenant is a promise that God makes between Himself and His people that cannot be broken. This covenant-making God spoke to Moses that day in the desert.

Reread Exodus 3:7-10.

What did God say that He had seen? (vv. 7-9)

What did God call Moses to do? (v. 10)

From this encounter at the burning bush, Moses received His call to deliver the Hebrew nation from slavery. From that moment on he would answer that call, and he would never be the same. Moses was building a foundation—a relationship with God that was so solid and immovable that later when he stood before Pharaoh, Moses was not shaken or swayed, regardless of threats.

Like Moses, your response when God speaks is directly determined by that same kind of foundation—the depth of your relationship with the Lord Jesus. Though what you know is important, it's *Who* you know that makes the difference. Once you establish Jesus as the foundation of your life, everything else will fall into place.

> Though what you know is important, it's *Who* you know that makes the difference. Once you establish Jesus as the foundation of your life, everything else will fall into place.

Read Matthew 6:33 in the margin. What does the verse promise?

In what ways can you make God the first and final authority in your life?

God is still speaking today. He does not want you to live your life in *reaction* to what you see and feel. He desires that you live your life in *response* to what He has already said. This is where real confidence begins. As you learn to trust Jesus for who He really is, your faith adventure will take you places you've never been. The most successful way to establish trust for tomorrow is to get to know Jesus today.

You see, the only things in this life that we can be absolutely sure of are those unchanging truths founded on God's eternal Word. You can place all your confidence in God because He *never* changes. He will never, ever fail you. And when you determine that you will trust God's Word no matter what, that's when you realize God will take care of you *and* everything that concerns you.

Go to God

Ask

Knowing Christ personally leads to a greater level of confidence in Him. As you grow in Christ, you will realize more and more that your strength is not in your own abilities but in Christ who supplies your strength. As your confidence in the Lord increases, your desire to serve Him will also increase. But don't worry about your abilities or your lack of them. God equips and uses ordinary people to do extraordinary things in His name. Moses was an ordinary man with weaknesses like the rest of us, but God still chose to use Moses in miraculous ways.

Have you made Jesus Christ *Lord* of your life, and have you made yourself completely available to Him? If you are experiencing the joy of being used by God, describe those encounters and the joy that you are realizing.

If there are areas in your life that you have not fully surrendered to Jesus, present those concerns to Him now, asking for His forgiveness and direction. Realize that Jesus is ready, willing, and able to help you in any and every area of your life.

Seek

Our study today revealed that God heard the cry of the Hebrew people and had compassion on them because of their oppression. Compassion is being concerned about another's difficult situation—feeling his or her pain.

In what ways do you hear the cries of others? How have you helped others in the past?

Is there a need for change or growth in this area? Search your own heart and then act upon what you discover.

Knock

Do you find it difficult to trust God? If you want to experience joy in your relationship with the Lord, then you must make the decision to fully trust Him. Continue to trust God this week—moment by moment and circumstance by circumstance. You will soon find that the joy of the Lord will become your strength.

Dear heavenly Father,

Thank You for the promise that I can completely trust You. I never have to worry if You will come through for me, because You always do just what you say You will do. Experience has taught me that placing confidence in myself is empty and vain. Putting confidence in You, however, will make me stronger each day as I trust in You. Your Word makes a world of difference in my life. Sometimes I feel so inadequate, but my weakness is a reminder of how strong You will show Yourself to be in and through me. I'll not only listen for Your voice today, Lord, I will obey. In Jesus' name. Amen.

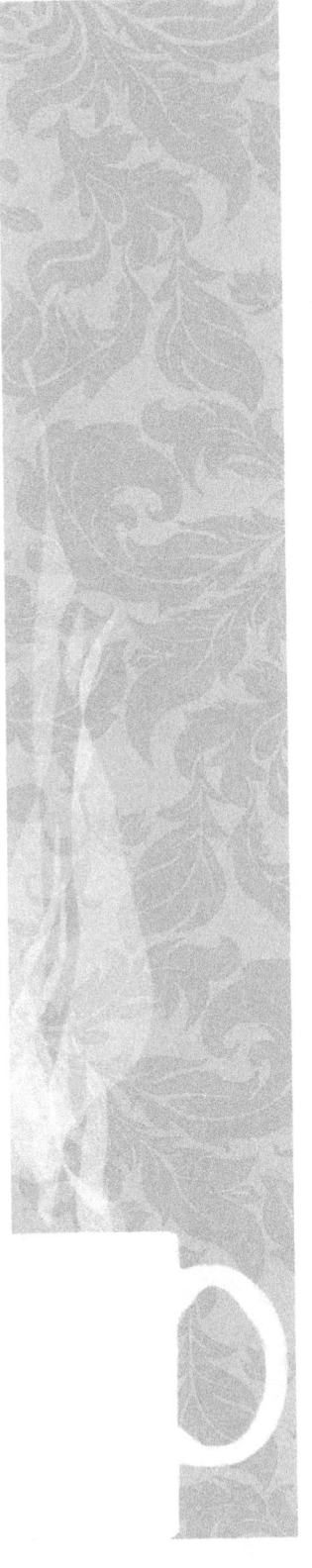

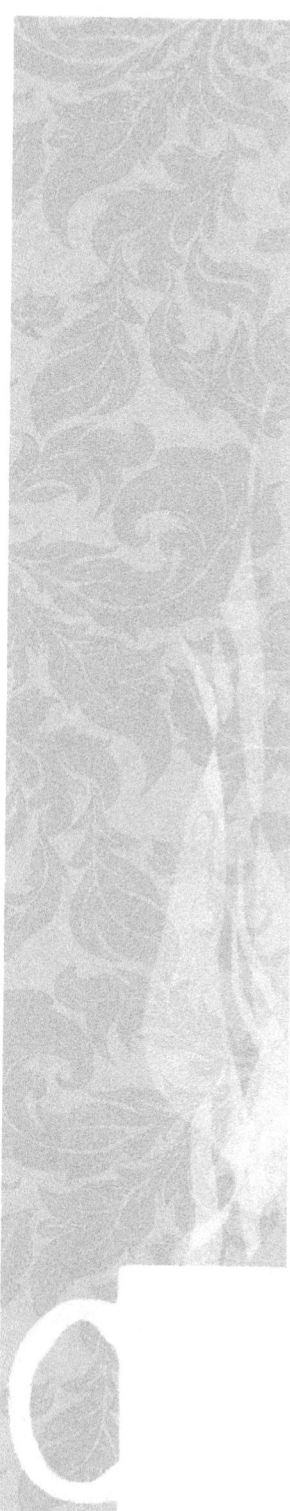

Day 3: Knowing God Leads to a Changed Life

Read God's Word

¹ *Now Moses was tending the flock of Jethro his father-in-law, the priest of Midian. And he led the flock to the back of the desert, and came to Horeb, the mountain of God.* ²*And the Angel of the LORD appeared to him in a flame of fire from the midst of a bush. So he looked, and behold, the bush was burning with fire, but the bush was not consumed.* ³*Then Moses said, "I will now turn aside and see this great sight, why the bush does not burn."*

⁴*So when the LORD saw that he turned aside to look, God called to him from the midst of the bush and said, "Moses, Moses!"*

And he said, "Here I am."

⁵*Then He said, "Do not draw near this place. Take your sandals off your feet, for the place where you stand is holy ground."* ⁶*Moreover He said, "I am the God of your father—the God of Abraham, the God of Isaac, and the God of Jacob." And Moses hid his face, for he was afraid to look upon God.*

⁷*And the LORD said: "I have surely seen the oppression of My people who are in Egypt, and have heard their cry because of their taskmasters, for I know their sorrows.* ⁸*So I have come down to deliver them out of the hand of the Egyptians, and to bring them up from that land to a good and large land, to a land flowing with milk and honey, to the place of the Canaanites and the Hittites and the Amorites and the Perizzites and the Hivites and the Jebusites.* ⁹*Now therefore, behold, the cry of the children of Israel has come to Me, and I have also seen the oppression with which the Egyptians oppress them.* ¹⁰*Come now, therefore, and I will send you to Pharaoh that you may bring My people, the children of Israel, out of Egypt."*

¹¹*But Moses said to God, "Who am I that I should go to Pharaoh, and that I should bring the children of Israel out of Egypt?"*

¹²*So He said, "I will certainly be with you. And this shall be a sign to you that I have sent you: When you have brought the people out of Egypt, you shall serve God on this mountain."*

Exodus 3:1-12

Reflect and Respond

Knowing Jesus not only leads to faith and confidence in God; it also leads to a changed life. In other words, it makes a difference in how you live. From the inside out, your relationship with Jesus reflects in your thought life, relationships, conversation, behavior, and compassion for others. The beautiful prayer of Psalm 19:14 becomes the cry of your heart:

> *Let the words of my mouth and the meditation of my heart,*
> *Be acceptable in Your sight,*
> *O Lord, my strength and my Redeemer.*

It's not just *what* you know that matters but *how* you apply what you know so that it changes the way you live.

No matter how well you think you already know Christ, there is still the capacity to know Him in a deeper, more meaningful way. There is always room for a greater level of growth and intimacy with Christ. This richer, fuller life is accessible to every believer. However, many Christians never realize a more intimate walk with Jesus because they don't know or believe it's even possible. It's like being presented a beautifully wrapped gift but never opening it up to reveal what's inside. Too many Christians have yet to discover that Jesus makes this rich and satisfying life available. And that, my friend, is a real tragedy. My prayer is that you will not miss out on anything that God has in store for you.

With this in mind, I'd like us to revisit the story of Moses' encounter with God at the burning bush and consider the power of a changed life—a life that is separated, submitted, and sold out to God.

God calls those who are *separated* to him. As you will remember from our study yesterday, Moses ran from his life in Egypt to the backside of the desert in Midian. After forty years, he met God at the burning bush. God called out to Moses from the bush that would not be consumed, and Moses answered. Moses realized this was a moment like no other—that he was in the very presence of Almighty God.

Moses would learn that God's timing is perfect. Forty years earlier he had been burdened for his people, and now God was calling Moses to the front to give him his marching orders. You see, God uses whomever He wishes whenever He chooses. It's not so much the one God chooses to use as it is what God can do with the one who is separated to Him—who surrenders her or his heart and life. When one encounters the very presence and power of God, any old bush will do!

Reread Exodus 3:4 and fill in the blanks:

> *So when the Lord saw that he _____ _____ to look, God called to him from the midst of the _____ and said, "Moses, Moses!" And he said, "_____ ___ _____."*

No matter how well you think you already know Christ, there is still the capacity to know Him in a deeper, more meaningful way.

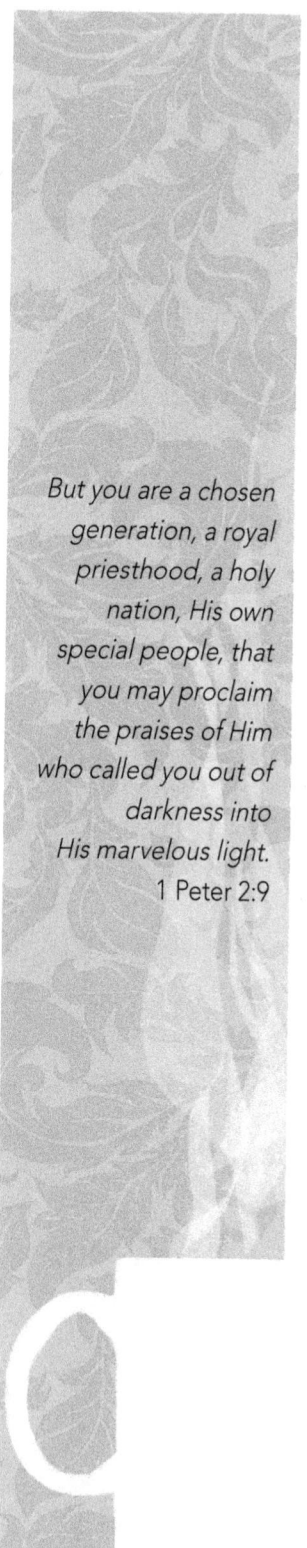

But you are a chosen generation, a royal priesthood, a holy nation, His own special people, that you may proclaim the praises of Him who called you out of darkness into His marvelous light.
1 Peter 2:9

God spoke to Moses in a desert—a place that was barren, stark, and desolate. It was a place where God could have Moses' full attention. Even on the backside of a stark, barren desert, Moses was precisely where God wanted him to be; and God met Moses and spoke to him there. Moses thought he was in a place where no one could find him. But in the quietness of this barren place, God had Moses all to Himself. There were no distractions to dim his view, no vain ambitions to tempt him, no applause of people to fluff his ego, no palace servants to do his bidding. Only God's voice could be heard. Only God's divine presence was there.

Sometimes it may appear that God has taken you to a station in your life that is barren and stark. It may feel like a desolate place—like a dry, parched desert. Could it be, though, that your desert is not a place of loneliness and desolation but a place of intimacy and isolation? Think of this situation in your life as one where God can have you all to Himself. Like Moses, God wants you to live a life that is dedicated solely to Him. He does not want your heart to be divided or contaminated by the thoughts and ways of the world. He wants your heart all to Himself.

Read the following Scriptures and note what each says about being separated or dedicated to God.

Leviticus 20:26

2 Chronicles 19:9

1 Peter 2:9

Are there distractions in your life that keep you from giving God your whole heart? If so, what are they?

What about your relationships? Are there people in your life who draw your heart away from God instead of encouraging you to grow in the Lord?

These areas require thoughtful prayer and consideration. Write a prayer, asking God to do His work in your life.

God calls those who are *submitted* to Him. When Moses heard God's voice, he did not hesitate but immediately answered, "Here I am." God is looking for those who will not ignore the slightest prompting but will be quick to answer His voice and humbly submit to His lordship. Complete and total abandonment to Christ is what God asks of us.

I've mentioned that when I was a young college student, the music of the world became very enticing to me, and I began pursuing a secular music career. I sang in bars and clubs on Friday and Saturday nights while still playing for my dad's church on Sundays. More and more, I could feel the ways of the world tugging at my heart, luring me away from the Lord. I could see how my friends in the club were impacting me more than my faith in Christ was impacting them. I was distracted by the things of this world, and my relationship with Jesus suffered because of it. I tried to live for Christ while pursuing worldly ambitions, but it was impossible. The two desires are like oil and water. They can never mix.

One of the greatest life lessons I've learned is that God is looking for a life that is totally committed to Him. You see, God is not as concerned about delivering you out of the messes you've made of your life as He is about you growing from those messes. Even when I was unfaithful to Him, He was faithful to me. I thank God that He kept me on the path that would lead my heart right back to Him. The Lord led me to a Christian college where my faith could grow and flourish. It was on that campus that I obeyed God's voice and submitted my life completely to Him.

I look back on that season of my life and see how compromise is deadly to the believer's walk of faith. Compromise is a gradual process. Perhaps there is an area of your life that once was strong and vibrant, such as your prayer life or Bible reading. Over time, these daily practices become relaxed and neglected because of a lack of discipline or worldly distractions. Think of a beautiful green lawn that was once well kept and manicured but because of neglect is now overtaken with weeds. There is not a day that goes by that we are not tempted. How we handle those temptations either shapes and conforms our character so that we resemble the character of Christ, or it draws us in the other direction.

Is there evidence of compromise in your life right now? Is there a mindset or behavior that once was fully submitted to Christ but over time has been neglected, allowing compromise to creep in and take over?

How did you gradually come to that compromised mindset or behavior?

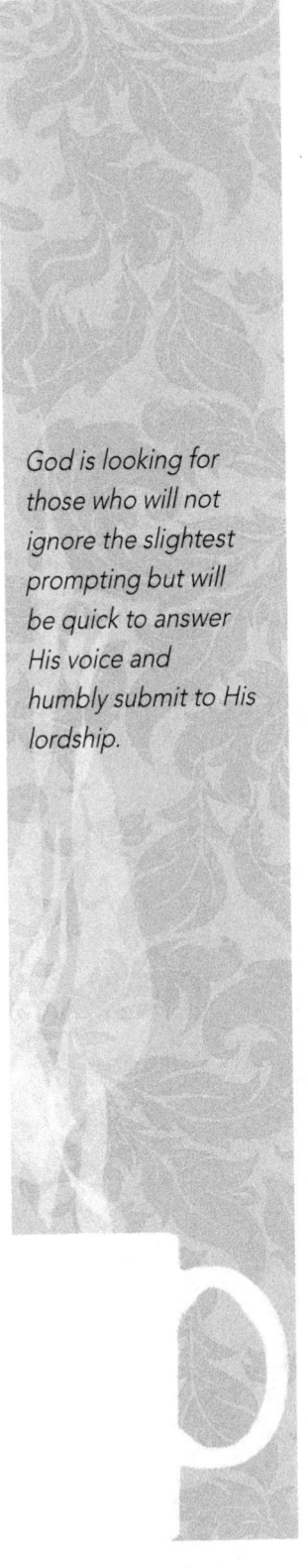

God is looking for those who will not ignore the slightest prompting but will be quick to answer His voice and humbly submit to His lordship.

God calls those who are *sold out* to Him. The call to serve God "no matter what" will always be a countercultural call. While other people are looking for ways to make *themselves* famous, God is looking for those who will make *His* name famous in the earth. God is searching for people who would rather celebrate His name than celebrate their own. Right now, God seeks those who would rather serve than be served. God is pursuing those who will advance His kingdom rather than advance their selfish agendas.

God knew that Moses was a man who fit that description. Of course, there was no way Moses could know all the details of God's call on his life to deliver the Israelite nation from the oppression of Pharaoh. Moses was hesitant at first, but God in all of His wisdom knew that he was the right man for the job.

Reread Exodus 3:11.

What did Moses say to God?

Have you ever received instructions from the Lord and, like Moses, responded essentially, "Who am I?"

What was God's response to Moses?

"I will be with you." What a powerful promise! Beginning with the encounter at the burning bush, God requested that Moses perform what seemed impossible. In his own strength, Moses could never accomplish the monumental task of leading an entire nation from bondage to freedom. Do you remember the conditions under which Moses had left Egypt? He had killed an Egyptian and buried the man in the sand. Then he had fled to another country. Moses knew that he was just a man with weaknesses and faults. The great feats involved in this call could not be accomplished without the help of a great God.

God empowered Moses to perform miraculous exploits that allowed this remarkable leader to go down in history as one of the greatest men who ever lived, all because Moses was willing to put God's desires ahead of his own. Moses is a prime example of what can happen when the Lord is with us. Let's look at some of the God-sized feats that took place throughout the course of Moses' leadership of the Hebrew people.

Draw a line to match each description with the corresponding Scripture.

Moses told Pharaoh to let God's people go.   Exodus 16:1-5

Moses and Aaron performed miracles before Pharaoh.   Exodus 14:21-23

God used Moses to initiate plagues.   Exodus 20

Moses led the Israelite army through the Red Sea.   Exodus 17:8-13

God fed the tribe of Israel with manna and quail.   Exodus 5:1

God led the Israelites to defeat their enemies.   Exodus 7-11

Moses brought the law of the Ten Commandments.   Exodus 7:8-9

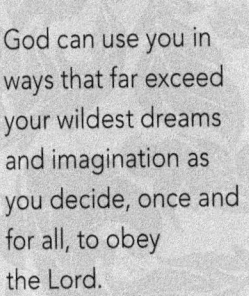

> God can use you in ways that far exceed your wildest dreams and imagination as you decide, once and for all, to obey the Lord.

Moses played the key role in leading God's chosen people through the desert right up to the edge of the land of promise. Add to that the responsibility of dealing with the mounting needs of an entire nation of people. Moses never could have done it alone. And he didn't have to, for the Lord was with Him.

Dwell on this for a moment, my friend. Moses' decision to obey God and lead His people originated from his heart. The future of an entire nation rested upon one decision of one man's obedience. Do you see what God can do with one person's willingness to obey Him? God can use you in ways that far exceed your wildest dreams and imagination as you decide, once and for all, to obey the Lord.

God is looking for those whose lives are separated, submitted, and sold out to Him. Be determined that you will open up your heart to receive the ways that Jesus wants to create this more intimate life with you. When you do, your life will be changed and will reap wonderful rewards. You will see doubts vanish. You will realize a new level of faith. You will see the Word of God come alive in your life. You will sense heartfelt compassion for those who are hurting. And you will experience a newfound excitement to share your faith with others. As we make ourselves available to God, there's no telling how He will use us to bring His love to the world!

Go to God

Ask

Remember, it's not just *what* you know that matters but *how* you apply what you know until it changes the way you live. You can start to apply what you

know before your feet hit the floor in the morning. Do you begin the day by thinking about your to-do list, worries, or old wounds from the past? Why not start tomorrow morning with a new routine. Ask the Lord to help you commit your first thoughts to Him. Start by thanking and praising Him for the blessing of a new day. Then submit your day—and your life—to Him.

Seek

All too often we look for ways to gratify our own needs and desires. Think about how Moses submitted his needs and desires to the Lord; then think about what God did through the obedient life of Moses as a result. Today, try this exercise. Instead of putting your need in the spotlight, put your desire to please the Lord in the spotlight. In your prayers and in your actions, offer your time, energy, and resources in a way that pleases God and brings Him glory.

Knock

The life God uses is separated, submitted, and sold out to Him. This is the example that our Lord Jesus set for us when He laid down His own desires to fulfill the will of His Father by going to the cross. By the world's definition, the word *servant* conjures up a negative connotation. But from God's point of view, a servant is one who desires to be just like Jesus. In God's kingdom, the servant will become the greatest of them all.

What will you do today to demonstrate to those around you that you are separated from the world, submitted to the lordship of Christ, and passionately sold out to Jesus?

Dear heavenly Father,

Please open my eyes so I may see the true condition of my heart. Teach me, Lord, what it means to separate myself from the world and submit my life to You in service, not selling out to the world and its emptiness but dedicating my life to be used for Your glory. It sounds like such an impossible task, and it would be without Your help. Forgive me, Lord, for trying to go it on my own. There is no life in that. I know where my help comes from. You are so pleased to help me, and I am so pleased to allow You. Change me, Lord, from the inside out so that I can become more like You. In Jesus' name. Amen.

Day 4: Knowing God
Leads to a Life of Peace

Read God's Word

¹*Now about that time Herod the king stretched out his hand to harass some from the church.* ²*Then he killed James the brother of John with the sword.* ³*And because he saw that it pleased the Jews, he proceeded further to seize Peter also. Now it was during the Days of Unleavened Bread.* ⁴*So when he had arrested him, he put him in prison, and delivered him to four squads of soldiers to keep him, intending to bring him before the people after Passover.*

⁵*Peter was therefore kept in prison, but constant prayer was offered to God for him by the church.* ⁶*And when Herod was about to bring him out, that night Peter was sleeping, bound with two chains between two soldiers; and the guards before the door were keeping the prison.* ⁷*Now behold, an angel of the Lord stood by him, and a light shone in the prison; and he struck Peter on the side and raised him up, saying, "Arise quickly!" And his chains fell off his hands.* ⁸*Then the angel said to him, "Gird yourself and tie on your sandals"; and so he did. And he said to him, "Put on your garment and follow me."* ⁹*So he went out and followed him, and did not know that what was done by the angel was real, but thought he was seeing a vision.* ¹⁰*When they were past the first and the second guard posts, they came to the iron gate that leads to the city, which opened to them of its own accord; and they went out and went down one street, and immediately the angel departed from him.*

¹¹*And when Peter had come to himself, he said, "Now I know for certain that the Lord has sent His angel, and has delivered me from the hand of Herod and from all the expectation of the Jewish people."*

¹²*So, when he had considered this, he came to the house of Mary, the mother of John whose surname was Mark, where many were gathered together praying.* ¹³*And as Peter knocked at the door of the gate, a girl named Rhoda came to answer.* ¹⁴*When she recognized Peter's voice, because of her gladness she did not open the gate, but ran in and announced that Peter stood before the gate.* ¹⁵*But they said to her, "You are beside yourself!" Yet she kept insisting that it was so. So they said, "It is his angel."*

¹⁶*Now Peter continued knocking; and when they opened the door and saw him, they were astonished.* ¹⁷*But motioning to them with his hand to keep silent, he declared to them how the Lord had brought him out of the prison. And he said, "Go, tell these things to James and to the brethren." And he departed and went to another place.*

Acts 12:1-17

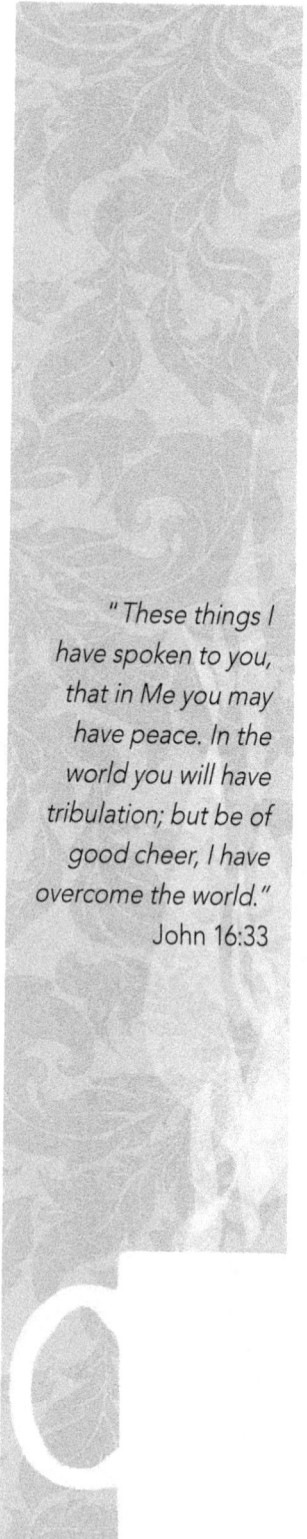

Reflect and Respond

Walking with the Lord brings a foundational stability and an inner strength that we wouldn't know otherwise. Even in the face of tremendous difficulty, trusting in the Lord brings us a peace that cannot be explained.

Have you ever been in a crisis? We all go through a rough patch every now and then, but I'm not talking about the daily problems we experience—things like a flat tire, a busted water heater, or a bounced check. I'm talking about coming face to face with a super-sized, acme-strength, larger-than-life crisis.

The disciple Peter experienced this kind of crisis, and he demonstrated indescribable peace in the midst of it. As we examine his story, we'll see that for every great crisis we may face, there is an almighty, mountain-moving, miracle-working, ever-present God who has a solution.

Reread Acts 12:1-6. Where do we find Peter in verse 5? What do these verses tell us about the level of security and the nearness of Peter's execution?

"These things I have spoken to you, that in Me you may have peace. In the world you will have tribulation; but be of good cheer, I have overcome the world."
John 16:33

King Herod, a despicable man, hated the church and wanted to destroy its people and the work they were doing by torturing and executing the leaders of the church. He had already put James, the brother of John, to death. By executing Peter, one of the church's greatest leaders, Herod hoped to stifle the growth of the church and put fear in the hearts of Christ's followers.

Peter was in prison under heavy security. Four squads of soldiers guarded him, and he was chained to guards on his left and right. Guards also stood at the prison entrance. Herod wanted to assure that Peter would stand trial the next day. Within hours, Peter was to be put to death, most likely to be beheaded.

Scripture tells us that Peter was thrown in prison for preaching the good news of the gospel. He was sentenced to death for doing good—for helping people come to the knowledge of Jesus Christ.

Every day God is at work through those who put their lives on the line for the sake of doing what is right. It leads us to ask *why*. Why are people treated so badly for doing good? You may find yourself in a difficult situation right now and have the same question. Why do bad things happen to good people? God does not promise us a life of ease. Jesus faced challenges just like the rest of us.

Read John 16:33 in the margin. What does Jesus tell us?

When bad things happen to you, be reminded that God, in His sovereignty, is always working. Sovereignty means that God has supreme authority. He rules and reigns independently. God is always in control and working on behalf of those He loves. Just because you don't see evidence of God working doesn't mean that He isn't working. And just because you don't feel God moving doesn't mean that He isn't moving. God is not tripped up by our problems or our circumstances no matter how great they may seem to us. He is not taken back by catastrophic events or seasons of darkness.

Read Psalm 139:12 in the margin. What does this verse tell us?

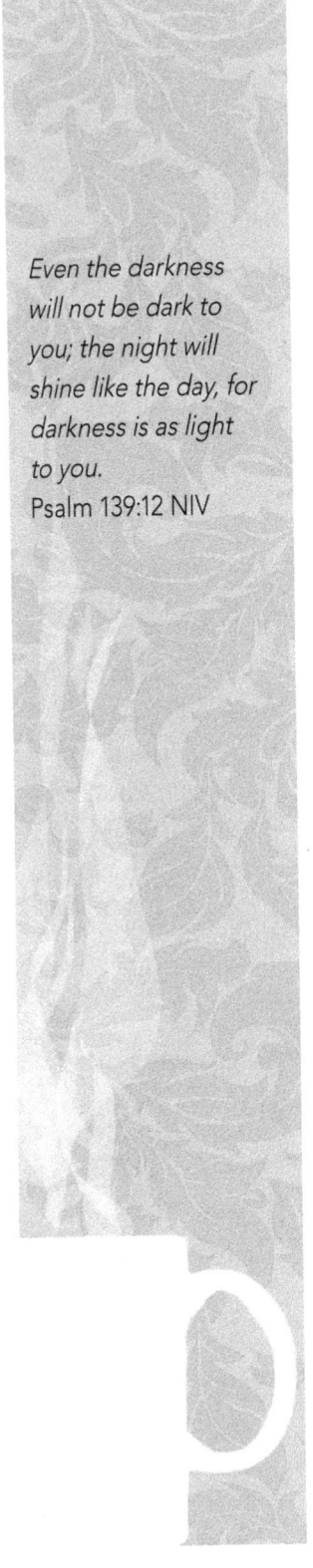

Even the darkness will not be dark to you; the night will shine like the day, for darkness is as light to you.
Psalm 139:12 NIV

Your situation may take you on a journey filled with pain and problems. You may have said something like, "Lord, I'm living according to Your will. I've done my best to obey You. Why is everything turning out so badly for me?" As I've said in various ways throughout our study, there will be many times in life when we don't understand the situation we are facing, but God is always working. Don't worry if it doesn't make sense. Just because it doesn't make sense to you today doesn't mean it won't make sense tomorrow. The possibility is great, though, that the circumstance you are in may never make sense. This is when you must trust God. From your perspective, your circumstances may seem out of control—even bleak. However, God sees the big picture. To understand this point a bit more clearly, try this simple exercise.

Find a penny and hold it at arm's length, between the thumb and index finger of your right hand. Close your left eye and place your left hand completely over your left eye so that you are looking at the penny with your right eye only. With the penny at arm's length, what can you see?

Now, with the left eye still covered, focus only on the penny and gradually bring the penny closer and closer to your eye. Note below how your vision changes.

When the penny was at arm's length, you could see the coin and everything in the background in proper perspective. But as you brought the penny closer and closer to you, the background dropped out and all you could see clearly was the

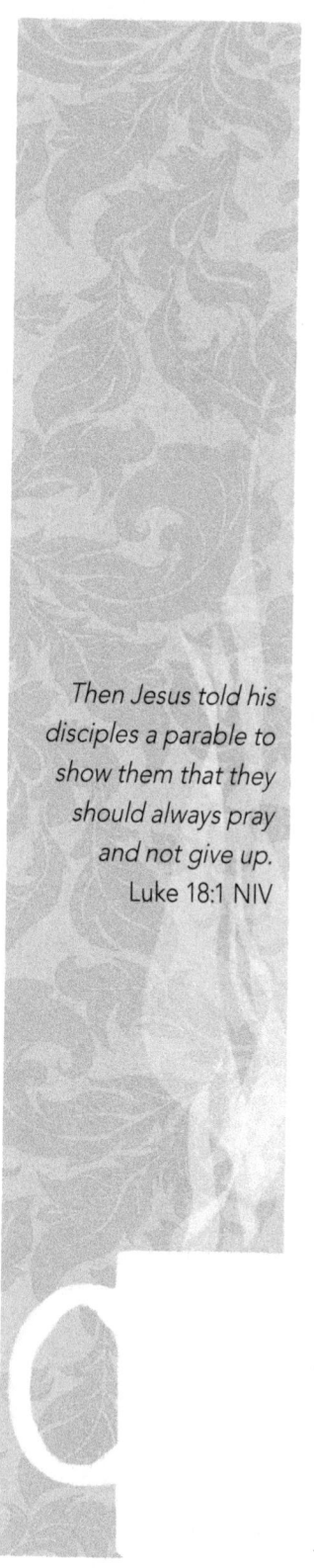

penny. Isn't it amazing how something as small as a penny can consume your entire line of vision?

Life is like that sometimes. We can get so consumed with the smallest details of life until they occupy all of our time and attention. Then we begin to obsess over these small, sometimes insignificant details. God does not want you to worry over the details of your life. If God is big enough to keep the entire universe spinning, He is big enough to provide an answer for your problems. Lean on the comfort of Romans 8:28: "And we know that all things work together for good to those who love God, to those who are the called according to His purpose." You may not know how it will work out, but rest assured, God will work it out for good—just as He worked it out for Peter.

Read Acts 12:5 again. Who was praying for Peter—and how often?

Do you recall when I said this earlier in our study: "When you are down to nothing, God is up to something"? While Peter was locked up, the people of God were praying for him *constantly*. There seemed to be no hope for Peter. Every door that led to his freedom was closed and locked tightly. Every door was blocked except heaven's door. Heaven's door is never locked. When you are facing a crisis, you should pray, pray, and pray some more.

Read Luke 18:1 in the margin. What does this verse tell us?

When we pray, we must pray and not lose heart. When my husband, Charles, was hospitalized after a stroke, I sat by his bed for days and prayed. I stayed awake throughout the night, watching over him and praying for him. I prayed *constantly*.

I also got on the phone and called family members. I sent text messages to friends. I sent e-mail messages to ministry partners overseas. Messages poured in from all over the world. People everywhere wanted us to know that they were praying with us and for us. Charles and I were undergirded by the prayers of the saints of God. I learned what it was like for the people of God to pray concertedly. Even though people were in different parts of the world, they were praying as a body of believers for us. God is pleased when his people pray together.

During that season, I found that prayer is hard work. Romans 15:30 tells us to "strive together" in prayer. Prayer is a labor of love, and we must labor in prayer with intention.

Read Philippians 4:6. What do we learn from this verse about how to pray with intention?

Praying with intensity is praying *consciously*. Present every single request you have to the Lord, giving thanks to God and believing that He will answer your prayers. Do you have a specific need? Then pray a specific prayer. Is there sickness in your body? Pray that you will be healed. Is your marriage in trouble? Pray that your marriage will be restored. Is your child going away to school? Pray for your child's protection. Do you need a job? Pray for the type of job you desire. Our own resources are powerless unless they are accompanied by the power of prayer.

Are you in a crisis situation today? Have you asked another believer to pray with you? Don't allow fear or pride to keep you from asking someone to pray with you for an answer to your problem.

A woman called one of her dearest friends on the phone one day. When her friend asked how she was, she replied, "I'm fine, under the circumstances." The friend, full of faith, responded, "What in the world are you doing under there?"

I like that response. Remember, dear one, you are never a victim of your circumstances. Because of Christ, you are a victor *over* your circumstances! When God is on your side, you will never go under. You are going over! Because you are an overcomer, you will never come out on the losing end. Romans 8:37 reminds us that we do not have to be discouraged or afraid because we are more than conquerors through Christ.

Let's continue now with the miraculous account of Peter in prison.

Reread Acts 12:6-9.

What does verse 6 tell us that Peter was doing?

What was God's rescue plan? Write the details below.

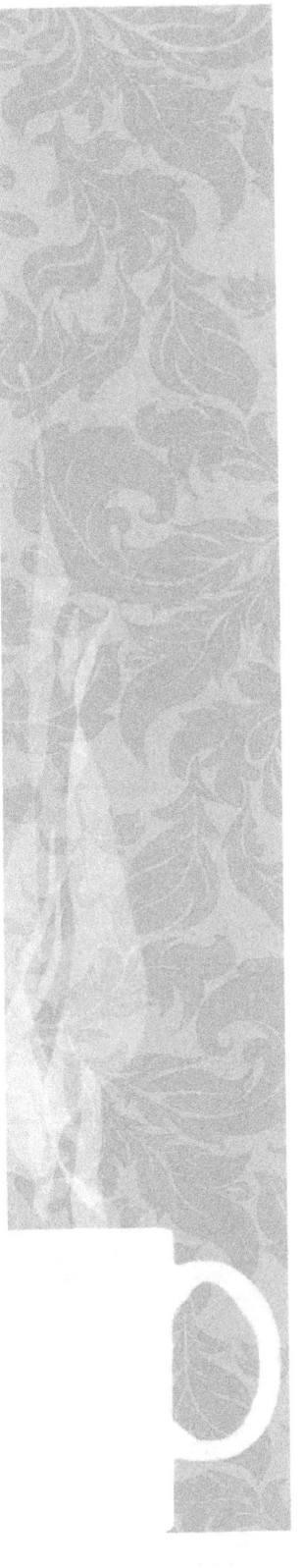

Not only was Peter not worrying; he was fast asleep! While Peter was sleeping, God sent an angel to rescue him. A deep sleep came over all the guards. Peter himself was a sound sleeper—so sound that the angel had to give Peter a punch in the ribs to awaken him. His ability to rest completely undisturbed on the eve of his scheduled execution is evidence of his faith and complete trust in the Lord.

Accompanied by a brilliant light, the angel helped Peter to his feet, and immediately his chains fell off. The angel instructed Peter to get up and fix his robe about him, tucking it into his belt so he wouldn't trip on his garments on the way out. The angel told Peter to put on his sandals because Peter would be taking a walk. Then the angel told Peter to grab his cloak to warm himself against the chilly night air.

Friend, do you see that God thinks of everything? No stone is left unturned when it comes to your care.

Pause for a moment and think of all the ways that God has shown His care for you since you got up this morning. List them below. Then thank Him for being attentive to all of your needs.

The angel led Peter past all the sleeping guards and past the outer iron security gate. Miraculously, the gate opened on its own. If you think the automatic door is a twentieth-century invention, think again, dear one! Once Peter was outside the prison walls and a few blocks in the clear, the angel vanished.

Reread Acts 12:11. What did Peter say once he had "come to himself"?

I love that it says Peter knew "for certain"—some versions say "without a doubt" or "for sure"—that God had rescued him.

When you find your back against the wall, do you cower in fear? Do you lay awake at night tossing and turning with worry? Do you get on the phone and rehearse the problem over and over with your friends? Or do you, like Peter, determine in your heart that you know that God is on your side and find peace in that? Peter knew this for sure. God may use people, places, things, and even angels to bring His intended purpose to pass. But when all is said and done, we must agree with Peter that "without a doubt" it was the Lord who moved on our behalf.

Picture Peter out on the street in the middle of the night. I remember an old Motown song by Martha Reeves and the Vandellas called "Dancing in the Street." If only for a moment, Peter had every reason to cut a rug and dance for joy right there on the street corner. God had delivered him from the hands of his enemies. But before the guards at the prison discovered that he was missing, Peter thought it best to run for cover and inform the church of his deliverance. So he headed to the home of John Mark's mother. It was there the church was praying for him in an all-night prayer meeting.

Reread Acts 12:12-16. What difficulty did Peter encounter when he arrived at the house?

The saints were inside the house praying as Peter stood outside the house, banging at the gate, trying to get in. It wasn't until after much persistence that the residents believed the servant girl named Rhoda, who told them that Peter was at the door, and finally let him in. While Peter found it rather easy to break out of the prison, he found it next to impossible to break into the prayer meeting!

Despite the weakness of their faith to believe God would answer their prayers, God in His great love and mercy answered their prayers anyway. This speaks to the greatness of God to answer prayer. Go ahead and ask God for the impossible. Then believe that He will come through for you. Luke 18:27 reminds us that "what is impossible for humans is possible for God" (CEB). So don't allow what you don't know to keep you anxious and depressed. Rejoice in what you know for sure.

Read these verses from the Psalms and note how each lifts your faith.

Psalm 46:10

Psalm 56:9

Psalm 135:5

*"Be still, and know that I am God;
I will be exalted among the nations,
I will be exalted in the earth."*
Psalm 46:10

Peter was not alarmed or afraid during this whole ordeal because he was confident in the prayers of God's people, convinced of God's presence, comforted by God's peace, and certain of God's power; and he celebrated God's name with praise. Thanksgiving is perhaps the most powerful key to peace. As we replace our anxiety with the joy of the Lord—the joy of His presence—we find strength.

There is never a reason to fear when you know for sure that Jesus is with you. As we established earlier in our faith adventure, Jesus promised that He would never leave or forsake us. The word *never* means *not ever*! Build your inner strength on this promise from Psalm 9:10: "And they that *know* thy name will put their trust in thee: for thou, LORD, hast not forsaken them that seek thee" (KJV, emphasis added). What a great truth to stand on at all times, especially when life doesn't make sense!

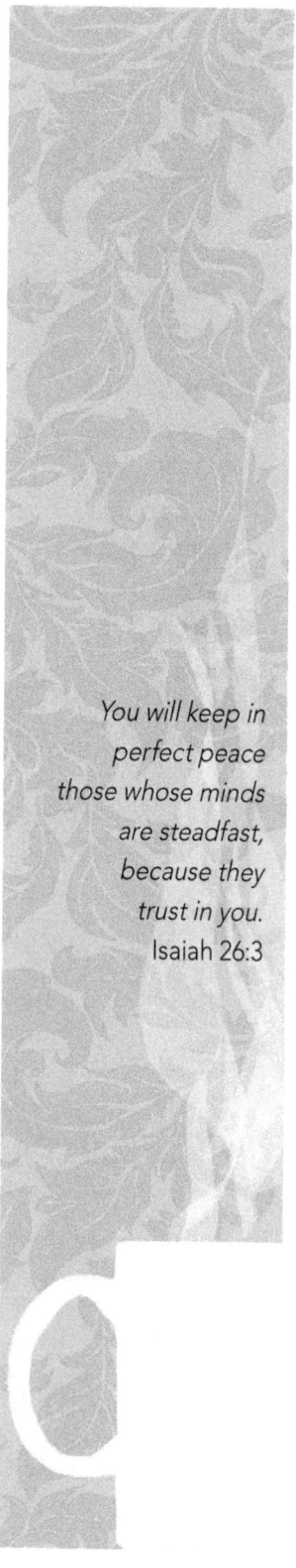

Go to God

Ask

Has your back ever been against a wall like Peter's was? Maybe your crisis is not a physical one but an emotional one. Perhaps you have been hurt by someone you trusted. Unlike people, God is trustworthy. No one can believe this for you. You must learn to trust God for yourself. Oswald Chambers said in his book *Bringing Sons to Glory* that we have to find the shadow of the Almighty for ourselves and then abide there. Have you found that abiding place, dear friend? Begin by entrusting your hurts and disappointments to the Lord now.

Seek

When we are in a real crisis, our desperation has a way of driving us to the feet of Jesus, and that's the best place we can go. We stand tallest when we are on our knees. There, in prayer, we can bring our specific needs to the Lord. Make a short list of your specific needs and present them to Jesus. He wants you to know that it may not be okay right now, but it *will* be all right. You have His Word on it!

Knock

Peter stood at the door and banged with persistence. He didn't stop until the door was answered. This is a powerful picture of prayer. It is not that God is hard of hearing or that He is stubborn. Far from it! The persistence is for our strength for the long haul. The Lord knows that you will need great faith for the days ahead, and He does not want you to give in or give up. Standing your ground builds faith and courage to face what lies ahead. Is there a closed door in your way? Have you exhausted all earthly options? Make prayer your first option, not your last resort.

Write Isaiah 26:3 on an index card and put it in your purse or pocket. Throughout the next few days, meditate on this powerful truth.

Precious Father,

Even though I am facing a challenge today, I choose to be joyful. In Your joy, I will always find my strength. Yes, people have let me down and disappointed me. Thank You, Lord, that You know all the hurting places in my heart and can heal them all. I roll all my cares on You today and receive Your strength. In Jesus' name. Amen.

Day 5: Knowing God
Leads to a Heart of Hope

Read God's Word

For we were saved in this hope, but hope that is seen is not hope; for why does one still hope for what [one] sees? But if we hope for what we do not see, we eagerly wait for it with perseverance.

Romans 8:24-25

Reflect and Respond

It's hard to believe, but here we are at the last day of our study. What an incredible journey of faith this has been. I wish you could see me at this very moment. I am on my feet cheering you on because you made it right up to the finish! I have envisioned you studying and pouring over God's precious Word with this study as your guide. You, dear friend, have worked your way into my heart. I have asked Jesus to speak to you wherever you are on your journey. My prayer is that your faith will find buoyancy, causing you to soar above the cares of this world like never before. Oh, how I praise Jesus for the life change that only the Word of God brings! My dear sister, when tough times come, may you be found believing in God's Word and the Living Word, the Name above all names: Jesus.

As believers, we never, ever need to lose heart because our hope is not in people or the economy or the world's systems. Our hope is in Christ. In the Bible, you'll find all the right answers for all that is going wrong in the world. Because Jesus finished His perfect work at the cross, no matter what your present situation may look like, you have a great hope and an anchor for your soul. Always remember, your best and brightest days are still ahead.

One afternoon, a man was out for a walk when he happened upon a Little League baseball game. He asked one of the young players in the dugout what the score was. The young boy responded, "We're losing eighteen to nothing."

"Wow," said the spectator. "I'll bet you guys are really discouraged."

"Why should we be discouraged," said the young boy. "We haven't even gotten up to bat yet."

That young ballplayer believed that the best was yet to come. His heart was filled with hope. That's the kind of outlook we should have as faith-filled believers.

It's easy to feel hopeful when everything is going well. But when you seem to be fighting a losing battle, it can be difficult to hold on to hope. The apostle Paul teaches us how to not be discouraged when things don't turn out the way we think they should. Anything is possible for the one who hopes in the Lord. When we reach the place where we realize all we really have is our hope in God, it is then that we arrive at the place of our miracle. And with the power of hope operating in our lives, we can go from merely existing in our circumstances to prevailing over them. Let's take a look at the difference hope can make.

The apostle Paul wrote the Letter to the Romans to underscore the truth that salvation is found only through the gospel of Jesus Christ. In the first four chapters, he builds the case that we are not saved through our own good works but through faith in Christ alone. In chapters 5-7 he talks about how our faith in Christ gives us life and frees us from sin. Then we come to chapter 8, which describes our new relationship with God through Christ.

Read Romans 8:15-17, 24-25 and fill in the blanks:

For you did not receive the spirit of bondage again to fear, but you received the Spirit of _____, by whom we cry out, "Abba, Father." The Spirit Himself bears witness with our spirit that we are _____ of God, and if children, then heirs—heirs of God and joint heirs with Christ. (vv. 15-17a NKJV)

For we were saved in this _____, but hope that is seen is not hope; for why does one still hope for what [one] sees? But if we hope for what we do not see, we _____ _____ for it with _____. (vv. 24-25 NKJV)

What does Paul mean by "this hope"?

What a great hope we have! As we considered in Week 4, Almighty God saves us and adopts us as His children. Regardless of where we come from, the color of our skin, our economic background, or our abilities or disabilities, God wants us to be a part of His family. It is mind-boggling to think that a holy God would want to be connected to unholy people. He didn't wait for us to get our act together. It wasn't up to us to make the first move. He was the initiator in this relationship, loving us first, pursuing us relentlessly, drawing us to Himself, giving us His name.

Because of Jesus, we are in right standing with a holy God. We are holy as He is holy. What's more, through Jesus we have an intimate, personal relationship with God and the deep love that grows as a result. He draws us close to Himself, inviting us to trade our sorrow for His joy, our cloak of sin for His robe of righteousness, our sickness and disease for His healing and well-being, our ashes of despair and mourning for His countenance of beauty and life, our poverty for His abundance. I love how my good friend Pastor Tony Ashmore describes this exchange: "We swap the worthless for the priceless."[3]

How would you describe what this exchange has meant in your own life? Respond by completing one or more of the following statements:

I have swapped...

my _____ for His _____.

my _____ for His _____.

my _____ for His _____.

Paul ends Romans 8 by reminding us that God's love will never fail.

Read Romans 8:31-39.

According to these verses, what can separate us from the love of God? Is there anything that God cannot do for us?

What does verse 37 say we are through Christ who loves us?

Because God's love will never fail us, we can trust God for the big things...as well as for the everyday things.

Because God's love will never fail us, we can trust God for the big things, such as our eternal salvation, as well as for the everyday things, such as the income to pay our bills, the needs of our families, and the issues we have with our health. Our only hope for all of these things, great and small, is Jesus Christ.

As we saw earlier in our study, the hope we have in Christ—biblical hope—is not the same as the world's definition of hope. You may have heard someone use the word *hope* in this context: "The economy has taken a turn for the worse. I sure hope things get better soon," or "My friend's health hasn't been that great lately. I sure hope she pulls through." The hope we read about in the Bible is not the same as the world's understanding of hope, which is a cross-your-fingers way

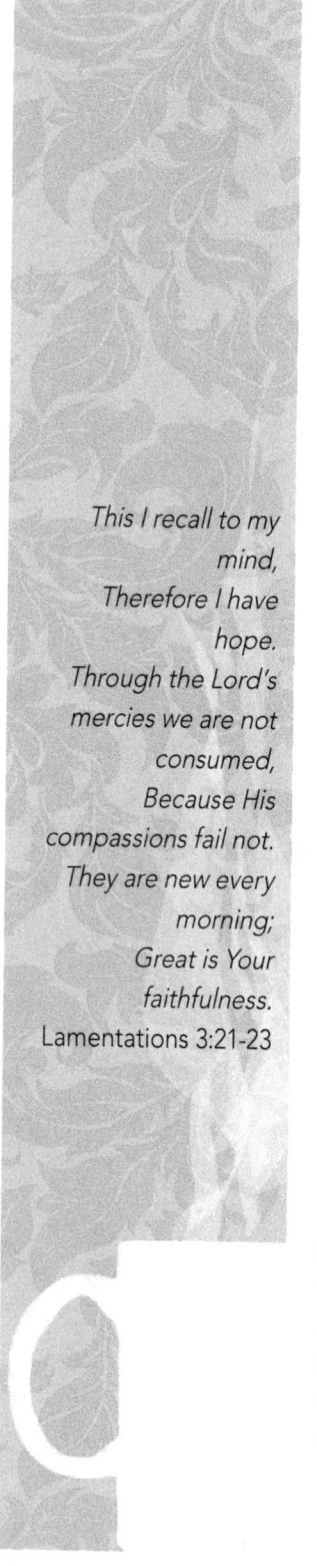

This I recall to my
mind,
Therefore I have
hope.
Through the Lord's
mercies we are not
consumed,
Because His
compassions fail not.
They are new every
morning;
Great is Your
faithfulness.
Lamentations 3:21-23

of thinking. Biblical hope is not wishful thinking or betting and wagering as in a game of chance. It is complete confidence in God, believing Him for a favorable outcome. It is a confident expectation of good. It is waiting with anticipation. The Greek word for hope is *elpis*, which means to anticipate, usually with pleasure, expectation, or confidence.[4] When this kind of hope makes itself at home in your heart, you will find that this is precisely where Jesus is.

Why do you think many Christians think and operate in terms of the world's definition of hope rather than the biblical understanding of hope?

Have you ever been faced with a situation so painful that, after the dust settled and the smoke cleared, all you had left were questions? Tragedy always leaves behind aching hearts with gnawing questions. This must have been the prophet Jeremiah's experience as he surveyed the smoldering ruins of Jerusalem in the year 586 B.C. The Babylonians came in with a vengeance and destroyed the city, including Solomon's Temple along with the ark of the covenant. Jeremiah, known as the weeping prophet, recorded his thoughts in the Book of Lamentations.

Read Lamentations 3:4-9. How did Jeremiah describe his pain?

Now read Lamentations 3:21-23 in the margin. What hope do we find in these verses?

In some translations, verse 21 begins with the conjunction *but*. We must not let this little three-letter word go by unnoticed. As a matter of fact, it should make us want to respond with a shout of praise. You might be in the middle of a tremendous trial, *but* there is always hope!

You may be low on funds today, *but* Jesus will provide for you. You may be sick in your body, *but* Jesus is the Great Physician. Your marriage may be in trouble, *but* Jesus is able to reconcile all differences. You may be very discouraged right now, *but* Jesus is the lifter of your head.

Complete the following statement, describing a situation you are faced with currently and the hope you have in Jesus:

I_____,

but Jesus_____.

We can always look on the bright side of life because God is able to see us through to certain victory. Hope is what enables us to wait for that victory.

Reread today's Scripture, Romans 8:24-25. According to these verses, how are we to wait?

No matter how long it takes, hope enables us to wait with patience and perseverance. Hope causes us to believe that God will continue to work in our lives today, tomorrow, and into the future.

I find hope for the future by reviewing what other faith-filled people have done in the past. Over the past six weeks we've studied the lives of many people from God's Word—people like Abraham and Sarah, Moses, Rahab, Ruth, David, Mary the mother of Jesus, and Peter. We consider them superheroes of the faith, but they were ordinary folks just like you and me. Their decisions to believe God in the face of trying circumstances give us hope to face the coming days with faith and confidence.

These great men and women of the past demonstrate that hope is not crossing your fingers. Hope is a decision to fill your heart with a confident expectation of good even when the situation doesn't necessarily look good. They would be the first to tell you that hope is not a feeling. In fact, regardless of their feelings, they trusted God, knowing that their feelings would catch up.

You might say, "Babbie, you don't know what happened in my life." No, I don't know your story, but Jesus does. Although your story may be mingled with pain and loss, hope causes you to come out a winner every time. Biblical hope reminds us that regardless of what has happened, our future will always be better than our past.

Read Zechariah 9:12.

What do you think it means to be a "prisoner of hope"?

How much does God promise to restore to us?

> We can always look on the bright side of life because God is able to see us through to certain victory. Hope is what enables us to wait for that victory.

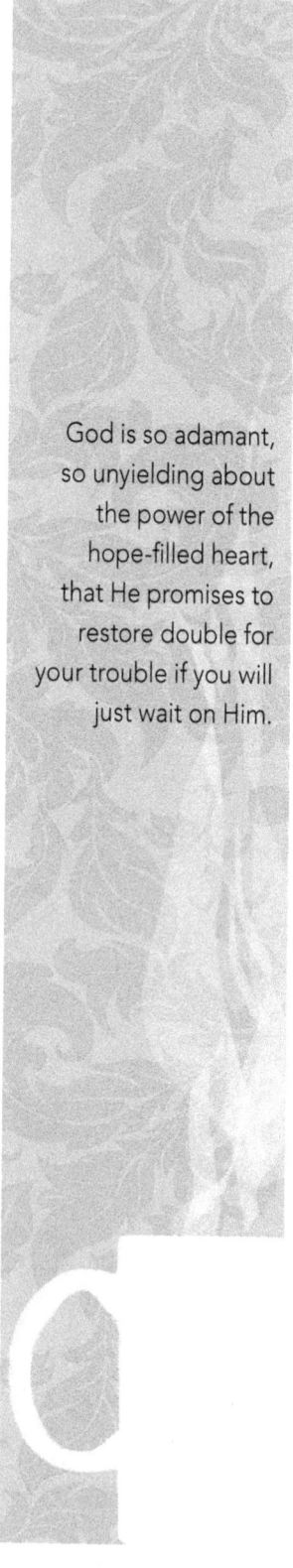

God is so adamant, so unyielding about the power of the hope-filled heart, that He promises to restore double for your trouble if you will just wait on Him.

When I think of being a prisoner of hope, I think of an expectant mother. With each month, she grows more and more expectant. Pretty soon, her life is centered around the anticipation of bringing the baby she is carrying into the world. She gets everything ready, decorating the baby's room and packing her bag. And she waits. She can hardly think of anything else until that baby is born. In the same way, when your life is filled with hope, it consumes you. Everywhere you look you see hope. Every thought you dwell on is a hope-filled thought. God is so adamant, so unyielding about the power of the hope-filled heart, that He promises to restore double for your trouble if you will just wait on Him.

Friend, I hope that after our weeks of study together, you are *fully* persuaded that God will do what He has promised He will do. Now that we've reached the grand finale, join me in affirming that our God is able to keep every promise in His Word. We've worked on memorizing the words of 2 Timothy 1:12 throughout our weeks together, and I invite you to affirm them again now by either reciting or singing them:

> *I know whom I have believed, and am persuaded that he is able to keep that which I have committed unto him against that day.* (KJV)

In the days and weeks to come, I encourage you to revisit the five landmarks we've studied and keep them in your heart as a reminder to put your faith completely in Christ. My prayer is that as you do, you will be reminded all over again just how faithful and trustworthy God really is. If you're anything at all like me, you'll probably need to be reminded before this day has even ended! In the meantime, would you lift your voice with mine to celebrate the landmarks of our journey by singing the chorus of our theme song one more time? This is one moment that this alto is happy to be singing to the choir, because my faith is increased just knowing that you are standing with me. As you sing, you will be declaring that you will no longer be controlled by your circumstances or moved by your feelings but will be motivated by your faith in Jesus, the One who has given you all these promises and more. He will be faithful to carry out His plan and purpose for your life.

> *There is a God in heaven*
> *And I am in His plan*
> *He will forsake me never*
> *My life is in His hands*
> *His boundless love will lead me*
> *As long as time endures*
> *Oh, this I know*
> *This I know for sure*
>
> *Amen.*

Go to God

Ask

Could your heart use some hope? Read Psalm 146:5-6. Share your concerns or burdens with God in prayer, expecting Him to answer. Pray with expectancy and hope today.

Seek

Renowned preacher and author Warren Wiersbe has said, "The safest place in all the world is in the will of God, and the safest protection in all the world is the name of God."[5] As you draw near to God, He will tell you what you are to let go of—worry, doubt, unconfessed sin. Whatever it is, you cannot experience the hope and the joy of being in the will of God while carrying these weights.

What do you need to let go of in order to take hold of the hope of God?

Knock

Recall the phrase "prisoner of hope" from Zechariah 9:12. When I roll that phrase around in my mind, I think of the word *relentless*.

Do you have a relentless, persistent, unyielding, uncompromising, and determined hope today? Can you think of another word to add to this list?

How will you become a prisoner of hope today?

Dear heavenly Father,
What a joy and privilege it is to pray for my precious sister once more. I know you have great plans for her. May she never settle for less than Your very best for her. May she realize success in every area of her life. Teach her to walk in faith, trusting You with everything that concerns her. May she always remember that You love her just as much as You love Your Son, Jesus. Make her a beacon, a living testimony of Your hope and grace in a dark and hopeless world. As she walks in Your ways, remind her that nothing will be impossible for her. May she always be a woman of the Word, allowing Your truth to guide her in all her ways. Bless her now and always. In the name of Jesus, I pray. Amen.

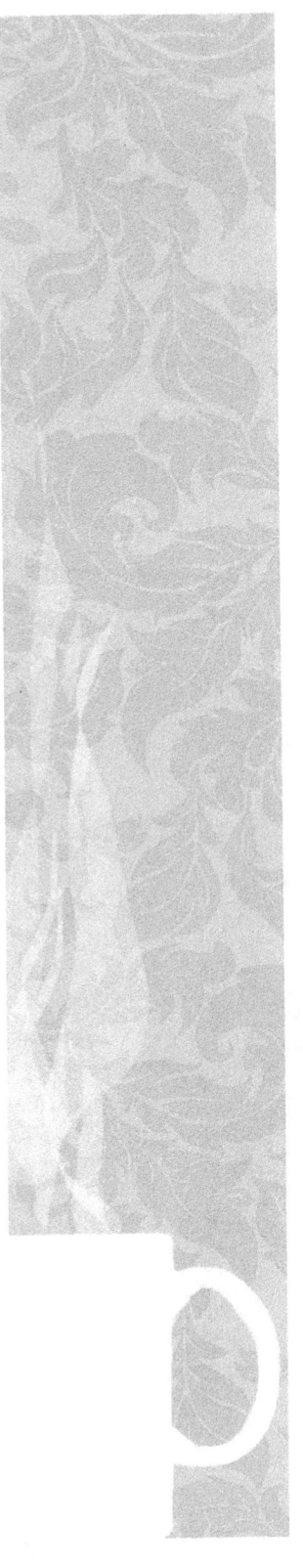

Week 6

Video Viewer Guide

Though there were many things in Moses' life that he did not _____ ...this man of great faith stepped out and said, "God, _____ me."

Even though they would wander in the desert for forty years because of their _____...Moses continued to _____ God.

It's your responsibility to _____ on _____ you know. And you get to know this Almighty God by reading His _____.

God does not want you to live your life in _____ to what you _____; He wants you to live your life in _____ to what you _____...in His _____.

No matter how well you think you already know _____, there is a capacity to know him _____.

Jesus in His great _____ will help you put what you already know into _____.

His divine power has given to us all things that pertain to life and _____, through the _____ of Him who called us by glory and virtue.

2 Peter 1:3 NKJV

He did not waver at the promise of God through unbelief, but was strengthened in _____, giving glory to God, and being fully _____ that what He had promised He was also able to perform.

Romans 4:20-21 NKJV

206

Notes

Week 1: There Is a God in Heaven

1. *Nave's Topical Bible*, edited by John R. Kohlenberger III (Grand Rapids: Zondervan, 1992), 819.
2. *Nave's*, 819.

Week 2: I Am in God's Plan

1. "Tiqvah," accessed May 6, 2013, http://www.biblestudytools.com /lexicons/hebrew/nas/tiqvah.html.
2. "Baqash," accessed May 6, 2013, http://www.biblestudytools.com /lexicons/hebrew/kjv/baqash.html.
3. "Darash," accessed May 6, 2013, http://www.biblestudytools.com /lexicons/hebrew/kjv/darash.html.
4. Acton Bowen, *Escape the Noise* (Lincoln, NE: iUniverse, Inc., 2007), 6-8.
5. From "Brainy Quote," accessed May 7, 2013, www.brainyquote.com /quotes/quotes/b/billygraha161989.html.
6. "Mathétés," *Strong's Greek*, accessed May 7, 2013, www.bibleapps.com /greek/3101.htm.
7. "Worship," last updated in 2009, http://www.thefreedictionary.com /worship.
8. Tony Sutherland, *Graceworks* (Atlanta: Tony Sutherland Ministries, 2011), 20.

Week 4: My Life Is in God's Hands

1. "Stay Up on the Wall," Babbie Mason and Turner Lawton, © 1999 BMM Music, Praise & Worship Works (ASCAP), administered by Music Services; Turner Lawton Music. All rights reserved. Used by permission.
2. Adrian Rogers, "Six Principles to Fortify Faith," Speech excerpt from Sunday, November 11, 1012, accessed May 7, 2013, http://www.lightsource.com /ministry/love-worth-finding/six-prinicples-to-fortify-faith-307514.html.

Week 5: God's Boundless Love Will Lead Me (As Long as Time Endures)

1. "The Story of Paul Gustave Dore," in *Our Daily Bread*, January 6, 1993.
2. Luke 15, *Matthew Henry's Concise Commentary on The Bible*, accessed May 7, 2013, www.biblegateway.com/resources/commentaries/Matthew-Henry /Luke/Prodigal-Son-Wickedness.
3. Max Lucado, *A Gentle Thunder* (Dallas, TX: Word Publishing, 1995), 15-16.

Week 6: This I Know for Sure

1. "Hagah," *Strong's Hebrew*, accessed May 7, 2013, http://www.biblestudy tools.com/lexicons/hebrew/nas/hagah/html.
2. "Ginosko," *Strong's 1091*, accessed May 4, 2013, http://www.biblestudytools .com/lexicons/greek/nas/ginosko.html.
3. From a eulogy delivered by Pastor Tony Ashmore at Life Gate Church, Villa Rica, Georgia, May 25, 2013.
4. "Elpis," *Strong's Greek*, accessed May 7, 2013, http://www.bibletools.org /index.cfm/fuseaction/Lexicon.show/ID/G1680/elpis.htm.
5. "Safest Protection in the World," Warren Wiersbe, accessed May 7, 2013, http://articles.ochristian.com/article10227.shtml.